The Metaphysics of Love

The Metaphysics of Love

Gender and Transcendence in Levinas

STELLA SANDFORD

THE ATHLONE PRESS
LONDON AND NEW BRUNSWICK, NJ

First published in 2000 by
THE ATHLONE PRESS
1 Park Drive, London NW11 7SG
and New Brunswick, New Jersey

© Stella Sandford 2000

Stella Sandford has asserted her right under the Copyright, Designs and Patents Act
1988, to be identified as the author of this work

British Library Cataloguing in Publication Data
A catalogue record for this book is available
from the British Library

ISBN 0 485 11566 2 HB
0 485 12163 8 PB

Library of Congress Cataloging-in-Publication Data
Sandford, Stella, 1966–
The metaphysics of love : gender and transcendence in Levinas / Stella Sandford.
    p.   cm.
Includes bibliographical references and index.
ISBN 0-485-11566-2 (alk. paper) – ISBN 0-485-12163-8 (pbk. : alk. paper)
1. Levinas, Emmanuel.   2. Love.   3. Sex.   4. Transcendence (Philosophy)   I. Title.

B2430.L484 S255   2000
128'.46 – dc21

00–031309

Distributed in The United States, Canada and South America by
Transaction Publishers
390 Campus Drive
Somerset, New Jersey 08873

Typeset by RefineCatch Limited, Bungay, Suffolk
Printed and bound in Great Britain by
Short Run Press Ltd, Exeter

Contents

Preface

Details of all of the works cited or referred to in this book are listed in the bibliography at the end. After the first citation (with full publication details) works are referred to with abbreviated titles and page numbers. Sometimes both English and French editions are cited; if notes use 'ibid.', the English edition page numbers are followed by a semicolon and then the French. If English translations are available I have used those listed in the bibliography; any modifications are indicated in the notes with 't.m.'. Otherwise, translations are my own.

Earlier versions of parts of Chapters Two and Three were previously published as 'Writing as a Man: Levinas and the Phenomenology of Eros' in *Radical Philosophy* 87, January/February 1998. An earlier version of Chapter Five has appeared in *Angelaki* 4.3, December 1999.

I owe thanks to a variety of people for their support during the conception of this project and the writing of the book. My original debt is to Simon Critchley, for introducing me to Levinas's work and for his continued intellectual support and friendship. Catherine Chalier, who was unwittingly so inspirational in Paris in 1993, has been more encouraging and kind than I fear I have deserved. I have debts of a more general kind to the members, past and present, of both the *Radical Philosophy* Editorial Collective and the UK Society for Women in Philosophy, especially Kate Soper, Christine Battersby, and Alessandra Tanesini. Thanks also, and love, to my mother, Maureen Deverall, and my friends Lisa Millard, Josephine Grosset, Christopher Wilbert and Olivia Rooney. My thanks, finally, to Peter Osborne, who read everything and kept me going.

Stella Sandford

Introduction

Levinas's place in the popular philosophical imagination can be summed up in the phrase 'ethics as first philosophy'.[1] In the Anglo-American philosophical world Levinas is best known for having reintroduced the question of ethics into the so-called 'Continental' philosophical tradition. Furthermore, it is through Levinas's profound yet often hidden influence that the 'Other' has become one of the key concepts in much contemporary work, not only in philosophy but also, for example, in feminist and postcolonial theory. However, the main thesis of this book is that a description of Levinas's fundamental philosophical project is by no means exhausted by any reference to 'ethics'; indeed that the emphasis on 'ethics' and 'the Other' in the reception and dissemination of Levinas's thought has served to cover over both the basis and the specific details of this project.

Levinas speaks, notably in *Totality and Infinity*, of ethics – the relation with the Other – as a metaphysical relation, as 'metaphysical desire', or even as metaphysics itself.[2] These statements are sometimes made according to a traditional subject–predicate structure – the relation with the other *is* metaphysics – and sometimes, perhaps more often, by way of a textual contiguity which avoids the copula in favour of other conjunctions, or even avoids the conjunction entirely: 'the desire of the absolutely other or nobility, the dimension of metaphysics'; '[t]he relation between the same and the other – or metaphysics'; '[m]etaphysics, transcendence, the welcoming of the other by the same, of the Other by me'. Even more curiously: 'Metaphysics approaches without touching. Its *way* is not an action, but is the social relation.'[3] These deliberate and careful formulations indicate that in any apparent identity statement such as 'ethics is metaphysics' the meaning of the 'is' is not to be taken for granted, any more than the meaning of 'ethics' or 'metaphysics' themselves. My contention – one not entirely absent in the existing literature on Levinas, but here elaborated in much greater detail – is that for Levinas ethics is the *way to* metaphysics, that 'ethics' is the phenomenological elaboration or experiential attestation of a more fundamental metaphysical claim that would reassert the necessity of a thinking of 'transcendence' as a first principle.

The elaboration of this thesis gives an importance and a centrality to certain themes in Levinas's work which have often been sidelined, when not wholly overlooked: eros, sexual difference, 'the feminine', maternity and the masculine family of terms associated with fecundity (paternity, filiality, fraternity). My original decision to focus on these particular themes was primarily informed by a feminist approach to the history of philosophy, more particularly by my first shocked reading of the passages on the feminine in Levinas's *Totality and Infinity* which appeared to me – as parts of Levinas's work had appeared to Simone de Beauvoir, I later learned – almost parodically exemplary of the crass, unthinking sexism so familiar in this history. The failure of many of Levinas's commentators to mention, let alone criticize, these passages was equally exasperating to this feminist reader, and spurred the work that has culminated in this book. The result, a critical reading of the Levinasian project, is thus also a demonstration of one aspect of the often misunderstood relation between feminism and philosophy, or of that strange hybrid 'feminist philosophy'. The work remains, importantly, a feminist critique of Levinas, and one which demonstrates the dependency of much of his philosophical argumentation on the specific details of the discussion of, for example, 'the feminine' such that the more obviously unpalatable aspects can neither be excised nor reinterpreted in a way that would exonerate Levinas from this sort of critique. The feminist orientation has made it possible to understand the centrality to Levinas's philosophy of the themes of the feminine, and eros, and enabled a reading which claims the attention of everybody interested in Levinas's work, feminists and others. It is also the aim of this book to question the idea of 'the feminine' as either a useful or a meaningful category, both as it appears in Levinas's work and more generally. This is most fully articulated in the Coda. I would also be inclined to indicate this scepticism throughout by referring to 'the feminine' always in inverted commas, but due to the frequency with which the word appears it would be cumbersome. Readers are therefore invited to imagine the inverted commas each time for themselves.

Emmanuel Levinas, who died in late 1995, was evidently a man who provoked more than philosophical admiration amongst those who knew him,[4] and his work has given rise to an unusually sympathetic body of literature. For whatever reason, it appears that the appropriation of aspects of Levinas's work in philosophy and other disciplines has been largely uncritical; at its worst the mere reproduction or intonation of terminology. Levinas's philosophy is not well served by this approach, any more than it is by the immanentism which would inoculate it against serious critique. On the other hand, his severest critics tend to judge him with a set of external criteria that often fails to take into account the way in which Levinas's philosophy is constructed as a complex and erudite critique of precisely those criteria. This does not mean that Levinas was unaware of the objections his work would invite; often, indeed, they are pointed out in the texts themselves. Nor did he fail to respond to others' criticisms, as the progress of his philosophical career illustrates. In an attempt to avoid both of these extremes, what follows offers an immanent critique based on a sympathetic attempt to understand the overall project and internal workings of Levinas's philosophy.

Chapter One introduces some of the main themes of Levinas's thought in a chronological study of some key texts, and argues for an understanding of his project in terms of a metaphysics of transcendence. The developments in Levinas's increasingly critical relationships with the philosophies of Husserl and Heidegger are taken to demonstrate the working out of the priority of metaphysics in relation to Levinas's specific understanding of phenomenology and ontology. This project, according to Levinas, was to be understood as the retrieval of a certain Platonism, but one which Levinas's commitment to the insights of his immediate predecessors prevents from becoming a form of antiquitism. It is this peculiar combination of the ancient and the modern – the retrieval of an ancient idea of transcendence through a modern phenomenological method – that is characteristic of Levinas's philosophy (as of Heidegger's), something that an over-emphasis on ethics has failed to take into account. Although Levinas's relationship to Plato has often been acknowledged, it is argued here that the location of influence in the categories of 'the same' and 'the other' in Plato's *Sophist* is mistaken. Emphasized instead is the inspirational and enigmatic idea of the 'Good beyond being' in the *Republic*, an emphasis which highlights the perhaps unexpected neo-Platonist aspects of Levinas's thought.

If this describes Levinas's fundamental project, the chapters which follow show *how* the project is elaborated and justified, that is, how Levinas attempts to make good the basic metaphysical claim for transcendence through various phenomenological and/or ontological analyses. Chapter Two traces the changing roles of eros, sexual difference and the feminine in Levinas's philosophy. An initial privileging of the erotic relation as the site of transcendence (a privilege explained by Levinas's comments on the formal structure of sexual difference and the absolute alterity of the feminine) gives way, it appears, to the importance of the idea of infinity and an account of ethics in which the latter is distinguished from – even opposed to – eros. This shift, for which Levinas himself gives no explanation, is here understood in terms of the negotiation of the relation between metaphysics and phenomenological ontology. Even taking this shift into account, in Levinas's work up to and including *Totality and Infinity* (1961) and the other texts of that period, the feminine nonetheless appears consistently, operating as a *philosophical* category which Levinas increasingly tries to distance from any empirical referent. Discussion of it requires an investigation of the origin and the implications of its use, especially given the tendency, notable in *Totality and Infinity*, to use the phrase interchangeably with *la Femme*. Chapter Two considers this question in relation to Levinas's texts, their philosophical inspiration, and the commentaries, both critical and apologetic, to which they have given rise. Despite the changing role of the feminine, which runs parallel

with the demotion of the importance of eros, some elements remain remarkably consistent. The association of the content of the feminine with the mark
of sexual difference sets up an opposition between the feminine and the
human, where the latter is associated with the alleged linguistic and conceptual neutrality of the masculine. Arguing this point against Levinas's
apologists (those, for example, who would see his 'masculine standpoint' as an
honest and admirable admission of the sexed specificity of his subject position), this chapter introduces the position, maintained throughout, that
Levinas's discussions of sexual difference and the feminine have nothing to
offer an appropriative feminism. If feminist theorists and philosophers have
argued otherwise, this makes the demonstration of the point all the more
urgent.

Chapter Three develops these conclusions further in a discussion of
Levinas's notion of fecundity and its elaboration as paternity, filiality and
fraternity. The idea of fecundity, explored in most detail in the final section of
Totality and Infinity, is the most important term in the thinking of transcendence in this period of Levinas's work. Arriving at fecundity through the
phenomenology of eros – and thus subordinating eros *to* fecundity – not only
explains the otherwise puzzling emphasis placed on this phenomenology, but
also relocates ethics in relation to the metaphysics of transcendence, dis-
placing the apparent priority of ethics in the previous sections of *Totality and
Infinity*. A consideration of the related discussions of the role of the third, *le
tiers*, in fraternity and the idea of the trace, or illeity, shores up this point and
suggests a way of understanding the relation between ontology and metaphysics in Levinas's work at this time. As in the previous chapter, these
analyses also show – against the various attempts to argue otherwise – that
the gendered vocabulary of these discussions (this time masculine) is integral
to Levinas's philosophical argument and cannot be rendered innocuous
through redescription.

By the time of the publication of his last major work, *Otherwise Than Being
or Beyond Essence* (1974), it is unlikely that Levinas was unaware of the feminist unease with aspects of his earlier work. For this reason, some commentators have read the introduction of the notion of 'maternity' in *Otherwise Than
Being* as an attempt to redress the overly masculine vocabulary of paternal
fecundity with a term that marks a philosophical innovation in Levinas's
thinking of subjectivity as responsibility. Connected to the albeit brief references to maternity, *Otherwise Than Being* also reflects a new emphasis on
sensibility, related to the earlier account of *jouissance* or enjoyment in *Totality
and Infinity*, but in a more complex way. Chapter Four argues, however, that
the idea of maternity, far from replacing the masculine parental term, is
conceived and elaborated within the terms of the priority of paternity and is
ultimately subordinated to the latter. Highlighting the discussion of fraternity and the third in *Otherwise Than Being*, maternity is understood as occupy-

ing the same position as eros in the earlier work. As expressive of the ethical relation, maternity lacks the moment of universality that, for Levinas, would ensure justice. Like eros and the feminine in *Totality and Infinity*, maternity is overcome in the universality of fraternity, now also elaborated in terms of the 'wisdom of love'. When *Otherwise Than Being* is thus seen – despite its undoubted originality and stylistic novelty – in terms of its continuity with the basic structures of *Totality and Infinity*, maternity is neither a philosophical innovation nor a cause for feminist celebration.

In Levinas's later work from the period of *Otherwise Than Being*, the distinction between erotic and non-erotic love, which comes to be figured terminologically as the distinction between 'eros' and 'love', makes explicit a tendency which is already discernable in the early texts. Levinas's phenomenology of eros and the idea of fecundity clearly owe much to Plato's two main discussions of love in the *Symposium* and *Phaedrus* dialogues. A comparative reading of Plato and Levinas shows how Levinas's avowed philosophical affinity with aspects of Plato's philosophy of love (in particular Socrates's report of Diotima's speech in the *Symposium*) operates according to the same sublimation of the sensuous or the physical in a philosophical-spiritual realm, the subordination of 'eros' proper to 'love', or to the wisdom of love: philosophy as fecundity or, as Plato says, spiritual procreation. Despite feminist and other attempts to laud the female figure of Diotima and her metaphors of gestation and birth, the argument of the *Symposium* testifies to the subordination of the maternal-physical to the paternal-spiritual, a transcendence of the feminine by the masculine. This same trajectory performs for Levinas's philosophy a subordination of the phenomenology of eros to the metaphysics of love. Refusing to follow this trajectory, however, one might still pause to consider the plausibility of Levinas's phenomenological analyses. Although Levinas himself rejects the comparison, a 'Levinasian' interpretation of Aristophanes' speech in the *Symposium* reveals that the strengths of Levinas's phenomenology of eros lie in precisely those elements which the metaphysics of love and fecundity would overcome.

Drawing together the book's main thesis with the various thematic explorations of the previous chapters, Chapter Five looks in greater detail at exactly *how* – that is, according to what conceptual mechanism – the phenomenological aspects of Levinas's work are mobilized in the service of his metaphysical claims. Locating both eros and ethics in a region of *affectivity*, Levinas's phenomenological analyses point to an order of intelligibility irreducible to the structures of cognition and which attests to an 'experience' of transcendence. The metaphysical claims 'borrow' their proof, as it were, from this affective intelligibility. In this emphasis on affectivity, however, the problem of the relationship between eros and ethics resurfaces. Characterized by their affective, rather than cognitive, nature, the descriptions of eros and ethics are often indistinguishable. At the same time, Levinas's insistence on the distinction between them becomes more and more pronounced. Given that, textually, the distinction tends ceaselessly to collapse, what then accounts, philosophically, for Levinas's attachment to it? What role is the distinction between eros and ethics called upon to play in the philosophy of transcendence, and what are the consequences of its collapse? In answering these questions this chapter examines the complex implicit distinction between two different sorts of affectivity – a distinction upon which Levinas's argument is shown to hinge. As this distinction is explicitly manifested in the opposition between eros and ethics, the collapse of the latter is symptomatic of the failure of the phenomenological analyses to 'prove', in whatever sense, the metaphysical claims at the core of Levinas's philosophy.

The results of the conjunction of philosophy and feminism are as multifarious as its aims, and each particular instance gives rise to a very specific set of questions. Even so, two broad areas of concern often suggest themselves: what does this conjunction mean for feminism, and what does it mean for the philosophy under interrogation? These questions, whose presence hangs heavy in the background of this book, are faced head on in the Coda. Giving rise, in this case, to a determinately negative answer, the first of these questions is more easily dealt with. Despite, perhaps because of, the claims that feminists have made for the usefulness of Levinas's notion of the feminine, my discussion ends with a demonstration of the contrary. The question of the significance of this for Levinas's philosophy dovetails with the critique of his metaphysical claims and is therefore more complicated. The Coda ends with some suggestions as to how we might now conceive this relation between feminist critique and Levinas's philosophy, and with a warning as to how we should not.

There is always, of course, with any relatively short study of an oeuvre of the size and complexity of Levinas's, the problem of justifying what one has *not* said. This means both explaining why certain things have been left out and why other possible readings have been closed off. It is traditional at this point to cite the exigencies and constraints of time and space. All I will say here (the point is elaborated in the Coda) is that granted other interpretative possibilities, one writes because a certain interpretation either imposes or recommends itself, or because the times are such that this interpretation appears necessary (and this is also true, perhaps especially so, of those interpretations which insist on the impossibility or multiplicity of interpretation). What follows is what I take the time of philosophy and the time of feminism to demand now of a reading of Levinas.

CHAPTER ONE
The Metaphysics of Transcendence

If *Totality and Infinity* may be taken as representative, in broad sweep, of the articulation of Levinas's philosophical project, it needs to be explained what it means for him to describe it as an attempt to *'retrouver le platonisme'*:[1] to rediscover, recover or re-encounter Platonism, to find or meet it again, but also to find oneself back in the place of Platonism, to recuperate it. This 'Platonism', it transpires, has little to do with those specific theories, epistemological or otherwise, that, taken together, constitute 'what Plato said', to use Shorey's over-confident phraseology.[2] With regard to the most general elements of any Platonic epistemology – the theory of anamnesis and, such as it is, the more labile theory of Ideas or Forms – Levinas will be consistently and unambiguously critical. Rather, 'Platonism', for Levinas, refers more generally to that thread in Western philosophy committed to the idea of transcendence. As such, its most general articulation is primarily negative, a response to what Levinas calls 'contemporary anti-Platonism',[3] that is, the assumption of the immanent origin and extension of all meaning and value in human language, culture or society, the denial of a transcendent Truth which may also be glossed as the death of God. In the same way, Levinas's identification of and with specific, positive moments in the history of philosophy – notably the Platonic 'Good beyond being' and the Cartesian idea of infinity – is more an appeal to a general idea of transcendence than a profession of allegiance to any particular transcendent content.

At the same time, this appeal to an ancient, some would say archaic, philosophy is wedded to a thoroughly modern philosophical method applied to modern themes and concerns. The terms in and on which Levinas refers to a certain Platonism are conditioned by the achievements of his philosophical contemporaries. In particular, Levinas's work would have been unthinkable without that of Husserl and Heidegger, who had, for Levinas, determined the terrain on and against which contemporary philosophy must operate. In any discussion of Levinas's work, one of the first difficulties lies in negotiating this complex conjunction of the ancient and the modern. One might begin, however, with the observation that Levinas's early philosophical career was dominated by his modern teachers.

With his first book-length publication, *The Theory of Intuition in Husserl's Phenomenology* (1930),[4] and his collaborative French translation of Husserl's *Cartesian Meditations* (1931), Levinas was largely responsible for the introduction of Husserl's work into the French philosophical scene. To a lesser but still significant extent, the same was also true *vis-à-vis* Heidegger's early reception in France. (Levinas had studied at Freiburg under both Husserl and Heidegger.) As might therefore be expected, Levinas's early work on both thinkers was largely expository and uncritical, albeit with a decided Heideggerian bent. *The Theory of Intuition* is a thoroughly Heideggerian reading of Husserl, specifically of *Ideas 1* and the *Logical Investigations*. In it, Levinas reads Husserl's phenomenological 'reduction' ontologically as revealing the absolute existence of consciousness, such that the *cogito* 'is no longer a reflection on consciousness that constitutes its existence; the former is made possible by the latter.'[5] That is, if consciousness did not already exist, one would not be able to reflect on it: I am, therefore I think. Although, on the whole, Levinas avoids the distinctive terminology of, for example, *Being and Time*, the priority of ontology is asserted, and for the greatest part the critique of Husserl rests on Heideggerian ground.

But, tantalizingly, Levinas already affords an inkling of his own original critique of Husserl at the end of the last chapter of *The Theory of Intuition*. Phenomenological reduction, Levinas says, will not be 'fully concrete' until it has tackled the issue of intersubjectivity, and he hints that this is indeed what Husserl is undertaking in his as yet unpublished work. In the event, one may speculate, the much-expanded fifth *Cartesian Meditation* failed to deliver this to Levinas's satisfaction. For Husserl 'the problem of the other' could be incorporated into egology leaving the latter, and the primacy of consciousness, intact. According to Levinas, however, egology is only a first step in phenomenology.[6] The force with which Levinas later criticizes 'philosophy as egology' can be seen as resting on this one fundamental disagreement.

Levinas's commitment to Heideggerianism is clearly evident in another early text, 'Martin Heidegger et l'ontologie' (1932),[7] a more or less uncontentious exposition of the main themes of *Being and Time* which reveals Levinas as the champion of Heidegger's return to the question of Being. Faithful to the tradition of Western philosophy which, since Descartes, has taught that subjectivity occupies an exceptional and important place in the 'economy of being', Heidegger, Levinas argues, nevertheless resists the tendency of that same tradition to think Being (*l'être*) in terms of beings (*étants*), to think Being in general as an absolute or transcendent being (*étant*). This tendency arises, in part, from the belief that Being cannot be defined.[8] Heidegger's achievement, Levinas says, is to have shown that the reverse is true, and that to understand Being has become the most fundamental philosophical task. More, he has shown that this task itself constitutes the very essence of human being: 'The comprehension of being is the characteristic and fundamental fact of human existence.'[9] By the time of the appearance of *Existence and Existents*, however (first published in 1947 but written for the most part whilst in captivity, between 1940 and 1945),[10] Levinas's turn away from Heidegger begins to emerge. The philosophical debt is still clear, but no longer unambiguous:

> If at the beginning our reflections are in large measure inspired by the philosophy of Martin Heidegger, where we find the concept of ontology and of the relationship which man sustains with Being, they are also governed by a profound need to leave the climate of that philosophy, and by the conviction that we cannot leave it for a philosophy that would be pre-Heideggerian.[11]

Heidegger's failure even to speak of, let alone retract, his practical and ideological involvement with Nazism, contributed immensely to this 'profound need'. Yet Levinas was writing against what he called 'Hitlerism' as early as 1934,[12] without this entailing a critique of either Heidegger himself or ontology as such. The years leading up to the publication of *Existence and Existents* will have brought knowledge both of Heidegger's involvement with Nazism and of the full extent of Nazi crimes, and later remarks in the essay 'Signature' (1963) indicate the influence of political events on Levinas's intellectual biography, dominated, he says, 'by the presentiment and the memory of the Nazi horror'.[13] However, Levinas's critical relationship to Heidegger would not be philosophical if these historical – and to an extent personal – considerations were alone determinant. Rather, one begins to see here the complex interrelationship between philosophy, history and politics that is the motivating presupposition of Levinas's distinctive contribution to Western philosophy. If this presupposition was inspired, in a positive sense, by Heidegger's philosophical work, it is at the same time the basis of the necessity to escape Heidegger's influence. Levinas always maintained the incomparable contemporary importance of Heidegger's philosophy, implicitly against those who would see it as nothing more nor less than a theoretical or mystical apologia for Nazism. That he nevertheless insisted on its mutual philosophical and political implications – Heidegger's position, after all – should also caution against any cultish Heideggerianism.

In *Existence and Existents*, the Heideggerian influence is, as one might expect, most obvious in the insistence on thinking beings in their relationship to Being, and positing this relationship as essential. Like Heidegger, Levinas here attempts to think Being without resorting to notions such as 'concept', 'category' or 'substance',[14] but he still produces an analysis that 'leave[s] the climate' of Heidegger's philosophy, phenomenological aspects notwithstanding. For despite Heidegger's methodological privileging of *Dasein* (in *Being and Time*), it is Being itself which remains his theme, whereas for Levinas Being is here invoked and thought in order to reflect more adequately on beings, or existents. The English translation loses the sense in which the title of *De l'existence à l'existant* itself articulates this 'reversal'. Nor does Levinas fight shy of the more 'psychological' aspects of the relationship between Being and beings; indeed he announces his preoccupation in this text with 'this relationship between the self [*le moi*] and its existence' when it becomes particularly poignant in certain situations 'which philosophical analysis habitually leaves to psychology, but to which we shall pay particular attention: fatigue and indolence.'[15] Heidegger may have paved the way with his analyses of, for example, fear or curiosity, but the pains he took to avoid speaking of anything like 'human existence', specifically through the use of the term *Dasein* (which, of course, also foregrounds *Sein*), is not apparently deemed necessary by Levinas[16] indeed it will later be deemed pernicious.

Furthermore, when Levinas thinks Being in *Existence and Existents* nothing of what one might call Heidegger's 'affection' for Being remains. Being, that is, Being in general, undifferentiated into beings, is, Levinas says, thought and experienced as *horror*. Echoing (in translation) Heidegger's *es gibt*, Levinas calls it the *il y a*, the 'there is': '*There is* in general, without it mattering what there is, without our being able to fix a substantive to this term. *There is*: impersonal form, like "it is raining" or "it is warm".'[17] In *Existence and Existents* Levinas describes insomnia in terms of the experience of the horror of the *il y a*, of the space not empty but filled with darkness, in which consciousness is given over to the night, submerged, depersonalized. In the night the things of the day are reduced to indeterminacy, they 'sweat being' as Levinas says in one particularly graphic formulation, and the 'I' (*le moi*) experiences not the horror of death, that is the horror of nothingness but, on the contrary, the horror of Being.[18]

The *il y a* is an important category in Levinas's work not only because of its thematic persistence but also because it forms part of the early thinking of subjectivity, refined and reworked but still recognizable in the first major study, *Totality and Infinity* (1961). In *Existence and Existents* Levinas characterizes the appearing of the subject or of an existent as the event of taking up a position within the *il y a*. *Contra* Heidegger, existence in the world is not to be thought as a 'fall' into the world, but as the possibility of extracting oneself from anonymous Being, an event Levinas calls 'hypostasis'.[19] In 1963 Levinas restates this general position with explicit reference to Heideggerian philosophy:

An analysis which feigns the disappearance of every existent – and even of the *cogito* which thinks it – is overrun by the chaotic rumbling of an anonymous 'to exist', which is an existence without existents and which no negation manages to overcome. *There is* – impersonally – like *it is raining* or *it is night*. No generosity which the German term 'es gibt' is said to express showed itself between 1933 and 1945. This must be said! Illumination and sense dawn only with the existing beings' rising up and establishing themselves in this horrible neutrality of the *there is*. They are on the way which leads from existence to the existent [*de l'existence à l'existant*] and from the existent to the Other [*autrui*] – the way which delineates time itself.[20]

In the 1951 essay 'Is Ontology Fundamental?'[21] – the title itself a contest-ation of Heidegger's 'fundamental ontology' – Levinas argues that, in stress-ing that the comprehension of a being (*étant*) unfolds within the horizon of Being (*l'être*) (the very gesture that Levinas praised in 1932), Heidegger belongs to 'the great tradition of Western philosophy wherein to comprehend the particular being is already to place oneself beyond the particular. Com-prehension is to relate the particular which alone exists, by knowledge, to the universal.' This, however, is no simple denunciation of this 'great [*vénérable*] tradition', for Levinas's point is that in our relationships with beings this attitude is for the most part unavoidable:

> From the moment one engages in reflection, and precisely for the reasons which since Plato have subordinated the sensation of the particular to knowledge of the universal, one is reduced, it would seem, to subordinat-ing relations between beings to structures of Being, metaphysics to ontol-ogy, the existentiell to the existential. How, moreover, can the *relation* with *being* be, at the beginning, anything other than its *comprehension* as being, the fact of freely letting it be inasmuch as it is being?[22]

This position remains a constant of Levinasian philosophy throughout. 'Reflection', thematizing thought which asks 'what is it?' or thinks ' "*ceci*" en tant que "*cela*" ' ('*this* insofar as it is *that*'), as Levinas often puts it,[23] is always and necessarily a subsumption of the particular being under a concept, much like the Platonic subsumption of all sensuous particulars under the guiding Idea. However, insofar as this is the very essence of thematization or con-ceptualization it is not in itself damnable; indeed this is the indispensable requirement for what Levinas, notably in *Totality and Infinity* but elsewhere as well, will call politics, equality or justice.

This universalizing gesture will often be metonymically invoked as 'ontol-ogy'. But in 'Is Ontology Fundamental?', the discussion is not so much a critique of ontology in itself, as an attempt to delineate its field of com-petence, or as the title suggests, to challenge its pre-eminent status. To repeat Levinas's question: 'How . . . can the *relation* with *being* be, at the beginning, anything other than its *comprehension* as being, the fact of freely letting it be inasmuch as it is being?' The answer: it cannot, unless this being 'is the Other' [*sauf pour autrui*].[24] Perhaps the most prominent (certainly the most notorious) term in Levinas's oeuvre, *autrui*, is introduced, then, as that which can curtail the pretensions of ontology, that which indicates something beyond ontology, or a something that confounds it:

Our relation with the Other certainly consists in wanting to comprehend him. But this relation goes beyond comprehension. This is not merely because knowledge of the Other, outside of all curiosity, requires also sympathy and love, which are ways of being distinct from impassive contemplation. Rather it is because in our relation with the Other, he does not affect us on the basis of a concept. The Other is a being and counts as such.[25]

As this last line clearly demonstrates, however, Levinas's work at this stage was, despite the critique of ontology, itself written in the language of ontology. In 'Is Ontology Fundamental?' the argument continues by answering an anticipated objection: is not to speak of a *being* of any sort already to invoke Being as that which lets that being be? This, recall, is the precise thesis that in 1932 Levinas defended as the profound truth of the priority of ontology. Now, however,

Our response is to ask whether the relation with the Other is in fact a matter of *letting be*? Is not the independence of the Other accomplished in the role of being called [*son rôle d'interpellé*]? Is the person to whom one speaks understood from the first in his being? Not at all. The Other is not an object of contemplation first and an interlocutor second. The two relations are intertwined [*se confondent*]. In other words, the comprehension of the Other is inseparable from his invocation. To comprehend a person is already to have spoken with him.[26]

In the relation that Levinas here calls 'calling' he does not deny that the relation with *autrui* consists *in part* in the comprehension of the being of the other ('I comprehend the being [*l'être*] of the Other, beyond his particularity as a being [*étant*]'), but he also insists that there is more to it than this:

The person with whom I am in relation I call being [*je l'appelle être*], but in so calling him I call to him [*j'en appelle à elle*]. I do not only think that the Other is, I speak to him. He is my partner in the heart of a relation which ought only to have made him present to me. I have spoken to him, that is to say, I have neglected the universal being that he incarnates in order to hold on to the particular being that he is.[27]

Familiar terminology is beginning to appear – the relation with the Other, explicitly distanced from ontology, is here called 'religion' or, for the first time, 'ethics' – but the language of Being still dominates: 'religion' is still the relation with a being as a being. The significance of this need to 'go through' ontology even in the act of undermining its primacy is one of the main themes of Derrida's 1964 essay on Levinas, 'Violence and Metaphysics'.[28] And the point was well taken. In the 1987 preface to the German edition of *Totality and Infinity* Levinas says, 'to avoid misunderstandings', that his last and possibly most impressive book, *Otherwise Than Being*, 'avoids, from the beginning, the ontological – or more exactly eidetic – language to which *Totality and Infinity* did not cease to have recourse.'[29] Even so, *Totality and Infinity*, and two companion texts of the same time – 'Philosophy and the Idea of Infinity' (1957) and the 1962 presentation of 'Transcendence and Height' – constitute a concerted attack on the 'violence and negation' of the ontological priority of Being over beings. Taken together, these three texts form something of a centrepiece,[30] in which unfolds the basic theoretical framework of the mature work prior to *Otherwise Than Being* and in which emerges, *contra* Husserl and Heidegger, the distinctively 'Levinasian' position.

The way of the same: egology, ontology and violence

It is in the emergence of this distinctively 'Levinasian' position that one sees the return, via Husserl and Heidegger, to a certain Platonism. In the opening section of 'Philosophy and the Idea of Infinity' Levinas distinguishes between two ways (*voies*) in which philosophy has searched for the truth. The first is explained with reference to Plato's location of the truth in the 'beyond', the *au-delà*, or *là-bas*, 'over there', 'up there'.[31] In searching for this truth '[p]hilosophy would be concerned with the absolutely other; it would be heteronomy itself . . . . Truth, the daughter of experience, has very lofty pretensions; it opens upon the very dimension of the ideal. In this way philosophy means metaphysics, and metaphysics enquires about the divine.'[32] The second way is, on the other hand, the way of 'the same', the path trodden by 'the philosophy of the same'. This is the way that ontology goes, a circular way, which, pragmatically speaking, is understood to be the path that will most often be taken. Again, it is not intrinsically bad, but its claim for the monopoly on philosophy must be challenged. In so doing, one of Levinas's characteristically idiosyncratic 'histories' of Western philosophy emerges via an emphasis on the philosophical presumption of the unquestioned value of liberty or autonomy. This is an instance in which it is difficult to assess Levinas's commitment to the details of the analyses of those philosophies against which he defines his own position. A marked tendency to over-generalization means that these analyses are unreliable and of little use as commentaries. Levinas's point, however, is to construct a broad context of opposition – a general characterization of the thrust of Western philosophy – in order to articulate the one principle of transcendence which all these philosophies lack. If details and differences are sacrificed to polemic, the discussion of philosophy's commitment to autonomy (in Socratic maieutics, Husserlian egology and Heideggerian ontology) is at least a subject that invites such a controversial articulation.

Autonomy, Levinas says, is 'a stage in which nothing irreducible would limit thought any longer, in which, consequently, unlimited thought would be free.'[33] *Vis-à-vis* Plato and Socrates, Levinas sees this played out in two seemingly different, but connected ways. The first rests on the distinction between true knowledge (philosophy) and opinion (doxa), and the association of the former with liberty. As Levinas asserts, rather than explains, this connection it is necessary to extrapolate what it might mean. If Western philosophy has most often leaned towards the side of the same and of liberty, Levinas does not seem surprised. Slightly facetiously he asks: 'Was not philosophy born, on Greek soil, to dethrone opinion, in which all tyrannies lurk and threaten?'[34] The Platonic war against doxa appears as a species of *xenophobia*. Doxa menaces because it threatens to invade thinking and impose itself as authority. It is in submission to doxa that 'the knowing subject goes astray and loses itself' as doxa is 'the heteronomy of inclination, where the person follows a law that it has not given to itself',[35] where the subject becomes alienated and inauthentic. The rigours of true philosophy must be pitted against the barbarian invasion of doxa to ensure the continued freedom of the soul. For Levinas this is equal to the efforts of the subject, *le moi*, to remain as it is, free from change, as if to maintain integrity of essence at the same time as integrity of thought:

> What else is this freedom but the thinking being's refusal to be alienated in the adherence, the preserving of his nature, his identity, the feat of remaining the same despite the unknown lands into which thought seems to lead? Perceived in this way, philosophy would be engaged in reducing to the same all that is opposed to it as *other*.[36]

Levinas reads the Platonic theory of knowledge (anamnesis) as based on the presumption of and the need to maintain the sufficiency of the self:

> The 'I think', thought in the first person, the soul conversing with itself,[37] or, qua reminiscence, rediscovering the teachings it receives, thus promote freedom . . . . This is Socrates' teaching, when he leaves to the master only the exercise of maieutics: every lesson introduced into the soul was already in it. The I's identification, its marvellous autarchy, is the natural crucible of this transmutation of the other into the same.[38]

Risking anachronism, Platonism is thus included in the conclusion that '[e]very philosophy is – to use Husserl's neologism – an egology.'[39] This refers, of course, to Husserl's apparent Cartesianism, to his claim to have laid bare, through the 'transcendental-phenomenological reduction', the structure of transcendental subjectivity as 'the ultimate and apodictically certain basis for judgments, the basis on which any radical philosophy must be grounded.'[40] This transcendental ego, the knowing 'I', is, Levinas says, 'the Same par excellence, the very event of identification and the melting pot where every other transmutes itself into the same. It is the philosopher's stone of philosophical alchemy.'[41] For despite Husserl's famous insistence on intentionality, 'this universal fundamental property of consciousness . . . to be consciousness *of* something',[42] in transcendental egology the 'something' is thought only as *noemata* or *cogitata*, that is, the 'contents' of consciousness. When everything belongs to consciousness, there can be nothing strange to it, nothing foreign, or nothing other. Once again this could be characterized as the triumph of xenophobia, the colonization of the other by the same which safeguards its identity without questioning its inalienable right to do so: 'This imperialism of the same is the whole essence of freedom.'[43]

Adequation between *idea* and *ideatum*, *noesis* and *noema*, is for Levinas the essence of egology *and* of idealism, to the extent that egology and idealism, while not synonymous, are at least aspects of each other.[44] Adequation implies an *a priori* 'fit' between the world and consciousness, such that consciousness embraces (*englobe*) the world with thought — nothing escapes and nothing surprises the 'I'. That this adequation entails the sovereignty of the 'I' is clear in Husserl. The phenomenological reduction reveals not that consciousness fits the world, but that the world fits consciousness:

> all the world, and therefore whatever exists naturally, exists for me only as accepted by me, with the sense it has for me at the time — that it exists for me only as *cogitatum* of my changing and, while changing, interconnected *cogitationes* . . . Consequently I, the transcendental phenomenologist, have *objects* (singly or in universal complexes) as a theme for my universal descriptions: *solely as the intentional correlates of modes of consciousness of them.*[45]

Granted, this is the 'artificial' attitude of the reduction but, to repeat, the transcendental subjectivity thus discovered is 'the ultimate and apodictically certain basis for judgments, the basis on which any radical philosophy must be grounded.'[46] The phenomenological reduction reveals the truth that, in some sense, consciousness constitutes the world for itself. In typically sweeping manner, Levinas even sees this privileging of consciousness as providing a model for Heidegger: '*Being and Time* has argued perhaps but one sole thesis: Being is inseparable from the comprehension of Being (which unfolds as time); Being is already an appeal to subjectivity.'[47] Levinas refers here to Heidegger's discussion of the 'pre-ontological understanding of Being', whereby Being is not only always already presupposed in propositional thought but also *understood*, albeit 'vaguely'.[48] Once again, a common measure between consciousness and Being unfolds as consciousness embracing Being, insofar as Being is comprehended.

This strained and reductive reading of Heidegger, which it would be well nigh impossible to maintain if elaborated, is again illustrative of that tendency in Levinas's work to read philosophical texts or positions so as to make them fit a general thesis. If this is Heidegger's fate here, his own general 'history of Western metaphysics' must, however, take some of the blame. Also according to the influence of such a history, Levinas will more commonly read Heidegger not as a philosopher of subjectivity or consciousness, but as the philosopher of Being, where Being itself (rather than consciousness of Being) is that which *establishes* adequation, within the same structure of thematization which, in 'Is Ontology Fundamental?' was characterized as 'reflection'. Once again, it is not difficult to challenge Levinas's reading. The parallelism between Heidegger's insistence on the priority of Being and the generality of the concept only works by ignoring Heidegger's explicit denials that 'Being' is a concept, his basic point that 'the "universality" of Being "*transcends*" any universality of genus',[49] and by aligning Heidegger with a predominantly epistemological philosophical tradition, when, in fact, *Being and Time* is partly conceived *in opposition to* philosophy as epistemology.[50]

Even so, the central tenet of the discussion in 'Is Ontology Fundamental?' appears unchanged in the later work largely because it is a thesis about the operation of thought upon which, since Plato, something like a consensus has been reached. That is to say, to make some thing, a particular being, an object or a theme for thought, that being is brought under the aegis of a necessarily general concept, in order that this being (*ceci*) be named or identified *as* that thing (*celà*). Its particularity is subsumed under generality, *and necessarily so*. It is not that Levinas thinks that this is an operation, which, all things considered, it would be better for us not to undertake. As he says in 'Is Ontology Fundamental?', it is not a question of preference. What is open to philosophy, however, is how to interpret the significance of this operation, and Levinas interprets it as *violence*. The relationship between the particular thing and the universal concept is, to put it another way, the identification of the diverse. The way in which this identification is accomplished assumes two main forms in Levinas's critique. First, it is the 'I' itself which acts as that which effects commensuration of the diverse; the Husserlian transcendental ego fulfils this function, likewise the Kantian 'I think' which accompanies all my representations.[51] Levinas also suggests that Heidegger's existential analytic of *Dasein* exhibits the same tendency, which perhaps goes some way towards explaining how ontology is understood, like egology, as a philosophy of freedom.[52] Knowledge (*connaissance*), or conceptualization, is for the subject *power*. The process of knowing is to domesticate, to take in hand or seize the thing for consciousness (*com-prendre*), and to make it a possession of consciousness: 'In a civilization reflected in the philosophy of the same, freedom is realized as a wealth. Reason, which reduces the other, is appropriation and power.'[53]

However, insofar as the critique of ontology as freedom refers to Heidegger in his originality, to his peculiar contribution to Western thought, Levinas probably has in mind Heidegger's 1930 essay 'On the Essence of Truth'.[54] There, Heidegger argues not so much that the 'usual concept of truth' as adequation between thing and intellect, or between thing and propositional statement, is wrong, but that philosophy has failed to think through the possible meaning, or the meaning of the possibility, of this adequation. In particular, Heidegger asks, how can there be adequation (or 'correspondence') between two completely dissimilar things – between a being and a statement? This is possible, he goes on to explain, because the statement 'presents' the thing in an 'open field', or an 'open region' 'within which beings, with regard to what they are and how they are, can properly take their stand and become capable of being said.' The relation of the 'presentative' statement to the thing thus appearing is a 'open comportment' within this same 'open region' such that the presentative statement 'subordinates itself to the directive that it speak of beings *such-as* they are. In following such a directive the statement conforms to beings. Speech that directs itself accordingly is correct (true).'[55] To the further question of how this pregiven directedness is possible Heidegger answers:

> Only if this pregiving has already entered freely into an open region for something opened up which prevails there and which binds every presenting. To free oneself for a binding directedness is possible only by *being free* for what is opened up in an open region. Such being free points to the heretofore uncomprehended essence of freedom. The openness of comportment as the inner condition of the possibility of correctness is grounded in freedom. *The essence of truth is freedom.*[56]

Now Heidegger insists that the objection to the proposition that 'the essence of truth is freedom' rests mainly on the preconception that 'freedom is a property of man'. Denying this, he says, is not to be understood as implying that truth is 'subjective', or subject to human caprice; indeed '[a]t best, the converse holds; freedom, ek-sistent, disclosive Da-sein, possesses man – so originally that only *it* secures for humanity that distinctive relatedness to being as a whole as such which first founds all history.'[57] The fact still remains, however, that *Dasein* and *Dasein*'s relation to freedom are essential to the essence of truth, and it is towards this that Levinas's critique is directed.

Once again, Levinas's interpretation is idiosyncratic and really rather unfair. One might, for example, point out that, despite Heidegger's attempts to delineate a conception of freedom that differs from the 'usual' conception, Levinas's inclusion of Heidegger within a general philosophy of the same seems to presuppose that a general conception of freedom is still operative within Heidegger's work. It is necessary to inflict a certain violence on Heidegger's text to make his 'freedom' resonate with the 'freedom' of the Husserlian transcendental ego. As a polemicist, such is perhaps Levinas's prerogative, although in so doing he would seem to be guilty of that very 'reduction to the same' which he allegedly finds in them. To understand this critique in a less straightforward (not to say naive) way, one needs to see it in the context of the second form of the identification of the diverse: mediation. For in 'Philosophy and the Idea of Infinity' Levinas shows how Heidegger rejoins the tradition despite his innovations: 'When he sees man possessed by freedom rather than possessing it, he puts over man a neuter term which illuminates freedom without putting it in question. And thus he is not destroying, but summing up a whole current of Western philosophy.'[58] Ontology is most often seen as the exemplar of this second form of the identification of the diverse:

> This identification requires mediation. Whence a second characteristic of the philosophy of the same: its recourse to Neuters. To understand the non-I, access must be found through an entity, an abstract essence which is and is not. In it is dissolved the other's *alterity*. The foreign being, instead of maintaining itself in the inexpugnable fortress of its singularity, instead of facing [me], becomes a theme and an object.[59]

What is more, Levinas says, Western philosophy has most often been just such an ontology. The meaning of this generalization is double-edged, for it is both an assertion of a necessary fact and a criticism: in its necessity it is the very accomplishment of Reason, but reason is accomplished as *violence*. In ontology the neutral/neuter, mediating, impersonal third term is Being itself, but that these words – neutral, impersonal, etc. – are suggestive of a harmless, even anodyne, philosophy is immediately contradicted. The being (*étant*) is not peaceably comprehended but ambushed:

> To know ontologically is to surprise in an existent confronted that by which it is not this existent, this stranger, but that by which it is somehow betrayed, given over and surrendered to the horizon in which it loses itself and appears, lays itself open [*donne prise*], becomes a concept.[60]

These two forms of the identification of the diverse – the mediation of the ego itself and the mediation of concepts – come together in such a way that explains Levinas's insistence that ontology affirms the primacy of the freedom of the subject, for '[t]he relation with the other is here accomplished only through a third term *which I find in myself.*' The understanding of Being which makes ontology possible allows for the neutralization of the being (*étant*), and is at the same time the free play of the ontologizing *moi*: to comprehend a being is 'not a relation with the other as such but a reduction of the other to the Same. Such is the definition of freedom: to maintain oneself against the other, despite every relation with the other, to ensure the autarchy of an I.'[61]

Ontology is thus an egology insofar as it fails to put the 'freedom' of *Dasein* to remain the same into question.

In 'Philosophy and the Idea of Infinity', in particular, the critique of 'the philosophy of the Neuter' is also, importantly, a critique of the Platonic interposition of the Ideas or Forms as the mediating third term through which the knower knows the known. Each particular thing *is* only insofar as it refers to or is a more or less imperfect copy of the perfect Idea of that thing, which is its universal form. The particular is never known in its particularity, but only in its correspondence to the universal. In fact, Plato goes further. The particular is never *known* at all: what one knows in the particular is the universal Idea, as the Ideas are the only proper and/or legitimate objects of (true) knowledge. This point connects back to the discussion of maieutics in such a way that what was originally in danger of appearing to be a rather simplistic account of the history of Western philosophy begins to emerge in some complexity. For according to the doctrine of anamnesis, knowledge of the Ideas is innate to the soul, learning is no more than remembering and, as stated above, philosophy is no more than the discourse of the soul with itself: the soul 'can not encounter anything really foreign to it.'[62] The freedom of the soul to remain as it is in itself, without encountering otherness or change, is never questioned. With regard to Plato this point is particularly resonant. For if there was one thing that the inquisitive soul of the freeborn Athenian male failed ever to question, it was precisely his inborn right *to be free* and to maintain his participation in the 'free' democracy of Athens at the price of the continued subjugation of others. It is not merely a matter of historical interest, therefore, to interrogate the roles of slavery and patriarchy as the conditions of possibility for Western philosophy. Levinas's critique has the merit of suggesting that the physical and political freedom of the aristocratic Plato might be more intimately bound up with the philosophical *concept* of freedom than has previously been suspected. We know now under what circumstances and with what hypocrisy the former was maintained; for Levinas the (unargued) case for maintaining the *a priori* and unexamined legitimacy accorded to the latter must now also be questioned.

That there exists such a connection between philosophical concepts (or philosophy itself) and their political elaboration is also suggested in the emotive terminology of *Totality and Infinity* and 'Transcendence and Height'. In these texts, the philosophy of the same is described in terms of 'totalitarianism' and 'imperialism', and the preferred word to characterize both the scope and the ambition of the philosophy of the same – 'totality' – echoes the first of these in a way that could not fail to evoke the political history of Europe and the USSR. Insistence on the (theoretical) role of 'history' as a neutralizing force, and references to 'violence' and 'war' beg for reference to relatively recent events in such a way that one cannot be sure that they are meant to be understood metaphorically. If, on the one hand, however, this forcible insistence on the relationship between philosophy and politics is part of the immediate attraction of Levinas's work – and that part which makes it *seem* as though it may be used as a resource in thinking every left-leaning or social-emancipatory (especially feminist and post-colonial) struggle – this sits, on the other hand, in extremely uneasy relation with Levinas's unwillingness to think history or politics in terms of anything other than 'the same'.

The way of 'truth': transcendence and infinity

According to the bipartite division of philosophy at the beginning of 'Philosophy and the Idea of Infinity', Levinas sees himself as having chosen heteronomy over autonomy. If Western philosophy has been predominantly a philosophy of the same, Levinas attempts to redress the balance by excavating from its history those points of opposition which, although well-enough known, remain unremarked and unelaborated. This does not involve the tracing of an alternative tradition or genealogy but spotlighting a few isolated instances in which 'the thinker maintains, in truth, a relationship with a reality distinct from him, *other* than him',[63] and developing them philosophically. For Levinas, whatever is truly and remains 'other than the thinker' is experienced or characterized as 'transcendence of the thinker' – not in the sense of a self-transcending, but as something that transcends the self, the same, or the self-same. The philosophy which breaks with the philosophy of the same is that which affords a glimpse of this transcendence, or at the very least does not rule it out *a priori*. The descriptions of the philosophy of the same in terms of the autonomy of consciousness, the totalizing and neutralizing horizons of the concept, of history and Being, whilst no doubt having a certain rhetorical force, actually obscure the point that it is fundamentally the inability or unwillingness to think what is in some ways a rather traditional philosophical conception of transcendence that constitutes for Levinas their fault.

Levinas's philosophical opposition to Heidegger, for example, makes more sense (which is to say, his reading is altogether more plausible) when it is seen as a response to Heidegger's refusal to think *Dasein*'s 'transcendence' according to the 'Platonic' metaphysical structure, that is, in terms of a 'beyond' *Dasein* towards which *Dasein* would nevertheless strive (basically, God).[64] Heidegger's conception of *Dasein*'s being-towards-death as a form of 'finite' transcendence (transcendence of the present towards an open future within the horizon of mortality) is opposed in Levinas's work by an insistence on *infinite* transcendence.[65] This is elaborated in relation to an idea of the Other quite absent from Heidegger's work.[66] Transcendence as infinity, also called 'exteriority' and 'height', is avowed or in some sense 'manifested' in the epiphany of the face of the Other (*autrui*), the relation with whom is 'metaphysical desire' or 'religion'. This relation is also, famously, called ethics – once again, a category conspicuously absent in Heidegger. Precisely because Levinas re-introduces 'the Other' and 'ethics' into the Husserlian-Heideggerian philosophical problematic in which they are so patently under-theorized, there appears to be something commonsensical – something so *right* – about it, like the correction of a very glaring error. Given that this seems so correct – and not a little bit heartwarming – it is easy to overlook the question of the precise status of the ideas of 'the Other' and 'ethics'. They are not, for example, simply empirical phenomena which, by their very obvious-ness, claim to have or are accorded the first and final word, as the phrase 'ethics as first philosophy' can suggest. If there is indeed a sense in which they constitute an appeal to a 'pre-philosophical' experience, phenomenologically elaborated, they are also, crucially, terms deployed in a philosophical project and as such need to be understood in their *philosophical* significance. As elem-ents of a philosophy presented as a 'return to Platonism', their relation to the aims and presuppositions of that philosophy needs to be made clear. 'The Other' and 'ethics' are not the only terms of a distinctively Levinasian phil-osophy, nor indeed are they the most important in the philosophical basis of the opposition to the philosophy of the same.

If what may be called the 'way of the same' constitutes a well-ensconced tradition of thought, its refutation, the 'way of truth', survives as a series of flashes or insights. To a philosopher of the anglophone tradition, especially, it might seem absurd that Levinas would develop a lifetime's work on the basis of a line here and there in Plato, and an idea in Descartes that the rest of Descartes' work seems to contradict. But for Levinas these moments are the re-emergence of profound truths – the return of the repressed of philosophy, one might say. And what has been repressed, what unfailingly returns, is 'transcendence'. In a slightly different idiom, Jean Wahl in *Existence humaine et transcendance* (1944), describes 'transcendence' or what he also calls 'the abso-lute' as having 'haunted the spirit of philosophers and writers since Plato.'[67] The metaphor of haunting is apposite in that it impedes one tendency in Levinas's philosophy, in the 'middle period' at least, to present the notion of transcendence as a 'victim' of the philosophy of the same. In this determin-ation transcendence *actively* haunts philosophy both in that it appears and disappears, and in its power to disturb. It unsettles philosophy because phil-osophy does not know what to make of it, is unable to fit it into traditional conceptual schemas. In reclaiming the name of 'metaphysics' to describe the philosophy of transcendence, Levinas evokes a series of both positive and negative philosophical relations to the idea or presumption of transcendence. According to one set of relations, for example, metaphysics, is the name given to that which is immune from empirical verification, that which positivist philosophy, broadly understood, would designate as meaningless. Meta-physics is that which the atheist Hume, scepticism notwithstanding, railed against with evangelical fervour: '*Does it contain any abstract reasoning concerning quantity of number?* No. *Does it contain any experimental reasoning concerning matters of fact or existence?* No. Commit it then to the flames: for it can contain nothing but sophistry and illusion.'[68] In certain empiricist discourses 'metaphysics' would similarly designate the (illegitimate) study of that which surpasses human understanding, that with which philosophy should not pretend to have any business. For a philosopher like Comte, for example, recognition of this would characterize the maturity of thought.[69]

This dismissal of metaphysics rests, from a Levinasian point of view, on the fundamentally mistaken premise that the limits of human knowledge are the limits of philosophy and the limits of any possible relation with what is other – be it the world, other people, or God. Anti-metaphysics (in effect, the privileging of a limited epistemology over all other philosophical forms) constitutes the tradition of the philosophy of the same, both in this styling of the human understanding as the limit of the *interesting*, and in its gesture of possession; for with the name meta-physics, it implicitly claims nature for its own. Now nothing in nature escapes the human/philosophy, since anything that escapes the human/philosophy is super-natural. Denial, however, is inverted recognition. The philosophy of the same would not need to protest so much were it not still haunted by its beyond, and nowhere is this more evident than in Kant's melancholy – but also more than half-admiring – account (especially in the Preface to the first edition of the *Critique of Pure Reason*) of the human compulsion to ask precisely those questions which cannot be answered philosophically – that is, rationally – but which it behoves the dignity of the human, nevertheless, to ask.

What 'haunts' philosophy – what is 'there' but escapes its gaze – according to Wahl is what one might inadequately call the objectivity of the objective:

> a certain density perceived behind concepts, an opacity, this interposition without a name and without an idea which could correspond to it – something like the primordial silt recalcitrant to every idea' of which Parmenides was perhaps thinking whilst he interrogated the young Socrates in Plato's dialogue.[70]

The difference between the two ways of philosophy is perhaps best illustrated by their choices when faced with the idea of this 'beyond'. It is either the least or the most interesting, the least or the most important: *false* philosophy or *first* philosophy. A few pages later Wahl continues:

> We have been studying some ideas – the idea of being, the idea of the absolute, the idea of transcendence, the idea of space – and we see that they lead us each time towards something which is beyond the ideas or even to the hither side of them [*en deçà*].[71]

Despite the lack of explicit reference to Descartes, it seems unlikely that Wahl would be unfamiliar with the corresponding passages in his compatriot's *Meditations*. Anti-metaphysically, one would read Descartes as, at certain points, woefully attached to scholasticism. Strange theses are asserted, as if self-evident, which cannot in fact withstand the onslaught of logical testing:

> Now it is manifest by the natural light that there must be at least as much reality in the efficient and total cause as in its effect: for whence can the effect draw its reality if not from the cause? And how could this cause communicate its reality to its effect, if it did not have it in itself? And hence it follows, not only that nothingness cannot produce anything, but also that the more perfect, that is to say that which contains in itself more reality, cannot be a consequence and a dependence of the less perfect. And this truth is not only clear and evident in the case of those effects which have the reality called actual or formal by the philosophers, but also in the case of ideas in which only the reality they call objective is considered.[72]

The conclusion then drawn is that as he, Descartes the imperfect, has an idea of God the perfect, this idea must have been put in him by God, who therefore exists, for his idea as effect could not have had any less real cause than God. No doubt this is, analytically speaking, an invalid argument; no doubt Descartes' notions of 'reality' and 'perfection' are too imprecise to bear the burden of proof that the argument demands of them; but that is not the point for Wahl or Levinas.[73] Such an analysis takes the human faculty of reason and its concepts, delineated in a system of logic, to be the measure of all things; a procedure not altogether surprising with regard to Descartes, widely held to be the father of rationalism. And yet, ironically perhaps, what Wahl and Levinas see as most important in Descartes is the transcendence of rationality or rationalism towards something 'beyond'. As the name suggests, in 'Philosophy and the Idea of Infinity' Levinas uses Descartes' discussion of the idea of the infinite, something which is put in me from outside, as a structural paradigm for transcendence.[74] Levinas sees in Descartes' philosophy that the subject who thinks, or the mental act of thinking, is always separated from the object of thought (even finite objects of thought), though not so much that it is impossible for the thinker to understand (*rendre compte*) those objects. There is always a distance between the idea and the object, but the distance between the idea of infinity and its ideatum is more profound:

> The intentionality that animates the idea of infinity is not comparable with any other; it aims at what it cannot embrace, that which is, precisely, Infinite . . . the alterity of the infinite is not cancelled, is not extinguished in the thought that thinks it. In thinking infinity the I from the first *thinks*

more than it thinks. Infinity does not enter into the *idea* of infinity – it is not grasped. This idea is not a concept. The infinite is the radically, absolutely other. The transcendence of infinity with respect to the ego that is separated from it and thinks it constitutes the first mark of its infinitude.[75]

The extraordinary thing about the idea of infinity is not only that it always remains fundamentally inadequate to its 'object', but also that the very *content* of the idea of infinity is constituted by this inadequation; it is an idea that can never be content with its content: an infinite idea can never be complete and adequate to itself. The idea of infinity is not just transcendent in origin, it is the idea of transcendence itself, the idea which always transcends itself, the idea that thinks more than it thinks, and thus confounds the adequation of the subject-object correlation.

The Other: face-to-face

That which is signalled in Levinas's work by the idea of infinity is also expressed in other ways. As will continue to be the case until the very end of his philosophical career, however, aphoristic assertion rather than decisive, explicative definition is the main mode of articulation. Despite the occasional hint of exasperation, Levinas's sympathetic readers have usually understood this apparent lack of precision, lack even of argument, as a conscious performative strategy.[76] If it is the impossibility of adequating thematization that is at issue, the refusal of conceptual mastery is not only apposite, it is necessary. One is not therefore in a position to say, for example, that infinity *is* transcendence, or that the other terms characteristically used in this 'middle period' – exteriority and height – are synonymous with infinity. These terms accrue such as to appear at times as aspects of each other, at times identical, building up a shifting picture which Derrida's description of Levinas's prose works very well to capture:

> the thematic development ... proceeds with the infinite insistence of waves on a beach: return and repetition, always, of the same wave against the same shore, in which, however, as each return recapitulates itself, it also infinitely renews and enriches itself.[77]

The notion of exteriority, for example, clearly owes much to the Cartesian idea of infinity (the thought of something put in me from *outside*), and also reinforces the critique of the Platonic idea of reminiscence. On the one hand, it seems to be a descriptive attribute of infinity, whilst on the other the subtitle of *Totality and Infinity* (*An Essay on Exteriority*) would seem to make it the main theme of that book, despite the fact that the actual word appears much less often than 'alterity', 'infinity' and 'transcendence'. The notion of distance (*l'éloignement*), of Platonic and Cartesian inspiration, signals much the same as exteriority, but otherwise. Again, the invocation of height performs much the same work, often spoken of in the same breath as infinity, although the implicit moral inflection of the word 'height' also signals its greater affinity with *Autrui*, the Other.[78] In its very concrete reference to the other person rather than simply another thing, this is a deceptively simple term. *Autrui* is said to be the absolutely other (*Autre*) as if to distinguish the two terms, or as if to inscribe the former as the limit case of the latter, the other *par excellence*. But Levinas also uses *Autre* or *autre* in this same capacity, even in the same paragraph,[79] as if to avoid the foregoing suggestion. The fact that *autrui* does not exist in the plural is certainly significant; when Levinas introduces the notion of *le tiers*, the third person, he will be forced to speak of *les autres* and thus to make a distinction between *autrui* and *autre* that was not before evident.[80] At the same time, however, the continued use of *Autre* will seem to stress that what is crucially at issue is precisely the *alterity* of the other, in a formal sense, rather than anything which could be said to be the specifically, empirically human of *autrui*. This is what prevents Levinas's philosophy from becoming an anthropology, or a sociology of the other person. At this stage, however, this absolute alterity, refractory to any totalization or subsumption in the same is *instantiated* as *autrui*, whilst the same is paradigmatically – but not only – *le moi*, the subject.

Even so, the elaboration of the 'experience' of this alterity in the apparently straightforward notion of the face begs for a literal interpretation. The immediacy, the uniqueness of the encounter with *autrui* described as the 'face-to-face' utilizes a phrase itself suggestive of the most unadorned human contact. Much that Levinas says reinforces such a reading. In 'Philosophy and the Idea of Infinity', for example, *autrui* is said to resist all the powers of the subject 'with the total uncoveredness and nakedness of his defenceless eyes, the straightforwardness, the absolute frankness of his gaze.'[81] In further distinguishing the human face from that of the animal, 'in which a being, in its brutish dumbness, is not yet in touch with itself', the literal interpretation seems to be endorsed. It is also stressed, however, that the face is not a phenomenon like any other, not a 'theme' or an image captured by my gaze, for example. The face is an event, a revelation, a mode of being of *autrui*, such that my relation to it could never be that of the knowing subject to the object: 'The transcendence of the face [*le visage*] is at the same time its absence from this world into which it enters, the exiling of a being, his condition of being stranger, destitute, or proletarian.' The face is also *expression*: 'The epiphany of the face is wholly language.' In *Totality and Infinity* this last thought is reiterated through the notion of discourse, but even when it is said that the face 'speaks', this is no simple exchange of words. This discourse is 'an original relation with exterior being' in which the essential thing is 'the interpellation, the vocative.'[82]

This literal interpretation of the notion of the face is, however, not incommensurable with the formal (non-anthropological) idea of alterity. The latter is 'experienced' in the face-to-face encounter, which is the phenomenological attestation of the metaphysical idea of infinity. The interplay between metaphysics and phenomenology finds expression in the (formal) asymmetry of the (actual) ethical relation.[83] Even so, the apparent simplicity or straightforwardness of the descriptions of the encounter with the Other are deceptive. This encounter, Levinas says, as if he were describing a relation of cause and effect, profoundly alters the ego. The freedom of the ego, its very egoity, is called into question:[84] confronted with the face (transcendence, infinity, height, exteriority) the ego is forced to account for itself, to offer an apology for itself. In measuring oneself against what Levinas calls, after Descartes, the 'perfection' of infinity, moral consciousness or conscience is born 'as shame, where freedom discovers itself murderous in its very existence.'[85]

Only after such an encounter and such a putting into question could the freedom of the ego be justified. The ethical relation does not simply strip the ego of its freedom, but invests it. The freedom of the ego is restrained not because it comes up against a resistance against which it struggles or to which it submits. It is revealed as 'arbitrary, guilty and timid; but in its guilt it rises to responsibility . . . this "action" upon my freedom precisely puts an end to violence and contingency, and, in this sense also, founds Reason.'[86] It is thus in refusing its own powers, in putting the same that it itself is into question that the ego enters into the ethical or religious[87] relation with the Other. Furthermore, in becoming self-conscious in this relation, in refusing the egoity of the same, the subject is invested as meaningfully *human*.

Although this relation is described from the point of view of the subject, what remains most important is always what eludes the subject. As a relation with what is absolutely other (transcendence and exteriority), ethics or religion is a relation that is never fully realized, it is a 'relation without relation' because of the abyss of separation which it cannot straddle. In describing this non-consummation as 'metaphysical desire', the ever yearning and ever burning nature of the never actualized relation with the other is emphasized. The idiosyncratic description of metaphysical desire as 'experience in the sole radical sense of the term' seems counter-intuitive, but Levinas insists on it. The face is, he says, 'pure experience, conceptless experience', or 'experience *par excellence*'.[88] That this experience, desire, is a relation without relation is thus meant to signal its superiority or its excellence; in its negativity (unfulfilment) is to be found its very positivity, for the separation or distance maintained between the self and the Other *is* respect for the Other.

These descriptions, assertions without argument, rely for their force on what one might call the phenomenological recognition of the reader. Early on in *Totality and Infinity* Levinas describes his philosophical task in the following way:

The effort of this book is directed toward apperceiving a non-allergic relation with alterity, toward apperceiving Desire – where power, by essence murderous of the other, becomes, faced with the other and 'against all good sense', the impossibility of murder, the consideration of the other, or justice.[89]

If it really is the case that the face of the Other, the eyes of the Other, forbid me first of all, and without pleading or reasoning, to commit murder, the force of Levinas's philosophical elaboration of this fact will most likely touch the reader in what one might call a 'pre-philosophical' way. Again, however, it must be stressed that this does not mean that the 'encounter with the Other' describes a purely empirical phenomenon, anymore than Hegel's dialectic of Lordship and Bondage describes any actual hand-to-hand combat. The reduction, indeed, of the encounter with the Other to an empirical phenomenon in which I experience the injunction not to commit murder is not only empirically incorrect (this is *not* how humans chiefly experience each other, and they often murder each other quite freely), it also removes the motivation of or for Levinas's philosophy: if this ('ethics') is how things are with us humans, then what's the problem? The point, surely, of the sustained critique of the philosophy of the same is rather the recognition of the opposite. As Levinas says in an interview from 1985:

> I have never claimed to describe human reality in its immediate appearance, but what human depravation itself cannot obliterate: the human vocation to saintliness. I don't affirm human saintliness; I say that man cannot question the supreme value of saintliness.[90]

'Truth', Levinas maintains, is only to be achieved when the starting point of philosophy is the face of the Other, which is not to say it is its content matter, but its motivation or presupposition. Again, this quasi-transcendental thesis is what distinguishes Levinas's philosophy from an anthropology of the human encounter. The point is that the experience of the Other is the condition of possibility for philosophy insofar as it is another way of referring to transcendence. This also means that 'ethics' as the presupposition of and motivation for philosophy *is not philosophy itself*. Not only is it not the case that Levinas's philosophy is *an* ethics, 'ethics' itself or 'the ethical' is not the main aim or even the main category of Levinas's philosophy. As he says, in a footnote to the essay 'God and Philosophy' (1975), '[i]t is the meaning of the beyond [being], of transcendence, *and not ethics*, that our study is pursuing. It finds this meaning in ethics.'[91] In other words, Levinas's basic philosophical project cannot in any way be summed up with the word 'ethics'. It is, instead, the attempt to reassert the possibility of the meaning of transcendence, or, an even stronger claim, the necessary presupposition of 'transcendence' if there is to be such a thing as meaning at all. Phenomenology, or the phenomenological description of the face-to-face encounter – ethics – is the *way to* metaphysics or Truth, the 'royal road', an experiential attestation or 'proof' (broadly understood) of the metaphysical (that is, speculative, undemonstrable) claim: metaphysics is 'enacted' in ethics.[92]

But what exactly is 'transcendence'? What does 'transcendence' mean? What does it mean to say that it is a 'metaphysical principle', for example? And what, for that matter, is 'metaphysics'? In the post-Kantian philosophical systems of the late eighteenth and nineteenth centuries a principle could be said to be 'metaphysical' insofar as it was posited as the necessary but undemonstrable – and hence speculative – presupposition, the first principle, on which the system was to be built. One might cite, as a more or less random example, Fichte's absolute subject or 'I'. In a sense, 'transcendence', for Levinas, points to the same sort of presuppositional, undemonstrable principle but with the two following, very important, differences. The presuppositional, undemonstrable principle to which 'transcendence' points will never, for Levinas, be located *in* or *as* anything (not even 'the Other'), and rather than being part of – even the most eminent part of – a system, 'transcendence' points to that which is outside of or beyond any system (outside of or beyond 'totality'), whilst still being its condition. If 'transcendence' appears to function as an empty signifier, this is not entirely incorrect. It refers to that which may not be referred to, in the sense of that which escapes but conditions reference itself.

This is worth stressing in relation to the idea of 'the Other', which has achieved such prominence in the reception of Levinas's work, as the compelling phenomenological aspect of the description of the ethical relation tends to obscure the formal, metaphysical principle which underlies it. The notion of the Other occupies a much more complex position than the main tendency in many current theoretical appropriations of Levinas's work would suggest. The Other is not a foundational category for Levinas. It does not appear fully-formed and un-birthed, as it were, as the unquestioned and unquestionable pre-philosophical ground of experience and thence of philosophy. The assumption that it does overlooks the fact that it is, precisely, a philosophical category, and, once again, risks mistaking Levinas's philosophy for an empirical – albeit philosophical – anthropology of the human encounter. Ironically, nowhere is this clearer than in a comparison with the Platonic text which is Levinas's inspiration. The origin of the terms 'the same' and 'the other' in Plato's *Sophist* is often remarked by way of introductory explanation.[93] The connection, however, is not at all clear. In particular, if one were to try to identify Plato's 'other' with or as a transcendent content then replicated or affirmed in Levinas's philosophical work, the connection appears to be virtually incomprehensible. These terms – the same and the other – have a content and a philosophical function for Levinas that can only be understood within the broader context of a philosophy of transcendence for which the 'Platonic' marker is the enigmatic 'Good beyond being' introduced in the *Republic*. Furthermore, as the general significance or aim of the *Sophist* dialogue is ultimately more consonant with Levinas's 'Platonism' than is its specific discussion of the other, it is worth looking at in some detail.

Plato's Sophist: *otherness, not-being and the One*

Plato's aim in the *Sophist* is to understand the conceptual and linguistic trickery by means of which the sophists of his day were able to argue untruths persuasively. In modern terms, the problem he believes he and his contemporaries to be facing is 'relativism': the sophists look likely to be able to convince us that there is no such thing as 'truth'. The *Sophist* is unusual in that its argument is led not by Socrates but by the 'Eleatic Stranger' (Elea being the site of the Parmenidean school). The significance of this is a matter of fruitful dispute in modern commentaries,[94] but at least one reason for it lies in the connection with the earlier *Parmenides*, in which a series of antinomical arguments from the mouth of Parmenides himself appear to show nothing except the impossibility of choosing between opposed philosophical positions. In the later dialogue, the sophist is defined as one who makes things seem true which are not, a charge which the sophist would try to avoid with the allegedly Parmenidean argument that, since it is impossible to say or think not-being, and to speak falsely is to assert or say what is not, it is impossible to speak falsely.[95] In revealing this argument as, precisely, sophistical, the Stranger both routs the sophist and reveals the true meaning of the Parmenidean thesis. If this involves the bold assertion, ostensibly *contra* Parmenides, that 'after a fashion not-being is and on the other hand in a sense being is not',[96] the necessity to get clear about what we mean by 'being' and 'not being' is clear. In attempting to avoid some of the confusions to which previous theorists of 'being' have been subject, the Stranger distinguishes between the 'classes' of being, motion and rest. Intrigued, however, by the necessity of the use of the verb 'to be' in phrases such as 'the universe "is" in motion, . . . it "is" at rest', the Eleatic Stranger is led to a theory of the combination of classes, or their mutual 'participation' in each other.[97] But in considering these 'most important' forms or Ideas (each of which is 'other than the remaining two, but the same as itself'), the Eleatic Stranger alights on further perplexity: 'But what do we mean by these words "the same" and "the other", which we have just used? Are they two new classes, different from the other three, but always of necessity mingled with them?'

The following proof that 'being' and 'the other' are indeed different classes rests on a distinction between that which is or can be absolute or absolutely, and that which is or can be relative or relatively. Asserted, but not argued, is the fact that while being may be both absolutely and relatively, 'other is always relative to other'. When being is thought absolutely, its opposite must be absolute not-being, or nothingness, and the absurdity of asserting that something both *is* absolutely and *is not* absolutely at the same time is apparent: this would be the truth of Parmenides' dictum. But to say that 'not-being is' is no longer contradictory when not-being is thought in other than absolutist terms:

> When we say not-being, we speak, I think, not of something that is the opposite of being, but only of something *different* . . . when we are told that the negative signifies the opposite, we shall not admit it; we shall admit only that the particle 'not' indicates something *different* from the words to which it is prefixed, or rather from the things denoted by the words that follow the negative. [Emphasis added.]

'Not-being' signifies not absolute not-being but rather 'other-being', and hence is 'as fully endowed with being as anything else', has 'an assured existence and a nature of its own'. Not-being is defined as or through other-ness, which is an Idea distinct from the Idea of being. The other is, otherwise said, the Idea of not-being, understood in a relative sense.

The suggestion that the provenance of the Levinasian use of the terms 'same' and 'other' may be traced back to this discussion in the *Sophist* is therefore curious. Firstly, Plato explicitly defines 'the other' as one of the Ideas or Forms or classes or kinds,[98] while for Levinas, the Platonic *eidos* functions as one of the great mediating and neutralizing tools of Western philosophy. The definition of otherness as 'difference' is similarly problem-atic. Not existing in-itself, it seems to Plato that 'the nature of the other is all cut up into little bits', 'distributed in small bits throughout all existing things in their relations to one another'. Accordingly, otherness only exists in the interstices of being or things, making the distinction of things *qua* things possible;[99] it is that which allows a system of differentiation to exist.[100] As Catherine Chalier points out, this is very far from Levinasian thinking.[101] In itself, the definition of otherness as 'not-being' reduces it to what Levinas would see as the dialectical opposite of being, unfolding, still, within the logic of being. Indeed, speaking specifically of the *Sophist*, Levinas says:

> Being and not-being illuminate each other, unwinding within a specula-tive dialectic which is a determination of being; the negativity which tries to overturn being is immediately overwhelmed by being . . . . Essence lays claim to recuperate and cover over every ex-ception: negativity, nothing-ness and, as far back as Plato, not-being which 'in a certain sense is'.[102]

This amounts, then, to what Levinas would call a subordination of the other to the same.

However, it is also the case that the possibility of another reading breaks through the ontological confinements of the text of the *Sophist*. The fact remains, for example, that Plato singles otherness out to give it an importance, an irreducibility and an independence which is unusual and cannot be said of Aristotle's or Plotinus's explicit treatments of otherness.[103] In insisting on the distinction between that which is the opposite of being and that which is 'something different', 'the other of being', one might wilfully understand Plato as straining towards that conceptual emancipation from the hegemony of being which Levinas was pushed to articulate as *autrement qu'être*, 'otherwise than being'. This might also be evident in the attempts of some commentators similarly trying to get to grips with the thought of something which 'does not at all designate the opposite of being, *but something different to being*.'[104] It is perhaps Plotinus who best illustrates this:

> By this Non-Being, of course, we are not to understand something that simply does not exist, but only *something of an utterly different order from Authentic-Being*: there is no question here of movement or position with regard to Being; the Non-Being we are thinking of is rather, an image of Being *or perhaps something still further removed than even an image*.[105]

The distinctness of the Idea of the other from the other Ideas gives it a positivity which not-being as the opposite of being would not possess.[106] It is as if an attempt is being made to rescue otherness from the relativity which is elsewhere affirmed to be its defining characteristic. But there is also a sense in which it would be wrong to be looking for an Idea of absolute otherness anyway. Perhaps, on the contrary, it is the 'absence' of the absolute other or the inability to grasp the other-in-itself conceptually that is most significant for a Levinasian reading. Paul Ricoeur, for example, describes the other as 'the most ungraspable category' ['*la catégorie la plus insaisissable*'].[107] Whether he intends this to refer simply to the *Sophist* or to have a wider application is not specified, but either way it presses upon an essential point. The Idea of the other in the *Sophist* is influential and radical precisely insofar as it eludes definition or eludes a place in the conceptual schema of the text. When Jean Wahl writes, in 1926, that the other in Plato is 'ungraspable ["*insaisissable*"] for purely conceptual thought'[108] it is a striking prefiguration of later Levinasian themes.

But looking further into Levinas's expressed debt to Plato the more interesting and often cited connection has nothing to do with this 'other', however it is construed. It is Plato's brief and extremely enigmatic reference to the 'Good beyond being' in the *Republic* that really appears to grip Levinas's philosophical imagination. Socrates (to the amusement of his interlocutors) describes the Good as 'the source not only of the intelligibility of the objects of knowledge, but also of their being and their reality; yet it is not itself that reality, but is beyond it, and superior to it in dignity and power.'[109] In Levinas's affirmation of this moment something rather unexpected emerges: a philosophical affinity with a Parmenidean-inspired neo-Platonism. The core of neo-Platonism rests almost exclusively on an interpretation of the so-called first hypothesis of the *Parmenides* dialogue, that the One exists,[110] and its negative articulation as the ineffable: 'Then the one has no name, nor is there any description or knowledge or perception or opinion of it . . . . And it is neither named nor described nor thought of nor known, nor does any existing thing perceive it.'[111] Aristotle, Plotinus and the neo-Platonists generally identified this ineffable One with the 'Good beyond being', and in 'The Trace of the Other', Levinas also explicitly makes the link between these Plotinian and Parmenidean philosophical moments and his own attempt to think 'beyond being':

> The One of Plotinus is posited beyond being . . . The One of which Plato speaks in the first hypothesis of the Parmenides is foreign to definition and limit, place and time, self-identity and difference with respect to oneself, resemblance and dissemblance: foreign to being and to the knowledge of which all these attributes constitute the categories. It is something else than all that, absolutely *other* and not with respect to some relative term . . . it is beyond being, wholly other than being.[112]

Also according to Levinas, the recognition of 'the place of the Good above every essence is the most profound teaching, the definitive teaching, not of theology, but of philosophy.'[113] The place of the Other and of ethics must therefore be understood *within* this 'definitive teaching'. Levinas's methodology – the very opposite of Hegel's beginning in his logic and in his philosophy of right – is to 'deduce' the abstract from the fully concrete, to reach metaphysics through phenomenology, transcendence through 'ethics'; that is, to retrieve a certain Platonism through contemporary philosophical means. If this is *what* Levinas attempts to do, the more detailed explanation of *how* – with precisely which philosophical resources – he attempts to do it is the subject of the following chapters.

CHAPTER TWO

*Feminine/Female/*Femme: Sexual Difference and the Human

In Levinas's metaphysics of transcendence what comes to be known as 'ethics' – the phenomenologically attested experience of the face-to-face relation – is not a philosophical end in itself but in some sense the revelation of 'transcendence', where the latter turns out to be both presupposed and produced by the former. An exclusive focus on the idea of 'ethics', therefore, would constitute an under-reading of Levinas's work and, while a recognition of this does not necessarily question the phenomenological force of 'ethics', it does problematize its place in the oeuvre and provoke an investigation into the underlying metaphysical claims. The genealogy of 'ethics' and its relation to the metaphysics of transcendence is further complicated by the place of the themes of eros and the feminine, not just in Levinas's early work, but also in *Totality and Infinity* and other texts of that period. If the goal of the Levinasian project – the retrieval and affirmation of a notion of transcendence – is described in terms of a certain metaphysical Platonism, it is worked out phenomenologically. To say that this peculiar conjunction of the ancient and the modern is, as I have argued, what is distinctive about Levinas's work is not, I think, contentious. But, for reasons which will be discussed, the importance of the role of eros and the feminine to this project is underestimated and misunderstood. In relation to the place of 'ethics', in particular, the difficulty is twofold. In the early work eros performs the phenomenological function of what will later be called 'ethics', and the idea of the Other is articulated through what would appear to be one particular sort of Other, the feminine. Increasingly, however, the erotic relation becomes *opposed* to ethics and, correlatively, the feminine becomes opposed to the Other strictly understood. In the absence of an explicit explanation, this shift needs to be accounted for. Furthermore, rather than there being a straightforward replacement of eros by ethics, of the feminine by the Other, at the end of *Totality and Infinity* the erotic relation delineates the way to transcendence *through* fecundity in a manner that apparently bypasses the discussion of ethics completely. How, then, does the changing role of eros and the feminine contribute to an understanding of the project of a metaphysics of transcendence, and what does it imply for the meaning of 'ethics'?

Eating/Loving

That the motivation of the phenomenological analyses of Levinas's early work lies in the attempt to think the possibility of transcendence is already clear in what is, in one sense, the *failed* attempt to do so in one of Levinas's least read works, *De l'évasion* (1935–6). This essay concerns the relationship between the subject and Being (or, more precisely, its own being) according to a problematic that will inform Levinas's philosophy to its end. According to *De l'évasion* the subject experiences itself as 'chained' to Being, experiences Being as 'an imprisonment from which it is necessary to free oneself [*dont il s'agit de sortir*].' The existence of the subject is, Levinas says, experienced as a burden, and the sense of the '*évasion*', the 'escape' of the title, is 'the need to "get out of oneself" [*sortir de soi-même*], that is, *to break the most radical, the most binding tie, the fact that the self is itself.*' Philosophy (and religion) bear witness to this need, translated into a desire to transcend the limits of human finitude and to commune with (the) infinite Being. The aspiration, if not the method, of idealism bears witness to this desire – perhaps even need – to get 'beyond Being' ['*dépasser l'être*']. In this context 'idealism' refers mainly, one surmises, to Plato – to the positing of a 'beyond' towards which the human aspires – the aspiration, indeed, which *is* philosophy. Idealism thus understood has failed, but the motivation behind it was a noble one, which leaves us with the task of 'leaving being *by a new route* [*voie*], at the risk of overturning certain notions which, to common sense and popular wisdom, seem to be self-evident.'[1]

If the 'old route', the hypostatization of another world – the intelligible world – no longer suffices, in *De l'évasion* no 'new way' is yet fully explicit, but the discussion of need and pleasure provides a clue. Traditionally, Levinas says, need, which seeks satisfaction in an object, has been seen as evidence of a lack. This overlooks, however, that there is something more, a 'malaise' that outlives the mere satisfaction of a need, an excess which will be elaborated in terms of *pleasure*. Pleasure is not, Levinas says, a determinate 'state' of being, but a movement or a *becoming* which is experienced as giddiness, light-headed drunkenness. In pleasure the subject experiences a certain loss of self, a movement beyond or outside of the self as the etymology of 'ecstasy' would suggest. Or this, at least is what pleasure *promises*, but without its being able to deliver. The *évasion* in pleasure is false (*trompeuse*), a failure accentuated by the phenomenon of shame. Here 'shame' is not introduced as a moral category, and hence is not a feeling related to the limitation of human being or its propensity to sin. Like need, it testifies not to a lack in being but rather to the plenitude of being, specifically the plenitude of *my* being, where 'what becomes apparent in shame is precisely the fact of being riveted to oneself, the radical impossibility of fleeing in order to hide from oneself'. This is most evident, Levinas says, in a certain experience of nudity, or more precisely nakedness, and whilst he does not elaborate on this it is not difficult to understand what he means. 'Shame', as an existential phenomenon refers to nudity as similarly 'interpreted', that is, the embarrassment of nudity as productive of shame refers only secondarily to socio-cultural mores and so on, and is more primordially a revelation of a mode of being. As such, one would not have to be literally naked; that nakedness experienced generically in dreams as a public spectacle, for example, might point to the same structure. For Levinas, however, nudity it is more profoundly a personal affair. Naked-ness is not only that which one would like to hide from others, but also from oneself, one's inescapable attachment to being or the scandal of the brute presence of one's being to itself.[2]

At the end of *De l'évasion*, then, whilst no 'new way' to the transcendence of Being has been discovered, the troubled nature of pleasure has been signalled as a point of interest. In the context of this existential-phenomenological analysis 'pleasure', however, is a peculiarly imprecise term, and Levinas does not indicate precisely *which* pleasures he has in mind. Presuming a reference to the sexual perhaps says as much about the reader as it does about the text: nothing Levinas says implies that these are not solitary pleasures (although, of course, there is a solitary eroticism) and the philosophical employment of the idea of nudity points to an experience which is not incompatible with being fully clothed.[3] Even so, in stressing the shameful experience of nudity as the accompaniment to the failure of pleasure, the promises, pleasures and failures of physical love (eros) are inevitably (albeit rather coyly) suggested. In this, the text prefigures the important discussion of eros in *Existence and Existents*, *Time and the Other* and *Totality and Infinity*. Echoes of *De l'évasion* resound most clearly in *Existence and Existents*, where the specificity and extraordinary potentiality of eros – its prospects, that is, as the subject of a phenomenology – are explained by distinguishing between the two pleasures of eating and love (*amour*). Love, Levinas says, is characterized by an essential and insatiable hunger. Unlike the desire to eat, amorous desire is not merely an agitation (*trouble*) that precedes the attempt at gratification, but is a desire *augmented* by such an attempt. In love, Levinas says, 'the burning bush which feeds the flame is not consumed'; or, rather, since it is the inexhaustibility of the flame that is at issue, 'the burning bush that feeds the flame does not extinguish it.' ['*Le buisson qui alimente la flamme ne se consume pas.*'] We can, however, be mistaken about the nature of our desire. We confuse love with the hunger for food, and as this hunger is satisfied through the consumption of a food object we attempt to sate desire with the consumption of a love object; thus, he says, 'the ridiculous and tragic simulation of devouring in kissing and biting.' Amorous desire can only be seen as a 'failure' when it is misunderstood in this way. If the inability to be satisfied by an object (or an act, one might add) – what Levinas calls the 'pathos' of love – is the essence of love it must also be the source of its pleasures: '*The very positivity of love lies in its negativity.*'[4]

Although the word 'ethics' has not yet arisen in *Existence and Existents*, many of the ideas which later accompany it have. The 'me–you' ['*moi–toi*'] relation, as it is called, is described as an unmediated, non-reciprocal face-to-face encounter with *autrui*, an experience of asymmetry which is said to be at the origin of intersubjectivity. The heterogeneity of *moi* and *autrui* is already posited as the primordial relation *presupposed by* the reciprocal relations of 'civilization', and in particular that reciprocal relation called 'fraternity'.[5] What is remarkable here, however, is the fact that this face-to-face relation is located in *eros*, that all relations of civilization are said to refer back to the relation of eros. Once again, however, the anthropological or sociological possibilities of this position are not to be confused with the more fundamental metaphysical point: 'It is in eros that the radical conception of *transcendence* becomes possible.'[6] The actual relation of eros – both the experience of it and its phenomenological description – are only important in relation to this possibility, which arises from the formal or structural dimension of asymmetry. In eros, however, the form of this asymmetry (paradigmatic or originary) is at the same time its content: *sexual difference*. In what reads as an ironic repetition of the opening paragraphs of *Being and Time*, Levinas cites Heidegger's philosophical misdescription of sexual difference in order to elaborate, through contrast, his own claim. Heidegger is charged with having failed to recognize the 'peculiar form of the contraries and contradictions of eros' because of his tendency to understand 'the difference between the sexes as a specification of a genus'[7]; that is, 'male' and 'female' would be 'species' of the genus (the general category) 'sex'. Failing to understand the extraordinary – possibly even unique – nature of the subject matter Heidegger fails to see the ontological priority of the question of sexual difference and fails to raise the question of the meaning of eros in its originality and profundity.

This explanatory priority is reversed in Levinas's actual discussion where, phenomenologically, eros is only important in its revelation of the originality of sexual difference – the Ur-form of difference itself, it would appear. This is elaborated through, or rather from within, a certain perspective on its content, such that sexed alterity appears as 'the feminine'.[8] This is more fully worked out in a series of lectures from 1946–7, published as *Time and the Other*. In many ways, this text is an extension of *Existence and Existents*. In the earlier text the themes of the feminine and eros, fecundity and paternity, are broached only for it to be announced that Levinas is anticipating later work, that these themes will concern him elsewhere. Towards the end, one section of *Existence and Existents* even bears the title 'Time and the other' and outlines what will be the main thesis of the later lectures. In fact *Time and the Other*, at less than one hundred pages, contains an enormous amount. As the title suggests, its main concern is ostensibly with time: 'The aim of these lectures is to show that time is not the achievement of an isolated and lone subject, but that it is the very relationship of the subject with the Other',[9] and the demonstration of this thesis involves a rehearsal of many of the concerns and concepts which will become familiar to the reader of Levinas. It is clearly stated at the beginning that the analyses about to be undertaken are *ontological* in the sense resurrected by Heidegger. The 'general economy of Being' is the unquestioned philosophical horizon throughout, such that even *autrui* will be encountered as a being (*étant*), albeit a privileged one. Even here, however, Levinas already begins to take issue with Heidegger, specifically with the analysis of *Mitsein*. For Levinas, *contra* Heidegger, the experience of solitude is philosophically prior to any Being-with. Furthermore, the analysis of Being-with as 'an association of "side by side", around something, around a common term and, more precisely, for Heidegger, around the truth' is supplanted by 'the original relation with the other', the asymmetrical 'face-to-face'. At bottom, though, the aim is not yet to get beyond Being, but to introduce a plurality into Being, or to think Being as plural, that is, as other than the blanket, amorphous 'oneness' which characterizes the allegedly Parmenidean understanding of being.[10]

Echoing the terminology and analyses of his earlier work, Levinas describes this amorphous being, 'existence without existents' in terms of the experience of the '*il y a*', and the event of taking up a position in anonymous Being is once again called 'hypostasis'. What is new, however, is the language used to describe the self, which appears in (or which *is*) the event of hypostasis. Hypostasis, characterized as 'the present', an evanescent moment of beginning (*commencement*) or rupture in the infinite fabric of existence, constitutes a *mastery* of Being: 'As present and "I", hypostasis is freedom. The existent is *master* of existing. It exerts on its existence the *virile* power of the subject. It has something in its power.' The key word is '*viril*'. Capable of being translated into English as both 'virile' and 'masculine', rooted in the Latin for 'man' (*vir*), the meaning of the French word retains its sexuate origin explicitly. When, therefore, Levinas constructs the self, *le soi*, as 'a virility, a pride and a sovereignty',[11] he constructs it as in some sense 'masculine', a tendency which persists, I will argue, throughout the whole of his career. Power (*pouvoir*), mastery, conquest, sovereignty, virility, activity and heroism are all attributes of the solitary subject which also characterize the intellectual and practical processes proper to it. In a sense, then, *it is the very economy of the same which is being coded as masculine*, a sense which remains to be investigated.

Also familiar in *Time and the Other* are the counterpoints to the above: the assertion that any true transcendence can only be accomplished in an event which interrupts this circular return to self, and the assertion that such an event is uniquely the face-to-face relation with *autrui*. In *Time and the Other* the phenomenon of death is also considered insofar as it, too, remains refractory to knowledge, the impossible object of any phenomenology which puts an end to the virility and heroism of the subject. Death is absolutely unknowable and, *contra* Heidegger, unassumable. The subject's relation with death is therefore a relation with mystery, and the event of death shows that the subject is, in fact, in relation with something absolutely other.[12] And yet death can tell us nothing about the event of transcendence, as death is an event of annihilation in which subject is crushed, wiped out (*écrasé*). The question driving *Time and the Other* thus remains unanswered:

> What can the other's relationship with a being (an existent) be? How can the existent exist as mortal and nonetheless preserve its 'personality', pre-serve its conquest over the anonymous 'there is', its subject's mastery, the triumph of its subjectivity? How can a being enter into a relation with the other without allowing its very self to be crushed by the other?
> This question must be posed first, because it is the very problem of the presentation of the ego in transcendence.[13]

Of course, the event in which the subject does not simply return to itself, and in which its integrity as self is nevertheless maintained, is the face-to-face relation with *autrui*. In *Time and the Other* this too is characterized as a relation with mystery, and as in *Existence and Existents*, the erotic relation is proto-typical. As it is also through the relation with the Other that the subject's relation with the future is made possible, the face-to-face with *autrui* is the very accomplishment of time.[14] It is then remarkable that for Levinas the erotic relation as the 'original form' of the relation with the Other offers *the only possibility for thinking transcendence* at this time, as this gives to eros a philosophical importance not attempted since the time of Plato, and no less audacious.[15] For Levinas at this time, however, this does not mitigate the philosophical abyss between them. Elaborating on similar passages in *Exist-ence and Existents*, he again suggests that the originality of eros lies in the experience of the sexed alterity of the Other. The passages are worth quoting in full:

> Does a situation exist where the alterity of the other appears in its purity? Does a situation exist where the other would not have alterity only as the reverse side of its identity, would not comply only with the Platonic law of participation where every term contains a sameness and through this sameness contains the other? Is there not a situation where alterity would be borne by a being in a positive sense, as essence? What is the alterity that does not purely and simply enter into the opposition of two species of the same genus? I think the absolutely contrary, whose contrareity is in no way affected by the relationship that can be established between it and its correlative, the contrareity that permits its terms to remain absolutely other, is the *feminine*.
> Sex is not some specific difference. It is situated beside the logical div-ision into genera and species. This division certainly never manages to

reunite an empirical content. But it is not in this sense that it does not permit one to account for the difference between the sexes. The difference between the sexes is a formal structure, but one that carves up reality in another sense and conditions the very possibility of reality as multiple, against the unity of being proclaimed by Parmenides.[16]

Searching for the possibility of a relation with the other in which the subject is neither returned to itself nor annihilated, the erotic relation is posited as primordial because the erotic relation is assumed to be heterosexual. The Levinasian subject, coded as masculine (or male; the Anglo-American sex/gender distinction is blurred in French), finds himself in the erotic relation face to face with alterity itself, the feminine, an experience with philosophical significance insofar as it highlights the formal structure of sexual difference as an opening onto the possibility of transcendence. At the same time, the disjunctive relationship between the two terms in or of sexual difference – the moment, precisely, of difference – has an ontological significance that should not be underestimated. The claim is not merely that the difference of sexual difference is ontological, but that it is the condition of possibility for onto-logical difference itself. As such it would not itself be ontological, but would be, to employ the terminology of Levinas's later work, 'beyond being'.

The changing face of the feminine

Despite the singular importance afforded the idea of the feminine, the structure of sexual difference and the relation of eros in the climax, as it were, of Levinas's position, these remarks in *Existence and Existents* and *Time and the Other* are in fact brief, unelaborated, and, argumentatively speaking, unjusti-fied. Anticipating Levinas's later work, it may also be noted that the elabor-ation of these themes will also be their *transformation*, to the extent that sexual difference, the feminine and eros will no longer be posited as primordial. Rather, their secondary or subordinate status will be signalled explicitly. What, then, accounts for this early emphasis, and why is it not sustained? Although Levinas himself offers no explanation, closer examination reveals a constitutive confusion with regard to the alleged status of the philosophical claim, the recognition of which forces the position apart in the way one sees in Levinas's later work.

Firstly, sexual difference (or, this not being a psychoanalytic discourse, 'the difference between the sexes') performs its philosophical function by virtue of its *formal structure*. The exclusively heterosexual erotic relation is important *qua* relation because in it the formal structure of sexual difference stands revealed in particularly stark relief. Although Levinas clearly believes that it is sexual difference itself that makes the relation precisely *erotic* – that is, homo-eroticism, as oxymoronic, is utterly disavowed – eros is philosophically instrumental, rather than an end in itself. The erotic relation highlights the formal structure of sexual difference as the possibility of *transcendence*. This is, in short, *a metaphysics of sexual difference*, or sexual difference as metaphysics. Only in this way is the philosophical, rather than the anthropological or personal, significance of eros attested. The difference of sexual difference is, according to Levinas, absolute, resisting all attempts to conceptualize it in terms of the specifications of a genus. There is no genus or concept to which the designations 'male' and 'female' both belong. Between them is not the distance between two points but the impossibility of measurement or commensuration, a radical conceptual diremption or the diremption of conceptuality itself. But why *sexual* difference, exactly? Is sexual difference an albeit felicitous but ultimately arbitrary example? And given that the formal structure of the idea of infinity becomes central to the elaboration of the idea of the possibility of transcendence in Levinas's later work, what is wrong with 'sexual difference' such that it has to concede this place?

Analyses of sexuality and eros constituted an important element in many of the major phenomenological investigations in France at this time (for example in Sartre's *Being and Nothingness*, Merleau-Ponty's *Phenomenology of Perception* and de Beauvoir's *The Second Sex*). The cultural-intellectual presence of psychoanalysis was undoubtedly partly responsible for directing attention to 'the sexual' as an existential, rather than simply biological phenomenon, and for relieving the discourse surrounding it of its knee-jerk moralism, thus making these philosophical analyses possible. But while this explains the opening up of the discursive space, the appropriateness of the subject matter, for Levinas especially, is quite specific, and this specificity explains both the choice of 'sexual difference' for philosophical investigation *and* its ultimate abandonment. What apparently allows sexual difference to perform its function here is also what compromises it. Levinas's problem, the elaboration of which will become one of the main themes of *Otherwise Than Being*, concerns the attempt to articulate the idea of the possibility of transcendence when this latter is, by definition, beyond the necessarily conceptual structure of any such articulation. As with the later elaboration of the experience of the Other – 'ethics' – the heterosexual erotic relation stands in, then, as the phenomenological witness to the strictly unthematizable metaphysical claim or 'truth'. Eros, both the revelation and the product of sexual difference, is not therefore a wholly arbitrary example insofar as its specific phenomenological content affords what in Levinasian language may be called a glimpse (a sideways, evanescent, indirect glimpse), in the formal structure of sexual difference, of transcendence, in a way that a phenomenology of eating, for example, does not.

That this *content* is crucial is evident in Levinas's slippage from the formal structure of sexual difference to what he will call the 'alterity content' of the feminine. In itself, the idea of sexual difference carries no phenomenological force. The idea of sexual difference must go down, as it were, to the level of eros, to the heterosexual erotic relation of one with another, and from this perspective the phenomenological subject must be sexed in order to experience the other as differently sexed. Unlike Hegel's 'phenomenologist', who as 'we' is meant to be universal, who sees and describes from a point of view above the fray, Levinas's lover has to *be there*, he has to *do it*. As this is a story told by a man, alterity will be the feminine; the feminine – specifically, concretely – will be the Other. But this being the case, sexual difference no longer functions as an abstract *formal* structure; it is identified with the *content* of the feminine, and in a sense compromised by it, or swallowed up by it in such a way that it can no longer perform its metaphysical function. The feminine *is* the content of sexual difference – or sexual difference *is* feminine content: in this identity sexual difference becomes absorbed, that is, made immanent to, its content and the formal structure of difference which articulated/produced the possibility of transcendence is lost.

It is interesting that in the relatively short Preface added to the 1979 reprint of *Time and the Other*, Levinas devotes a disproportionate amount of space to the feminine and its attendant themes when compared to the actual length of the discussion in the original text. Perhaps aware of the emergent feminist responses to the treatment of the feminine here and in his later work, and as if to reply to the above objection, Levinas says the following of *Time and the Other*:

> The notion of a transcendent alterity – one which would open time – is first of all sought starting with an *alterity-content*, starting with femininity. Femininity – and one would have to see in what sense this can be said of masculinity or of virility; that is, of the differences between the sexes in general – appeared to me as a difference contrasting strongly with other differences, not merely as a quality, different from all others, but as the very quality of difference.[17]

With this (belated) suggestion of the possibility of a reversal of terms Levinas would seem to be attempting to re-inscribe the formal structure of sexual difference in its metaphysical function, that is by distancing it from any necessary connection with the feminine, a connection which would now be seen as merely contingent upon a masculine subject position. If 'the masculine' functions in the same way for a feminine subject, both positions could be reinterpreted on the basis of 'the differences between the sexes in general', an abstract metaphysical principle to which both would have access and of which both would have phenomenological attestation in the experience of their sexual counterpart.[18] However, it is difficult to see how this arrangement is possible without understanding 'the difference between the sexes' in terms of the specifications of a genus – the exact move for which Heidegger was earlier criticized. This would be, moreover, to ascribe to the relation between the sexes a structure of symmetry and reciprocity that would negate the philosophical work that the formal (apparently asymmetrical) structure is meant to do.

Yet the suggestion of the possibility of reversal is disingenuous anyway. It overlooks the extent to which the association of the feminine with sexual difference is not so much an accident of the early Levinasian text as a presupposition of it, an important component of the definition of the feminine insofar as that term may be employed functionally at all. To the extent that this conflation is an historical (theoretical and cultural) commonplace it is easy for it to pass unnoticed. The attempt to re-present the feminine as a term occupying a space which may, under other circumstances, be filled by the masculine, is an attempt to void it of its content and make it function as an abstract signifier, whilst at the same time disavowing the historical association of the masculine with the unsexed universal or neuter. The only way to make sense of Levinas's suggestion is to transform it into the form of a statement about what *ought* to be (the feminine *ought not* to be identified with sexual difference; the masculine *ought not* to masquerade as the unmarked neuter), but this would be a curious beginning for an allegedly phenomenological analysis. The suggestion — parenthetical and phrased in the most tentative, even sceptical, manner — is also disingenuous in another sense. The fact is that, despite this apparent reinvigoration of the idea in the 1979 Preface, the formal structure of sexual difference drops out of Levinas's work after *Time and the Other*, except when used in negative comparison with the structure of the relation of 'ethics'. Read carefully, this passage from the Preface says as much, in its use of the past tense.

The notion of the feminine also undergoes a significant rethinking in *Totality and Infinity*. Levinas retrospectively describes this as the attempt to think 'the ontological structure proper to femininity',[19] but it appears more obviously as a full account of the role of the feminine in the 'economy' of lived life according to the novel analyses of the book. The second of the four sections of *Totality and Infinity*, 'Interiority and Economy', is a phenomenological description of the being in the world of '*le moi*', or the ego. In contrast to the following section, 'Exteriority and the Face', it details the fundamental relation of the ego to its environment *before* the irruption of the Other, that is, before the ethical relation. Although Levinas teaches, later in the same text, that the ethical relation is absolutely primordial and grounds all possible relations in/with the world, the section on interiority and economy does read, especially given its place in the book, as an account of the before-ethics, or an account of the conditions of possibility for the ethical relation. This is perhaps due to no more than the exigencies of composition — one has to start somewhere, one has to put things in some sort of order. In any case, it should not be read as a chronicle of man's life in and movement beyond the state of nature. Any 'priority' or relations of conditioned/conditioning need to be read philosophically, not as an anthropological history.

For Levinas a condition for, or an essential characteristic of, the ethical relation is the fact of the so-called 'separation' of the ego. This separation will be maintained in the ethical relation – in a sense it is the very description of the ethical relation – and it has to be shown how this separation 'comes about' (*s'accomplit*) in the ego itself, that is, without reference to a correlative or reciprocal other. Furthermore, the separation of the ego – something akin to the achievement of the event of hypostasis in *Existence and Existents* and *Time and the Other* – is not to be thought negatively, as a privation or a lack; it is not to be thought in terms of need. The first half of Section II describes this separated ego and its relation to the world primarily in terms of *jouissance*, translated by Lingis as 'enjoyment'. But to say 'relation to the world' is not quite right, for *jouissance* is more a '*vivre de . . .*', a 'living from . . .' in which the world and the things in it are not conceived as objects or themes for the ego, but rather 'nourish' it: 'We live from "good soup", air, light, spectacles, work, ideas, sleep, etc. These are not objects of representation. We live from them.' *Jouissance* and *vivre de . . .* obviously imply some sort of dependence on the world, and Levinas does not deny that the ego has needs. These needs, however, are not simply a 'lack', and they are not primarily lived as suffering or as a curtailment of freedom. The human being thrives on, and is happy for, his needs, Levinas says. They are, precisely, enjoyed. A human being without needs would not be more happy, but outside of happiness and unhappiness. The needy ego loves its needs – this is *jouissance*: '*love of life*'.[20]

Jouissance, moreover is not an attribute of the ego. There is not first an ego which then enjoys; the ego crystallizes *in* enjoyment, or *jouissance* is the very accomplishment of 'atheist separation'. The ego does not 'come about' dialect-ically, in opposition to the world or the things in it, because enjoyment is (like its philosophical model, Hegel's 'desire') the annihilation or exploitation of otherness. The otherness of the world is negated by the ego and turned (back) into itself:

> Nourishment, as a means of invigoration, is the transmutation of the other into the Same, which is in the essence of enjoyment: an energy that is other, recognized as other, recognized, we will see, as sustaining the very act that is directed upon it, becomes, in enjoyment, my own energy, my strength, me. All enjoyment is in this sense alimentation.[21]

The literal ingestion of food to become part of the body of the ego serves as the model for all its relations with what is other, including representation, thematization, knowledge, and so on. In *jouissance* or *vivre de . . .* the ego is therefore realized not in opposition to the world but always only in reference to itself; it is accomplished as 'interiority': 'The separation of the Same is produced in the form of an inner life, a psychism.'[22]

The ego lives its happy dependence on the world as independence because, able to fulfil its needs, it fulfils them as if there were no tomorrow, for the sake only of enjoyment. This does not mean that the possibilities of indigence and suffering do not arise, just that indigence and suffering are not the ego's primordial way of being in the world. The ego's relation to the elements is a case in point. The elements are not experienced primarily as objects of representation, but as a milieu: one 'bathes' in them. Nevertheless, today's joys have their morrows.[23] Stressing continually that the love of life is always stronger than any *'inquiétude'*, any worry or disquiet in the continuation of life (*'Encore une minute, Monsieur le bourreau!'*; 'One minute more, Mr. Hangman!'[24]), the uncertainty of the morrow must even so be dealt with. Not simply a question of prudence or providing for the future (as in the morality tale of the grasshopper and the ants) attending to this concern gives the ego the opportunity to engage itself in relations with (rather than incorporation/annihilation of) exteriority, and in that way to rise from the condition of the beasts. According to Levinas, it is work, and the gathering of possessions, that will overcome, or at least delay, this uncertainty, but these in turn have their own requirement:

> In order that this future arise in its signification as a postponement and a *delay* in which *labour*, by mastering the uncertainty of the future and its insecurity and by establishing *possession*, delineates separation in the form of economic independence, the separated being must be able to recollect itself [*se recueillir*] and have representations. *Recollection* and *representation* are produced concretely as *habitation in a dwelling* or a Home.[25]

Se recueillir is to recollect oneself, gather one's thoughts, like a transcendental unity of representation, but one with its own transcendental condition: the dwelling or the home. The intimacy of the home, the grant of extraterritoriality for the ego (exemption or protection from the 'laws' of the elements), is itself assured through the welcome of the Other, revealed not as a shocking alterity but as 'gentleness'. This gentle Other is 'the feminine'. At first blush this would seem to be an echo of the feminine from Levinas's earlier work, *Autrui* par excellence. But in *Totality and Infinity* her alterity is at once qualified. There is a contradiction in the idea that the gentle welcome which makes the separation of the human possible comes from 'a first revelation of the Other', for as Levinas himself explains a few pages later, according to the analysis of Section I, the Other disrupts the solitude of the ego, it does not produce it; it is the Other that paradigmatically *prevents* the return to self.[26]

The overcoming of this contradiction lies in the description of an Other who does not simply reveal themselves in/as face, but who simultaneously withdraws and is absent, a simultaneity called 'discretion': 'And the other whose presence is discreetly an absence, with which is accomplished the primary hospitable welcome which describes the field of intimacy, is the Woman. The woman is the condition for recollection, the interiority of the Home, and inhabitation.' This face-to-face is not a relation that opens up the dimension of height, or transcendence. Such a relation (ethics), 'coextensive with the manifestation of the Other in the face, we call language. The height from which language comes we designate with the term teaching.'[27] *Autrui* in such a relation one might call a 'true' Other, the indiscreet Other, the Master, therefore the male Other, respectfully 'vous', coming from the dimension of height and, through language, my teacher. The Other who affords a welcome in the home, on the other hand, is:

> not the *you* [*le vous*] of the face that reveals itself in a dimension of height, but precisely the *thou* [*le tu*] of familiarity: a language without teaching, a silent language, an understanding without words, an expression in secret. The I–Thou in which Buber sees the category of interhuman relationship is the relation not with the interlocutor but with feminine alterity.[28]

Now elsewhere, on more than one occasion, Levinas is keen to distance himself from Buber's *je–tu* relation precisely because that relation, in its intimacy and exclusiveness, does not have the dimension of exteriority that would make it ethical.[29] The *tu* of this relation is not the *vous* of the ethical relation, does not command the same respect. Aligning the feminine Other with Buber's *tu* amounts, therefore, to an admission that the feminine Other is not a 'true' Other, for, according to Levinas's own rigorous demands, an Other with qualifications, is no 'Other' at all. The 'Other' does not admit of any relative designation.[30] The status of this qualified feminine Other is then problematic. *La Femme*, also therefore the wife, does not recollect, she is a condition for an other's recollection. She is enough of an other to fulfil her function as welcomer and household settler, but not so Other that she unsettles the ego; an Other domesticated and rendered docile. And whilst she apparently exercises her function of interiorization only on the ground of a 'full human personality', this is a full human personality 'which, however, in the woman, can be reserved so as to open up the dimension of interiority.'[31] In opening up the dimension of interiority the woman makes it possible for him (the subject) to labour and acquire property. However,

> in order that I am able to free myself from the very possession that the welcome of the Home establishes, in order that I be able to see things in themselves, that is, represent them to myself, refuse both enjoyment and possession, I must know how to *give* what I possess . . . . But for this I must

encounter the indiscreet face of the Other that calls me into question. The Other – the absolutely other – paralyses possession, which he contests by his epiphany in the face . . . . I welcome the Other who presents himself in my home by opening my home to him.[32]

No human or interhuman relations are possible with empty hands (no gift to give) or closed doors. No ethical relation is possible without the home which she has opened up for the ego in order that he may labour, gather possessions, and then welcome the (true) Other (*'absolument autre'*) into what has become his house – for although she may have been the original inhabitant, he is the proprietor. 'She' is the condition for the ethical relation, but is not herself part of it,[33] or part of the business of giving birth to the world, to human culture and human sociality. She is a conduit, playing a supporting role in the philosophical drama of the self-realization of the subject/ego, who on this account must be masculine.

One hardly needs to point out that this frank and unselfconscious account of the nature and the place of the feminine in *Totality and Infinity* is gratingly and irritatingly conservative, at times to the point of risibility, at other times just plain offensive. It causes Levinas's readers some considerable embarrassment. It is for this reason, one imagines, that Silvano Petrosino and Jacques Rolland, for example, in *La vérité nomade: Introduction à Emmanuel Levinas*, manage a whole subsection on 'Maison, possession, travail'[34] without any reference to the feminine or *la Femme*. Others simply rehearse Levinas's position, refraining from any critical or explanatory comment, as if unaware that there might be any reason, feminist or otherwise, to consider it further.[35] As if to anticipate future objections, Levinas himself, however, adds the following disclaimer to his discussion of the dwelling and its feminine welcome:

> Need one add that there is no question here of defying ridicule by maintaining the empirical truth or countertruth that every home *in fact* presupposes a woman? The feminine has been encountered in this analysis as one of the cardinal points [*l'un des points cardinaux*] of the horizon in which the inner life takes place – and the empirical absence of the human being of 'feminine sex' in a dwelling nowise affects the dimension of femininity which remains open there, as the very welcome of the dwelling.[36]

With this Levinas clearly rejects the idea that the notion of 'the feminine' refers to empirical women, but offers only a very weak explanatory definition instead: 'a cardinal point of the horizon in which the inner life takes place'. Some twenty years later, in speaking of the legacy of Heidegger's *Being and Time*, Levinas uses a few of the same words:

> The Heideggerian notions of finitude, being-there, being-toward-death,

etc., remain fundamental. Even if one frees oneself from the systematic rigours of this thought, one remains marked by the very style of *Sein und Zeit*'s analyses, by the 'cardinal points' [*les 'points cardinaux''*] to which the existential analytic refers.[37]

This is interesting in that it would imply that Levinas's account of the dwelling and its feminine welcome is an 'existential analytic', but it clarifies the meaning of the feminine very little.

Some commentators have taken Levinas's disclaimer in *Totality and Infinity* to be a simple statement of the intended metaphorical meaning of the feminine, a state of affairs which would allegedly separate it out from any reference to any literal (empirical) woman. Adriaan Peperzak, for example, glosses Levinas's words thus: 'we must understand that the "feminine" presence by which a building becomes a home is a metaphor for the discreet and silent presence of human beings for one another that creates a climate of intimacy indispensable for a dwelling'.[38] And although he later adds that this assertion of metaphoricity 'does not yet answer the question of whether it is a good metaphor, and why or why not',[39] the question remains unanswered. Even so, quite what Peperzak means to assert in claiming metaphorical status for the feminine is unclear. Presumably he would not be foolhardy enough to argue that, as a metaphor, the trope of the feminine has no connection whatsoever, no linguistic or cultural reference at all, to empirically existing women, as this would deprive the metaphor not just of its rhetorical force, but of its very sense: of any possibility of it functioning with any intended meaning at all. It seems to me that it would be reasonable to ask of any metaphor how it derives its force and what the implications are of its presence in a philosophical text. To fail to ask this of a metaphor as complex and loaded as that of the feminine is more than careless.[40] An insistence on the metaphorical status of the feminine is also forced to overlook the fact that Levinas speaks just as often of *la Femme*. The alterity which opens the dimension of interiority only does so, he says, 'on the ground of the full human personality which, in the woman, can be reserved'. This is a statement that it is very difficult to read metaphorically.

John Llewelyn – whose bibliography in his *Emmanuel Levinas* reveals an acquaintance with some of the feminist literature – negotiates the question of metaphoricity somewhat differently. Alive – indeed sympathetic – to the possibility of a feminist critique Llewelyn argues that 'certain avoidable difficulties, though by no means all difficulties, will be circumvented' if the reader is continually reminded ('it cannot be too often repeated') that the feminine and other familial terms are not reducible to their biological signification.[41] For Llewelyn, however, this does not amount to any simple distinction between the literality of the biological ground of the trope of the feminine, for example, and its metaphorical employment. Llewelyn's discussion of Levinas goes hand in hand with a sophisticated account of metaphoricity based on Derrida's justifiably influential deconstruction of the presumed opposition between literal ground or origin and metaphorical derivation in 'White Mythology'.[42] Furthermore, Llewelyn quotes Levinas quoting Karl Löwith quoting Bruno Snell to the effect that, in Llewelyn's words, 'instead of thinking of the extended or metaphorical as opposed to the literal or natural we should think of each use as an extension or "metaphor" of the other.'[43] Applied to the notion of the feminine, this means that one could – perhaps even should – equally understand what Llewelyn calls the 'biological signification' as the metaphorical one.

However, neither the assertion of the metaphorical status of the feminine (Peperzak) nor the problematization of the literal/metaphorical distinction (Llewelyn) actually deals with the central problem of the relation between the notion of the feminine and actual women. First, in distancing the feminine from any empirical or sociological referent, Levinas is *not* in fact asserting its metaphoricity but rather its status as a *philosophical* category. In *Time and the Other* and *Existence and Existents* the feminine is explicitly introduced, for example, as an *ontological* category that introduces a plurality into Being itself. As such, it is (functionally) indistinguishable from the formal structure of sexual difference. But as the formal indicator of the metaphysical principle of transcendence, the idea of sexual difference is, as argued above, compromised by its identification with the feminine, that is, with the 'alterity-content' of the latter. In later work, particularly in *Totality and Infinity*, the description of the specific, concrete content of the feminine will be made into a philosophical virtue insofar as it will be emphasized, rather than denied. However, this does entail that the pre-eminent place of the feminine in the metaphysics of transcendence be ceded. The feminine in Section II of *Totality and Infinity* is still, Levinas would insist, a philosophical category. As the condition of possibility for interiority, and so on, it might not be difficult to understand the philosophical function of the feminine; like the relationship between actual historical experience and the 'experience' of consciousness in Hegel's *Phenomenology*, it might not even be difficult to grasp the point that the text need not be understood literally, that is, that in reading philosophically a certain level of *abstraction* is constitutive. At the same time, the feminine is not a category so abstract that it can function wholly in abstraction from the content that distinguishes it from a merely functional 'X'. This is true for both immanent and external reasons; that is, both because the intimately welcoming role of the feminine would be negated by the impersonality of an 'X', and because the feminine, as a word or a concept, is only meaningful (and hence only available for use) in terms of its descriptive and/or ideological content. This is why, of course, it is precisely the feminine and not 'the masculine' or 'the androgynous' that plays the role of welcoming gentleness.

Llewelyn's much more sustained engagement with the question of the feminine through the problematization of metaphoricity does not avoid the above conclusion; indeed it *supports* it. Levinas's reference to Snell, which Llewelyn quotes, concerns Snell's comments on an Homeric comparison between the resistance of an army to attack and the resistance of a rock to water. The meaning of resistance, Snell apparently writes, cannot be assigned originally or naturally to either the human or the rock (that is, the meaning 'belongs' to neither literally, to be transferred to the other metaphorically). In Levinas's words: 'Resistance is neither a human privilege nor a rock's, just as radiance does not characterize a day of the month of May more authentically than it does the face of a woman. The meaning precedes the data [*les données*] and illuminates them.'[44] If Levinas perhaps says more with the last line than Snell means, it is this 'more' that is interesting. It would mean, for example, that the meaning of the notion of the feminine does not derive unilaterally from empirical women but precedes our understanding of the latter and illuminates it. The difficulty of arguing for a separation between the feminine in its philosophical employment and any reference to empirical women is thus compounded. The descriptive and/or ideological content of the notion of the feminine cannot simply be dismissed as unrepresentative of empirical women because how we understand what it is to be an empirical woman is *influenced* – to some extent, that is, *constituted* – by this (and other) notions of the feminine.

As Llewelyn's position unwittingly reveals, further investigation of the descriptive and/or ideological content of the notion of the feminine is therefore crucial. One might ask, for example, what place unquestioned ideological assumptions have in a philosophical text, and what the uncovering of those assumptions means, philosophically, for that text. If it should turn out that the assumptions are, on the other hand, not unquestioned but consciously and purposively employed, one might ask what the employment of such assumptions tells us about the philosophical project under discussion, and what cultural or political consequences it might entail.

The phenomenology of eros: the ambiguity of love

As the impossibility of separating out the descriptive content of the feminine from its function as a philosophical category becomes more and more evident in Levinas's work, the metaphysics of sexual difference will give way to an unabashed phenomenology of eros and of the feminine beloved. The presentation of this in Section IV of *Totality and Infinity* presents the reader with the further difficulty that the nature and the role of the feminine there is, in one aspect in particular, significantly different to the presentation in Section II. In fact, this is part and parcel of a more general interpretative difficulty with *Totality and Infinity*. Section III, 'Exteriority and the Face', especially Part B, 'Ethics and the Face', comprises a discussion of those themes which have popularly come to be seen as most characteristically 'Levinasian': 'Infinity', 'the face', 'ethics', 'asymmetry', 'the Other', and so on. For any reading with a stress on the 'ethical', this would seem to be the climax of the book. And yet Section IV, with its very title, claims to move 'Beyond the Face'. For the ethical reading, accustomed to thinking of 'the face' and 'ethics' *as* the 'beyond', what exactly is, or can be 'beyond the face'?

'Beyond the face' is transcendence. In one sense, Section IV, through the phenomenology of eros and the introduction of the idea of fecundity, articulates the metaphysical principle that is phenomenologically attested in 'ethics', as described in Section III. To the extent that it is, then, the metaphysical articulation of the 'truth' of phenomenology, the narrative structure of the book is clear. What is unclear, however, is why the phenomenology of *eros* is necessary, given that the formal structure of the idea of sexual difference is no longer operative. Why are the phenomenology of 'ethics' and the formal structure of the idea of infinity not sufficient for Levinas's philosophical purposes?

In Section IV of *Totality and Infinity*, eros emerges as a much more problematic phenomenon in comparison with its role in Levinas's earlier work. Its now ambivalent role, moreover, finds its parallel in the similarly ambivalent status of the feminine, which is given a descriptive content far beyond that in Section II. In this account, eros is profoundly and essentially – that is, by definition – *ambiguous*. The French noun *ambigu(ë)* has two main senses, the second of which is less evident in the cognate English translation, but which is probably the most important here. In both languages it refers chiefly to linguistic expression and means the possibility of having more than one interpretation, or uncertainty in interpretation. In French the word also means that in which two opposing qualities are united, or that which participates of two different natures. For Levinas, the ambiguity of love (*amour*)[45] lies not in the possibility of more than one interpretation, but in the necessity of simultaneous and contradictory ones which are not, however, synthesized or united. 'The metaphysical event of transcendence', he says, 'is not accomplished as love. But the transcendence of discourse is bound to love. We shall show how in love transcendence goes both further and less far than language.' True, love is directed towards *autrui*, but there is also the inevitability that love 'throws us back this side of immanence itself'. Love is thus an event situated at the limit of transcendence and immanence.[46] Such a formulation would be impossible *vis-à-vis* the face-to-face relation, but any and every contradiction is possible in love.

The aspect of immanence is attributed to the fact that in love, now characterized as voluptuosity [*la volupté*] and eros,

> Voluptuosity . . . aims not at the Other but at his voluptuosity: it is voluptuosity of voluptuosity, love of the love of the other . . . . If to love is

to love the love the Beloved [*l'Aimée*] bears me, to love is also to love oneself in love, and thus to return to oneself.

In love both desire and need, metaphysical desire and erotic desire, transcendence and concupiscence, coexist. Furthermore, the suggestion is not that now one, now the other, prevails but that both prevail and that this ambiguity and simultaneity is the very essence of love, 'constitutes the originality of the erotic which, in this sense, is *the equivocal par excellence.*' The aspect of transcendence, on the other hand, is attributed to the fact that love is a relation which also goes beyond the Other: 'This is why there filters through the face the obscure light coming from beyond the face, from what *is not yet*, from a future never future enough, more remote than the possible.' Love looks beyond *autrui* to 'the infinitely future, which is to be engendered',[47] fulfilling itself in fecundity, the sense and implications of which remain to be explicated.

The ambiguity of love is also the ambiguity of the love object, l'*aimé*, or rather '[e]piphany of the Beloved [*l'Aimé*], the feminine': *l'Aimée*.[48] Love, Levinas says, is directed at *autrui*:

> in his frailty . . . . To love is to fear for another, to come to the assistance of his frailty . . . . The epiphany of the Beloved [*l'Aimée*] is but one with her *regime* of tenderness. The *way* of the tender consists in an extreme fragility, a vulnerability. It manifests itself at the limit of being and non-being, as a soft warmth where being dissipates into radiance . . . disindividualizing and relieving itself of its own weight, already evanescence and swoon, flight into self in the very midst of its manifestation.[49]

The description thus far invokes again the characterization of the feminine in Section II, especially in its (her?) status as 'an event in the oecumenia of being – a delightful "lapse" of the ontological order.'[50] But at the same time in eros *l'aimée*, or the feminine, is something gross, an 'exorbitant ultramateriality', or non-signifying raw being – the latter bringing eros into association with the notion of the *il y a*.[51] She is at once too frail for this world and yet too much (a part) of it. She is a mystery, hidden, modesty itself, but also openly displayed in 'the exhibitionist nudity of an exorbitant presence . . . profaning and wholly profaned', immodesty and indecency par excellence:

> *The essentially hidden throws itself toward the light, without becoming signification* . . . . It [*elle*] refers to the modesty it has profaned without overcoming. The secret appears without appearing, but not because it would appear half-way, or with reservations, or in confusion. The simultaneity of the clandestine and the exposed precisely defines *profanation*. It appears in equivocation. But it is profanation that permits equivocation – essentially

erotic – and not the reverse . . . . The simultaneity or the equivocation of this fragility and this weight of non-signifyingness, heavier than the weight of the formless real, we shall term *femininity*.[52]

The erotic caress also reveals the ambiguity of love, or reveals *l'aimée* in her ambiguity. Never quite catching hold of anything, the caress has its correlate in the carnality of femininity, where her body 'quits the status of an existent [*l'étant*]':

> The Beloved, at once graspable but intact in her nudity, beyond object and face and thus beyond the existent, abides in virginity [*se tient dans la virginité*]. The feminine essentially violable and inviolable, the 'Eternal Feminine', is the virgin or an incessant recommencement of virginity, the untouchable in the very contact of voluptuosity, future in the present . . . . The virgin remains ungraspable, dying without murder . . . . The caress aims at neither a person nor a thing. It loses itself in a being that dissipates as though into an impersonal dream without will and even without resistance, a passivity, an already animal or infantile anonymity, already entirely at death.[53]

As the very idea of a 'phenomenology of eros' simply does not make sense unless it is read as referring to the sensuous and sexual experience of one person's body on/in another's, the reference to the 'eternal feminine' is confusing in its seemingly pointless abstraction. In an earlier attempt to explain what is meant by 'the mystery of the feminine', the same idea surfaced:

> this mystery of the feminine – the feminine: essentially other – [does not] refer to any romantic notions of the mysterious, unknown, or misunderstood woman. Let it be understood that if, in order to uphold the thesis of the exceptional place and position of the feminine in the economy of being, I willingly refer to the great themes of Goethe or Dante, to Beatrice and the *ewig Weibliches* [the eternal feminine], to the cult of *Woman* in chivalry and in modern society (which is certainly not explained solely by the necessity of lending a strong arm to the weaker sex) – if, more precisely, I think of the admirably bold [*admirablement hardies*] pages of Léon Bloy in his letters to his Fiancée, I do not want to ignore the legitimate claims of the feminism that presupposes all the acquired attainments of civilization.[54]

The reference to Bloy is particularly interesting. Many of Bloy's later letters to his fiancée are taken up with a description of the book he wishes to write (but presumably never did):

The basis of my book is this. For woman, a creature temporarily, *provision-ally* inferior, there are only two sorts of existence [*deux manières d'être*]: the most venerable motherhood or the name and the character of an instrument of pleasure; pure love, or impure love. In other words, Sainthood or Prosti-tution . . . . Do you understand, my darling, what, to the astonishment of mediocre souls, I want to show? It is: the miraculous connection which exists between the Holy Spirit and the most despicable, most despised, most corrupted of human creatures, the Prostitute.[55]

One could have chosen other passages. Some letters reflect, for example, the theme of Goethe's 'Eternal Womanhood'[56]: 'You will be, darling of my soul, my conscience and my guiding light, because through you I shall always see my Saviour and the beloved Spirit of my God.'[57] Others bear witness to a less religious passion: 'My affection for you is boundless. I am drunk, I am mad with love for you, my adored darling.'[58] That Levinas refers to Bloy in the section on eros, in the context of a discussion of the alterity and the mystery of the feminine in eros, indicates that what is peculiar to Bloy and singles him out from the others in Levinas's list is his insistence on both sides of the coin, as it were. Out of these great authors only Bloy stresses not only the *Sainteté* of woman but also her relation to the profane. Like Goethe, Bloy evokes what he calls the '*Esprit Saint*'[59] of woman, but unlike Goethe never fails also to speak of the whore in her, thus confirming (or perhaps inspiring) Levinas's view of the essential ambiguity of the feminine:

> at the same time that the dignity of this principle restores, if one may put it thus, a soul to the spirit, the feminine also reveals itself as the source of all decline. This appears in an ambivalence in which one of the most profound visions of the ambiguity of love is expressed.[60]

In a sense, as a purely descriptive historical psychology or sociology there is some truth to this dichotomy; it is, after all, consonant with the representa-tion of women behind the two 'currents' (affectionate and sensual) described in Freud's 1912 essay 'On the Universal Tendency to Debasement in the Sphere of Love'.[61] Given that, it is particularly obvious in this discussion that no reversal of genders could turn it into an abstract point about sexual differ-ence, or, as Levinas says, the differences between the sexes in general (one could not, that is, seriously say 'The masculine essentially violable and inviol-able, the "Eternal Masculine" is the virgin or an incessant recommencement of virginity'). The way in which the discussion of the ambiguity of love slides ineluctably into a discussion of the feminine as the epiphany of the equivocal elides the difference between the two. The whole account of the phenomen-ology of eros depends on the description of the ambiguity of love, and this ambiguity is crucially manifested in the ambiguity/equivocality of the feminine. The particular details of the account of the feminine cannot be excised, as they are indispensable to the argument. Furthermore, what is ascribed to the feminine, both its role and its attributes, are ascribed precisely *to the feminine*. As in *Time and the Other*, where the feminine was said to bear alterity 'as essence', 'Judaism and the Feminine Element' uses similarly unequivocal language: 'Woman is *complete* immodesty, down to the nakedness of her little finger. She is the one who, *par excellence*, displays herself, the *essentially* turbulent, the *essentially* impure. Satan, says an extremeist text, was created with her.'[62]

The ambiguity of the feminine beloved (*l'aimée*) – analytically indistinguishable from the ambiguity of eros itself – means that her 'face' gets lost or shadows over. If the face is like the calm surface of a motionless pond, the movement of eros is a rippling and 'troubling' of this surface: 'In the feminine face the purity of expression is already troubled by the equivocation of the voluptuous. Expression is inverted into indecency, already close on to the equivocal which says less than nothing, already laughter and raillery.' Elsewhere, the feminine is described as effecting an 'inversion of the face', a 'disfigurement'.[63] Because the feminine does not signify as face, the relation of the lover towards her is not, apparently, one towards an adult human being at all. Levinas makes this particularly clear in the following extraordinary passage:

> The beloved is opposed to me not as a will struggling with my own or subject to my own, but on the contrary as an irresponsible animality which does not speak true words. The beloved [*l'aimée*], returned to the stage of infancy without responsibility – this coquettish head, this youth, this pure life 'a bit silly' – has quit her status as a person. The face fades, and its impersonal and inexpressive neutrality is extended, in ambiguity, into animality. The relations with the Other are enacted in play; one plays with the Other as with a young animal.[64]

Once again, the association of femininity with infancy and animality has a rich heritage, in the letters of Léon Bloy, for example, who repeatedly addresses his adult lover as 'my beloved child . . . . Be innocent (modest, pure, unaffected), my beloved, innocent like a child, a dove.'[65]

Of course, it would be ludicrous to ascribe to Levinas, the man, the view that he does not believe women to have human status. Nevertheless, the implication of these texts is indeed that the feminine is opposed to the human in a way that 'the masculine' is not.[66] To the extent that Levinas attaches an increasing importance to the distinction between the truly 'human' in its apparent sexual neutrality from the being of the human in his or her sexuate incarnation or the human being under the mark of sexual difference, the unequal status of the feminine and the masculine becomes more and more apparent. Only the feminine being appears in her sexuate incarnation or under the mark of sexual difference. As a consequence the human and the masculine are conjoined in such a way that the former loses its claim to neutrality.

Levinas's argument is, unsurprisingly, clearest in the two essays – 'Judaism and the Feminine Element' (1960) and 'And God Created Woman' (1972) – which take 'woman' or the feminine as their central theme. Speaking of the place of woman in Judaism (both theologically and culturally understood, it would appear), she will have, Levinas says 'the destiny of human being, in which her femininity will merely figure as an attribute . . . . The femininity of woman can neither deform nor absorb her human essence.' The explanation of this, however, works by aligning 'human essence' with the masculine: '"Woman is called *ishah* in Hebrew, for she comes from man – *ish*", the Bible recounts. The Sages seize on this etymology to affirm the unique dignity of Hebrew, which expresses the very mystery of creation, that woman is derived quasi-grammatically from man.' Now Levinas does not say that he agrees with the Sages on this point: 'A very different derivation from biological development!', he remarks immediately afterwards. But perhaps the main point of the essay, where it *is* clear that Levinas is expressing a view with which he agrees, is the idea that 'The relation of person to person precedes all relation.' In particular, he is concerned to affirm that this sociality precedes the erotic relation. In a quick gloss on *Genesis* 2, 21–23 (the creation of Eve from Adam's 'rib') Levinas says:

> Did she come from Adam's rib [*d'une côte d'Adam*]? Was not this rib rather a *side* [*un côté*] of Adam, separated while Adam, still androgynous, was sleeping . . . . 'Flesh of my flesh and bone of my bone', then, means an identity of nature between woman and man, an identity of destiny and dignity, and also a subordination of sexual life to the personal relation which is equality itself.[67]

This interpretation explains the apparent contradiction with the earlier *Genesis* 1, 27, where 'male and female created He them'. In creating Adam 'male and female' the priority of the human is affirmed over the sexual, which is the splitting of androgynous Adam into Adam and Eve. Accordingly, if, as the Sages maintain, Woman (*Isha*) is derived from Man (*Ish*), this would be to say not that masculine Man was primary, but generic Man, the human. This is consonant with conventional Hebrew usage, where '*Ish*' apparently refers not only to the masculine gendered person and the husband, but also to a person generically, without emphasis on gender, or to each person, everyone, or someone. '*Ish*' can also mean 'a mortal', and it was of course the curse of all mortals that they should know death as their proper punishment for disobedience. Adam is told that he will 'return unto the ground; for out of it wast thou taken: for dust thou art, and unto dust shalt thou return.' (*Genesis*, 4, 19.) Adam, which means 'man' before it comes to signify a proper name, is so called because he is of the earth ('*adama*'), to which he will return. Adam, as man, is therefore *Ish*, all mortals, and the derivation of Eve (or woman) from Adam (or man) is then woman's derivation from their common humanity.

The text of 'And God Created Woman' is also explicit in the assertion of the view that the human precedes the division into masculine and feminine, and is explained first of all with recourse to the same etymology: 'The meaning of the feminine will . . . become clear against the background of a human essence, the *Isha* from the *Ish*. The feminine does not derive from the masculine; rather, the division into feminine and masculine – the dichotomy – derives from what is human.'[68] Sexual difference is very clearly a designation of the human, which latter has priority: the sexual is only an accessory of the human. Accordingly, both Wyschogrod and Chanter would be right to argue that 'woman', shall we say, would appear both in her capacity as human and then, and only secondarily, *qua* feminine.[69] The role of the feminine in the dwelling, in which her full human personality is held in abeyance, and the non-signifying face of the feminine in eros would be secondary designations of the woman, primarily human.

This would only be right, however, if it were indeed the case that *Ish*, man, really did refer to the neutrality of the human, and was not compromised by the rather obvious fact that, being also the designation of the masculine man, it did not attest to a certain priority of the masculine. Such a reading would also have to overlook the surely not inconsequential fact that throughout this essay, and consonant with Levinas's work as a whole, woman is consistently aligned with sexual difference in such a way that the attempt to install her within the human is continually belied. 'Man' never appears in his sexual specificity, *qua* masculine man, and the arrival on the scene of sexual difference (and the erotic) coincides with the creation of woman, in her peculiarity.

In the creation myth of *Genesis*, despite 1, 27 – 'male and female created He them' – woman is very clearly created after man, second after the first. There is little that even the most subtle Talmudist can do to get around this fact. Indeed it is this fact that is the root of the essay 'And God Created Woman'. Having discussed two apparently contradictory Talmudic commentaries Levinas says:

> The problem, in each of the paragraphs we are commenting on at this moment, is in reconciling the humanity of men and women with the hypothesis of a masculine spirituality in which the feminine would not be an equal term but a corollary. Feminine specificity or the difference between the sexes which it manifests would not be, from the outset, on the same plane as the oppositions which constitute Spirit. Daring question:

how can the equality of sexes stem from the priority of the masculine? This, let us note in passing, removes us from the simple notion of complimentarity.[70]

The first sentence refers to a masculine spirituality; that is, a spirituality assumed to be masculine because the association between the feminine and the erotic, concupiscence, has already been presumed. In the second sentence the phrase 'feminine specificity' or 'the difference between the sexes which it manifests' further reinforces the troubling incompatibility between the feminine and (masculine) spirituality: masculine spirituality is 'the high', opposed to 'the low', or carnal concupiscence, or eros, or sexual difference, that is, the feminine. Given this incompatibility, a daring question arises: how can the equality of the sexes stem from the priority of the masculine? Answer: it cannot. Rav Abbahu (not Levinas) is said to explain it thus:

From the beginning [God] wanted two separate and equal beings. But that was impossible; this initial independence of two equal beings would no doubt have meant war.[71] It had to be done not strictly according to justice, which means, in effect, that one would have to be subordinated to the other.[72] There had to be a difference which did not affect equity: a sexual difference and, hence, a certain preeminence of man, a woman coming later, and as woman, an appendage of the human . . . . Society was not founded on purely divine principles: the world would not have lasted. Real humanity does not allow for an abstract equality, without some subordination of terms.[73]

Levinas's provisional conclusion is, then, that '[i]t is thus not in terms of equality that the entire question of woman can be discussed. From now on our text will seek to show the importance of a certain inequality, be it only a matter of custom.'[74] This inequality, the priority of the masculine over the feminine is affirmed, in essence, as the priority of the human, the social or the ethical, over the sexual or eros. In this hierarchy the feminine is in second place, but

[i]t is not woman who is thus slighted. It is the relation based on sexual difference which is subordinated to the interhuman relation . . . . Maybe man precedes – by a few centuries – the woman in this elevation. From which a certain – provisional? – priority of man. Maybe the masculine is more directly linked to the universal, and maybe masculine civilization has prepared, above the sexual, a human order in which a woman enters, completely human.[75]

Speaking as a man

There can be no doubt, then, that there is a significant shift in the role and the status of sexual difference, eros and the feminine in Levinas's work. Although the texts themselves give no explanation for this shift, it has already been suggested that it is the part that sexual difference and the feminine are called upon to play in the metaphysics of transcendence that provides the clue. It is as a formal structure of non-dialectical difference – in the exorbitant moment of this disjunctive and unassimilable difference, beyond the order of the genus – that sexual difference is first evoked as an approach to the affirmation of transcendence. Furthermore, it is precisely sexual difference and not just 'difference itself' that is evoked because the latter is too insubstantial a concept to play this role. Difference needs a content – an unsublatable relation – not only in order to be able to mark the infinite diremption between its terms, but also that it may signify phenomenologically in the text, in order to play its role convincingly as part of a philosophical argument. (If one were also to say, in other words, that difference needs a content in order to function here rhetorically, it would have to be understood that 'rhetoric' is not the other of philosophy.) Sexual difference apart, this same need conditions the use of the idea of the Other (*autrui*), as opposed to the more abstract 'otherness'.

Vis-à-vis sexual difference and its content, it becomes immediately clear, however, that this 'difference' is all on one side; this difference is, as it were, full of the feminine, or the feminine is this difference itself. As such sexual difference, identified with the *content* of the feminine can no longer function as a *formal* structure indicative of transcendence. The references to sexual difference – the metaphysics of sexual difference – give way to the much more detailed phenomenology of eros and the feminine, a phenomenology in which the specificity of content is no longer philosophically compromising but essential, indeed wholly constitutive. That the identification of the feminine and sexual difference is a presupposition rather than an achievement of the Levinasian text – a presupposition which signals not just a socio-cultural assumption but also the conceptual content of these words – means that Levinas's own brief (and, it must be said, rather half-hearted) suggestions that the analysis might work in reverse (in relation to the masculine) or in abstraction from its specific content (in relation to 'the difference between the sexes in general') fall flat. The impossibility – indeed the comedy – of any such reversal in the discussion of the feminine in *Totality and Infinity* is clear. Here, then, to avoid the very crassest reading of the place of the feminine in the dwelling as an affirmation that a woman's place is in the home, Levinas stresses the status of the feminine and even, we are to believe, 'the woman' as philosophical categories – a position that some of his commentators prefer to understand as the 'metaphorical' nature of the words. Even *as* philosophical categories, however, the feminine and the woman cannot be dissociated from the empirical content which makes them meaningful and available for philosophical employment. If this were not true then something – anything – else could function as substitutes for them without interfering with both the substance and the tone of the argument. This is obviously not the case; furthermore, it is interesting to note the extent to which here the tone *is* the substance of the argument.

But given the above, is it now so sure that Levinas's texts *can* avoid provoking the 'crassest' reading? Possibly the first and certainly the most famous feminist criticism of Levinas – one which appears to some as, precisely, crass – appears as a footnote to the Introduction of Simone de Beauvoir's *The Second Sex*[76]. Early on, her frank assertion of the state of the relations between the sexes as one in which man is posited as the Absolute, the subject, and woman as the Other[77] is justified and illustrated with reference to Levinas, quoting those passages from *Time and the Other* in which the prototypical alterity of the feminine is affirmed. Now at first sight these would seem to be criticisms easily dismissed by simply pointing out the fact that de Beauvoir has made a gross error of interpretation in failing to see that what Levinas means by the term 'Other' is not at all what de Beauvoir means by it. De Beauvoir equates the Other with the inessential, but, as Tina Chanter says, if 'we understand Levinas's statement that alterity accomplishes itself as the feminine in the context of the priority Levinas gives to alterity, otherness and exteriority'[78] we would see his text, *contra* de Beauvoir, as a prioritizing of the feminine over the masculine.[79] Failing to see this, failing to address the passages she quotes within this broader Levinasian context, de Beauvoir, says Chanter, 'shows herself unwilling to take up the challenge [Levinas] is making to philosophies of consciousness.'[80] Robert John Scheffler Manning similarly defends Levinas against de Beauvoir's attack, and in much the same way; that is, by trying to show how de Beauvoir has misunderstood the Levinasian project: 'Beauvoir is clearly mistaken when she accuses Lévinas of affirming "masculine privilege" by seizing the right to name and label what is female and feminine. This is, in fact, exactly what Lévinas's idea of the alterity and mystery of the feminine is attempting to oppose.'[81]

The resonances, however, of de Beauvoir's quarrel do not end here, and her seemingly naive complaints point to a more general problematic that these initial responses do not acknowledge. De Beauvoir's criticism of Levinas is in fact two-fold. First, she takes issue with him for writing from an explicitly masculine standpoint, 'deliberately taking a man's point of view', such that his description, which is intended to be objective, is in fact an assertion of masculine privilege. Second, and which she also takes to be 'an assertion of masculine privilege', she thinks that the role into which he has cast the feminine denies woman a full subjectivity. A slightly later passage from *Time and the Other*, also quoted in *The Second Sex*, is de Beauvoir's evidence for this second argument: 'The existent is accomplished in the "subjective" and in "consciousness"; alterity is accomplished in the feminine. This term is on the same level as, but in meaning opposed to, consciousness.'[82] What de Beauvoir means by Levinas's 'masculine standpoint' is perhaps not immediately clear. For some critics — and this would include Levinas's advocates on this point — de Beauvoir was mistaken in assuming that Levinas could have done anything other than to 'speak from a masculine standpoint', or 'take a man's point of view'. For has not the phantasmatic ideal of a pure stance of objectivity, uncontaminated by history, personality or prejudice, itself been revealed as perhaps the greatest of the prejudices of the philosophers? Yet while history, context and tradition, to name but a few, are readily avowed as essential to any understanding of any given philosophy, it is not therefore the case that philosophical discourse today is willing and eager to consider the gender of a text's author as a necessary, if not sufficient, condition for understanding — that is, when that author is not a woman. That much philosophy has been written from 'a masculine standpoint' has been covered over by the tendency of the masculine to represent the absolute human type from which the feminine is thought to be a deviation or upon which she is parasitic. Of course, de Beauvoir herself was not slow in recognizing this:

> A man never begins by presenting himself as an individual of a certain sex; it goes without saying that he is a man. The terms masculine and feminine are used symmetrically only as a matter of form, as on legal papers. In actuality the relation of the two sexes is not quite like that of two electrical poles, for man represents both the positive and the neutral . . . . it is understood that the fact of being a man is no peculiarity.[83]

Masculinity is allowed to remain largely unmarked precisely because 'he' represents an alleged neutrality or universality. A woman philosopher, on the other hand, is a different thing (as is a feminist one). Thus François Mauriac, on reading *The Second Sex*, was able to remark to an author from *Les Temps Modernes*, 'I have learned all about your boss's vagina',[84] while Sartre's misogyny and/or gynophobia in *Being and Nothingness* presumably did not warrant remark. Sartre's 'masculine point of view' is rarely mentioned (not even by de Beauvoir) as it is presumed to be everyone's point of view, whereas de Beauvoir's 'feminine point of view' is evidence enough of the partiality (non-universality) of her text.

These comments, then, point to a double fault: both the failure to remark on the specificity of the masculine, and the failure (shared by de Beauvoir) to see specificity as anything other than a regrettable failure of objectivity. De Beauvoir performs a necessary service when she points out the masculine specificity of Levinas's text (would that she had also turned her critical eye on Sartre), but for some she is not on strong ground in supposing that it could have been otherwise. Indeed, *contra* de Beauvoir, it could be argued that the obviousness of this specificity in Levinas's work (and not just in *Time and the Other*) marks him out as a honourable exception in a dishonourable and dishonest tradition.[85] Derrida, for example, in 'Violence and Metaphysics', asks the reader to note, 'in passing', that

> *Totality and Infinity* pushes the respect for dissymmetry so far that it seems to us impossible, essentially impossible, that it could have been written by a woman. Its philosophical subject is man (vir) . . . . Is not this principled impossibility for a book to have been written by a woman unique in the history of metaphysical writing?[86]

This and other questions, held in abeyance in 'Violence and Metaphysics', were to be taken up again by Derrida in his second essay on Levinas, 'At This Very Moment in This Work Here I Am' (1980).[87] For if this later piece is much more critical of Levinas *vis-à-vis* the feminine, the comments in the last footnote of 'Violence and Metaphysics' could be read as praise. If it was possible that any other book in the history of metaphysical writing could have been written by a woman, that would be because those books appear to be written from the objective, that is neutral, standpoint that de Beauvoir apparently demands. But this would be deceptive; the appearance of neutrality would in fact veil a covert masculine standpoint (assuming, as Derrida seems to assume, that those books were all written by men). Because of the treatment of the feminine as a mystery to him, Levinas, however, leaves us in no doubt that his books were written by a man, from a masculine standpoint, which is altogether more honest.

On the other hand, perhaps that is not what Derrida meant at all. It is hard to attribute such an unpersuasive argument to the author of 'At This Very Moment'. It would have taken a profoundly inattentive reader not to have noticed, until 1964, any other single text in the history of metaphysical writing that bore the stamp of its masculine provenance. To persist with a 'positive' reading of Derrida's last footnote, the best that one could say is that Levinas is not concerned to dissimulate the position from which he writes, to hide the fact that he is writing from 'a masculine standpoint'. But this would be an unreservedly positive move in only two scenarios: either if 'a masculine standpoint' was in itself a good thing, or if it was as well that the reader be warned about this 'masculine standpoint' because there was something further to say about it.

On balance, then, if it is impossible that either *Time and the Other* or *Totality and Infinity* could have been written by a woman, this is a matter deserving fuller investigation rather than congratulation. The obviousness of Levinas's masculine specificity in his philosophical texts might indeed make him something of an exception (though by no means as unique as Derrida suggests), but not necessarily an honourable one. De Beauvoir's first criticism of Levinas, then, still remains to be explored. Granted that he could not have written as if in a social-sexual vacuum, granted that he does write (amongst other things) as a man (this man), what is it that he says 'as a man'? Are there different ways to write 'as a man'? And what is the significance of his 'writing as a man' to his philosophy quite generally?

First, if the association of the feminine with sexual difference is one already in circulation – if the feminine is marked as sexual difference as it is in *Time and the Other* – the masculine must be or remain sexually unmarked and 'man' can lay claim to the universal representation of the human, as it very clearly does in, for example, 'Judaism and the Feminine Element' and 'And God Created Woman'. Thus it is not only the feminine which carries with it the weight of accumulated associations, but the masculine too, and when, as de Beauvoir claims, Levinas 'writes like a man' this does not necessarily mean, as Derrida suggests it could, that '[h]is signature thus assumes the sexual mark, a remarkable phenomenon in the history of philosophical writing, if the latter has always been interested in occupying that position without re-marking upon it or assuming it on, without signing its mark.'[88] In writing like a man in *Time and the Other*, Levinas rather *takes his cue* from the history of philosophical writing and, in sliding together the feminine and sexual difference, assumes the position of the unmarked, allegedly neuter 'man', in which there is no peculiarity.

Second, de Beauvoir's other complaint that Levinas denies woman a position of full subjectivity rings loudly in the ears when reconsidering Levinas's claim, in Section II of *Totality and Infinity*, that woman is able to (indeed, must) reserve her 'full human personality' in order to open up the dimension of interiority in the dwelling for the subject coded as masculine. Even if, as Levinas says, this is possible only because she does indeed have a full human personality to reserve, the consistently argued distinction between the feminine (as representative of sexual difference) and the human – the insistence that 'man' (*Ish*, Adam) represents the human as opposed to the specificity of the feminine/sexual difference – makes it difficult to see how this claim does not continually undermine and contradict itself. The fact is that the feminine is opposed to the human in a way that the masculine is not.

Third, *contra* Derrida, it is not at all impossible that *Totality and Infinity* could have been written by a woman, and there is no necessity that a man should write like this. If it is significant that Levinas 'writes like a man' this is an *ideological* rather than biological position, and thus one equally available to a woman. Its significance, then, concerns Levinas's philosophical project, not his sex. In other words, what is important is not that it is written by a man, but what it is that this man writes, although the 'writing as a man' defence tends to wash over this latter by diverting attention to the rather obvious textual fact of the former.

To return to an earlier question, if this analysis has uncovered that Levinas's 'writing like a man' reveals not that he is a man (that was hardly in question), but that he employs or enacts a certain ideological content (in particular the conflation of the feminine with sexual difference and with eros), it may now be asked what part this ideological content plays in his philosophical project and whether, in particular, it is essential to his philosophical claims. As previously noted, the climax of *Totality and Infinity* is 'Beyond the Face', and the phenomenology of eros and the discussion of the feminine, which appears in this section, seems to have a crucial role to play. Philosophically, the most important moment is the contention that '[t]he fecundity of the I is its very transcendence'.[89] The explanation of this assertion is the most explicit working out and justification of Levinas's central metaphysical claim. The role of eros and the feminine must now be re-examined in this context.

CHAPTER THREE

Paternal Fecundity: Sons and Brothers

Thus far, in speaking of a shift in the role and status of eros, sexual difference, and the feminine, the implication has been that these once enjoyed a philosophical priority in Levinas's work which is later ceded. Levinas's brief retrospective comments appear to confirm this. In an interview from 1985, for example, he reflects on the role assigned to the feminine in his early work in comparison with his contemporary position:

> At the time of my little book called *Time and the Other*, I used to think that femininity was this modality of alterity – this 'other genre'[1] – and that sexuality and eroticism were this non-indifference to the other, irreducible to the formal alterity of terms in a *totality*. Today I think that one must go back even further and that the exhibition of nudity and the imperative demand of the face of the Other make up this modality which the . . . feminine already presupposes: *the proximity of the neighbour* is non-formal alterity.[2]

As with the 1979 preface to *Time and the Other*, the use of the past tense is pointed.[3] Readers like Tina Chanter have wanted to stress Levinas's emphasis of the theme of femininity in the 1979 preface,[4] but the references there to masculinity and sexual difference in general in fact function more effectively as a de-emphasis. No longer unique, what Levinas once called 'the exceptional role and place of the feminine',[5] has now been abdicated. In a closely related move, the argument for a subordination of sexual difference to what one might call ethical difference[6] – already evident in 'Judaism and the Feminine Element' in 1960 – often plays itself out as a demotion of the feminine: 'the feminine as such is only secondary. Man and woman, in their authentic humanity, work together as responsible beings. The sexual is only an accessory of the human.'[7]

In terms of Levinas's fundamental project, this apparent shift was read in the previous chapter as the recognition of the failed attempt to locate the structure of transcendence in sexual difference, a failure explained by the compromising 'content' of sexual difference in its identification with the feminine. Accordingly, the structure of transcendence would now have to be sought elsewhere, and in *Totality and Infinity* it is found in 'fecundity'. It is also the case, however, that the notion of fecundity is already present – albeit inchoately – in the earlier texts, a fact which problematizes the alleged priority of the feminine, eros and sexual difference at any time. This is significant for two reasons. First, it bears witness to a remarkable continuity and philosophical consistency in Levinas's work over a 50 year period in terms of the basic project of a metaphysics of transcendence. Second, it casts a different, critical light on the various feminist appropriations of the early discussions of the feminine which now need to be examined in this light.

Paternity and filiality

The problem to which the notion of fecundity answers was already articulated in 1935, most explicitly in the final words of *De l'évasion*: 'It is a question of leaving being by a new route, at the risk of overturning certain notions which to common sense and popular wisdom seem to be self-evident.'[8] When this 'other way' is thought through the notion of *fecundity* it transpires that 'getting out of being' is not the impossible task of leaving being behind, but of abandoning a certain thinking of being which Levinas calls 'Parmenidean'.[9] The major exposition of how this takes place appears in Section IV of *Totality and Infinity*, immediately after the discussion of the ambiguity of love and the feminine. That these themes are linked is not in question, but *how* they are linked is, and commentators have interpreted the issue differently.[10]

Levinas himself often speaks of eros and fecundity as if the two were identical. He complains, for example, that its relegation to the sphere of biology has obscured the ontological importance of sexuality, and then characterizes the latter in almost the same terms as the 'ontological category' of fecundity.[11] But there is more evidence to suggest that they should be separated out as distinct structures. Even in *Existence and Existents*, where the distinction between eros and fecundity is perhaps the least clear, the text already suggests that the phenomenology of eros has in no way exhausted what it is possible to say about fecundity. It is in the erotic relation that intersubjectivity is achieved, Levinas says, but this asymmetric relation is different to the reciprocity of civilization, called 'fraternity', which is said to be dependent on 'the intermediary of the father', an as yet enigmatic reference. Again he stresses the originality of the erotic relation where 'transcendence can be conceived as something radical', but goes on to end this section (the last, before the conclusion) with another suggestive promise: 'Asymmetrical intersubjectivity is the locus of a transcendence in which the subject, while preserving its structure, has the possibility of not inevitably returning to itself, the possibility of being fecund and (to anticipate what we shall examine later) having a son.'[12]

As Levinas explains later in *Totality and Infinity*, this transcendence has never adequately been thought in the philosophical traditions of the West, and has always appeared as an impossible contradiction:

As classically conceived, the idea of transcendence is self-contradictory. The subject that transcends is swept away in its transcendence; it does not transcend itself. If, instead of reducing itself to a change of properties, climate, or level, transcendence would involve the very identity of the subject, we would witness the death of substance.[13]

To find a way of making this contradiction tolerable, or to find a way between the two stools of death and the egoistic return to the self-same, was, to recall, the project outlined in the untitled first pages of Section IV of *Totality and Infinity*. This transcendence is not achieved in the erotic relation with the feminine because love is ambiguous, 'an event situated at the limit of immanence and transcendence', where this aspect of immanence is ultimately compromising. Eros without issue oscillates between 'the beyond of desire and the "this side" of need [*l'au-delà du désir et l'en deçà du besoin*]', an ambiguity which must be decisively overcome if transcendence is not to be a sham. For Levinas, the overcoming of ambiguity is achieved in fecundity: '[eros] takes place beyond all pleasure, all power, beyond all war with the freedom of the other, because amorous subjectivity is transubstantiation itself. This unparalleled relation between two substances, where a *beyond substances* is exhibited, is resolved [*se résout*] in paternity.'[14]

'*Résoudre*' is a polyvalent word, but however one chooses to read it the implication is that, in some sense, eros 'terminates' in paternity or fecundity: 'Like need, *Eros* is bound up with a subject identical with itself, in the logical sense. But the inevitable reference of the erotic to the future in fecundity reveals a radically different structure.'[15] This movement *through* eros *to* fecundity was already signalled in the trajectory of *Existence and Existents*. In familiar fashion, the hint given there, 'in anticipation', is more fully worked out in *Time and the Other*, in the last section, in which the exposition of the achievement of transcendence in fecundity is clearly different in kind from the previous account of the erotic relation with the feminine.[16] The section begins with the now familiar problem of transcendence:

> I am going to return to the consideration that led me from the alterity of death to the alterity of the feminine . . . . How, in the alterity of a you [*un toi*], can I remain I, without being absorbed or losing myself in that you? . . . *This can happen only in one way: through paternity.*[17]

Again and again it is stressed that, while eros is indeed the necessary route to transcendence, only fecundity (the relation between the father and the son) is its achievement.

The originality of the relation of fecundity becomes evident in the details of its exposition, for which Levinas often uses the same words in both *Time and the Other* and *Totality and Infinity*. In the 1979 preface to *Time and the Other*,

Levinas says that the analysis there already pointed 'beyond being', but this, as mentioned above, refers not to an impossible 'beyond' in the sense of an outside of being, but the abandoning of an apparently 'Parmenidean' notion of being as One to which we owe 'our' logic and which is the primary of those notions named in *De l'évasion* as seemingly self-evident but nevertheless to be overcome. The apparently indissoluble tie between the One and being leads, Levinas says, to the tendency always 'to imagine existing in an existent, one existent. Being *qua* being is for us monadic. Pluralism appears in Western philosophy only as a plurality of subjects that exist. Never has it appeared in the existing of those existents . . . . Unity alone is ontologically privileged.'[18] In other words, unity and multiplicity are always thought as logically incompatible, hence the opposition dramatized in antiquity as the feud between the schools of Parmenides and Heraclitus. The radicality of fecundity lies not in an overcoming of this opposition, nor in a simple refusal of it. Rather, both unity and multiplicity will be conserved, such that the relation of fecundity or paternity is described with a flurry of 'logical' contradictions:

> Paternity is the relationship with a stranger who, entirely while being Other, is myself . . . . The son, in effect, is not simply my work, like a poem or an artifact, neither is he my property . . . . Neither the notion of cause nor the notion of ownership permit one to grasp the fact of fecundity. I do not *have* my child, I *am* in some way my child. But the words 'I am' here have a significance different from an Eleatic or Platonic significance. There is a multiplicity and a transcendence in this verb 'to exist', a transcendence that is lacking in even the boldest existentialist analysis.[19]

The child is a stranger to the father (is *l'autrui*), and yet he *is* the father; he is 'me a stranger to myself.' In the son the father both remains himself and yet becomes other than himself, accomplishing the demand of transcendence that the self be not annihilated (either in death or in the collectivity, the state) and yet not simply return to the egoity of the self-same. The relation with the son in fecundity effects the very *transubstantiation* of the subject. The two opposing poles of egoity and totality have seemed to be the only options only because transcendence has been thought according to the ontological hegemony of the One, which could also be called the ontological hegemony of the Same. Fecundity, however, 'evinces a unity that is not opposed to multiplicity, but, in the precise sense of the term, engenders it.'[20]

In the preface to *Totality and Infinity* Levinas describes the book as 'a defence of subjectivity' founded in the idea of infinity.[21] This not only refers to the idea of infinity opened up in the face of the Other, but also to the infinition of time opened up in fecundity. In the son there opens a new future for the father, a future for which the father cannot account (*rendre compte*) by himself. The relation with the son opens for the father an absolute future or infinite time which overflows the destiny of any self-same ego. The father outlives himself in the son but the time of fecundity, though infinite, is not thereby continuous: 'The reciprocity of paternity, filiality, the father-son relation, designates a relation of rupture and a recurrence [*un recours*] at the same time.' Infinite time is ruptured by birth and death, and yet because the son in a sense *is* the father each is not sealed in their own separate time or destiny: '[Eros] goes toward a future which *is not yet* and which I will not merely grasp, but I *will be*.' The future of the ego, then, lies in the possibility of its 'transcending absolutely in fecundity.' In this sense, paternal fecundity is also said to be that which makes a discontinuous history possible; the son (*le fils*) is the thread (*le fil*) of history The discontinuous but infinite time of the father and the son forestalls old age or senescence (*la vieillesse*) with an incessant renewal through the youth of the son:

> To be infinitely means to be produced in the mode of an I that is always at the origin, but that meets with no trammels to the renewal of its substance, not even from its very identity. Youth as a philosophical concept is defined thus.[22]

To the extent that the elaboration of the pre-eminence of fecundity over eros is also a downgrading, as it were, of the feminine, there is, as even the least perceptive reader will have noticed, a decisive shift into a masculine metaphoric. However, unlike the discussion of the feminine in the sections on dwelling and eros, the possibility of a reversal of gendered categories in the discussion of fecundity is at least not ridiculous; the words 'mother' and 'daughter' could very well be substituted for their masculine counterparts without the text then reading as a transvestite parody of itself. In a series of late interviews with François Poirié, Levinas demonstrates this. With fecundity it is not a case of the future conditional ('and one would have to see in what sense this could be said of masculinity or virility'[23]), but a present fact: 'One must first of all insist on the very analysis of filiality, the fact that the son *and the daughter too*, is other and is still . . . me.'[24] Acknowledging the fact of the gendered categories in the original account amounts to an admission that their blithe assumption was, shall we say, insensitive, and today's commentators – at least those of them not still similarly blithe – also feel the need to explain or justify them, primarily through the suggestion that the masculinity of Levinas's account of fecundity is neither essential nor integral but merely adventitious, an accident of expression. One finds, accordingly, repeated assertions that the concept of paternity is not only, or not primarily, or not at all a *biological* concept, amounting to its being characterized, sometimes only by implication, as a metaphor, interchangeable with other metaphors, and not the essential expression of the idea 'behind' it. Peperzak's view is exemplary:

If this means that, for instance, education, or writing, or fighting for human rights are equally forms of paternity, the whole metaphorics of fecundity seems to be detached from its biological connotations. Must we, then, also detach the 'eros' from erotic love in its narrow meaning and understand 'father', the 'feminine', 'beloved' and 'son(s)' as examples or illustrations of a history that is not essentially connected with procreation or the family?[25]

This point, however, is overstressed in comparison with what Levinas actually says. From its earliest elaboration in *Time and the Other*, the notion of fecundity is distanced from a purely biological signification in the following way: 'The fecundity of the ego must be appreciated at its correct ontological value, which until now has never been done. The fact that it is a biological – and psychological – category in no way neutralizes the paradox of its significance.'[26] Fecundity *is* a biological category, Levinas says, but one with other, non-biological significations, and much the same, in fact, was said of 'sexuality' in the discussion of eros. But in *Totality and Infinity* each time that fecundity is said to overflow its purely biological signification, the biological origin of the concept is nevertheless *affirmed*; each of these references is as much an emphasis on the ineluctably biological ground of fecundity, as its tendency to signify beyond this: 'If biology furnishes us the prototypes of all these relations, this proves, to be sure, that biology does not represent a purely contingent order of being, unrelated to its essential production. But these relations free themselves from their biological limitation.'[27] It is only later, after the shift from the 'metaphor' of paternity to that of maternity (in *Otherwise Than Being*), that the biological aspect of fecundity is more decisively played down. In the 1979 preface to *Time and the Other*, for example, the notion of fecundity is said, explicitly, to be 'non-biological', and in the 1981 conversations published as *Ethics and Infinity*, although biological fecundity is still said to be 'the first shape filiality takes [*la figure première de la filialité*]',[28] its non-biological significations are stressed much more.

In fact, though, the whole argument about metaphor and biology is a red herring if it is the meaning of the gendered categories *as gendered* that is at issue. The metaphorical status of 'paternity', for example, is asserted to bypass the question of gender according to the (mistaken) assumption that a metaphorical paternity is somehow less gendered than a biological one. The questioning of its biological specificity functions as a screen. Only then can paternity be treated (as some would treat the feminine) as a separable element that plays its part 'innocently', as if it did not play its part precisely *because of* its masculinity and the ideological associations of the latter. The meaning of the use of the masculine gender – the way in which the philosophical argument is pursued on the back of its ideological associations – is, however, by no means simple. It cannot be reduced, for example, to the analysis of any one specific term like paternity, because the latter plays its role as part of a constellation and within the problematic of the philosophical project as a whole. The situation is further complicated by the necessity to draw out two significantly different philosophical conclusions arising from the discussion of fecundity.

These two conclusions are elaborated from within – but also in a sense *as* – the scope or context of two different horizons which one might be tempted to call temporal. First, and more obviously, there is the immediate horizon of the philosophical elaboration of the *birth* of a son to a father. Phenomenologically, it is probably true that the profound experience of the sheer wonder of procreation – that I or we produced this other life – is most insistent in the early life of the child (and I would be prepared to bet that new fathers are Levinas's most engaged readers at this point). At this level, or in this context, Levinas's point is an unapologetically ontological one. In an essay from 1948, 'Pluralisme et transcendance' one finds another reference to the 'plurality of our existing' and its achievement in fecundity: 'Fecundity must be understood as an ontological category. In a situation like paternity, the return of the ego to itself, which the monist concept of the identical subject articulates, finds itself completely modified . . . . The fecundity of the ego is the very structure of transcendence.'[29] Fecundity, as a transubstantiation of the subject is an attempt to think identity – the *being* of the subject – as containing a multiplicity, not in the sense of encompassing (totalizing) it but as not strictly incompatible with it. Unlike some popular accounts of eros, in which two strive to become one, in fecundity one becomes two, and not two ones (one, one) but two-in-one without being a new One. In essence, Levinas seeks to describe an unmediated relation between two identities (and not, importantly, a relation between identity and difference) in which there is a mingling but not a merging of substance such that 'identity' itself is radically reconceived. In this sense the importance of the biological basis of the philosophical category of fecundity is, I think, clear. Feron, then, is only half right when he says that Levinas, in *Totality and Infinity*, 'is pointing to fecundity and paternity in an ontological sense, inasmuch as they are essential possibilities of existence or existentials, and not to biological paternity which is but its empirical expression.'[30] This amounts to the idea that biological paternity is the (adventitious) metaphorical clothing of the philosophical idea, which completely loses the sense in which the discussion is phenomenologically based and existentially intended – the elaboration of the philosophical (ontological) significance of biological paternity.

In this discussion fecundity as an ontological category is also said to outline the structure of the transcendence of the ego (that is, the ego as transcendence) precisely because, in common with the analyses of the previous sections of *Totality and Infinity*, it begins from the standpoint of the 'I' with its particular structure of identity. The irreversibility of the relation with alterity only becomes apparent from this standpoint; this appears to be presented both as a philosophical and a psychological necessity.[31] In fecundity, however, the ego transcends this structure of identity. To this extent, Section IV of *Totality and Infinity* redeems what might otherwise appear to be the monadic presentation of subjectivity in Section II, for example. The conclusions of the discussion of fecundity with regard to identity necessitate a re-reading of the whole book. Only in this way is it possible to see how the discussion of 'ethics' – which also begins from the standpoint of the ego – is based on this condition of possibility, that is, on the ontological structure of identity revealed in or as fecundity.

Third person transcendence: fraternity

The second conclusion to the discussion of fecundity is even less straight-forward. This conclusion, one might say, transcends the transcendence of the ego in that it transcends the starting point of/as the ego. In terms of scope or horizon, it is signalled textually by the way in which the analyses of fecundity and paternity in *Totality and Infinity* move the reader beyond the birth of a son to a father into the context of the adulthood of the son(s), into an extended horizon of reproduction and of the life of the son(s) outside of the relation with the father (Levinas's debt to Hegel's *Phenomenology of Spirit* is particularly clear here). The elucidation of this broader context moves beyond the text of *Totality and Infinity* and, as necessitating a further consideration of the role of eros, uncovers new layers of complexity.

Eros, according to the above, is philosophically important to Levinas by virtue of its role as the *way to* fecundity. But, it turns out, the place of eros – eros associated with the feminine – is more philosophically uncertain than this. In Levinas's work the word 'love' ('*amour*') is not used consistently, but rather with different meanings and associations over time. In the early work and at least up to and including *Totality and Infinity* '*amour*' and 'eros' are used synonymously. In later years, however, *amour* is dissociated from eros; the latter comes to mean sexual or romantic love, while the word 'love' itself begins to take on a whole new role. 'Love' becomes a new way of describing the ethical relation, or religion, to which 'eros' is progressively contrasted, almost to the point of opposition. 'Eros', however – truly sexual eros – is actually rather elusive. Even in *Existence and Existents* and *Time and the Other*, where the possibility of transcendence in the erotic relation is spoken of most warmly, Levinas always has an eye on the future of eros in fecundity. Eros as pure gratuitous expenditure, exhaustion, that which does not produce (engender) but rather uses up, is never really considered. Even that which is most carnal in erotic nudity – voluptuosity, the caress – always transcends the flesh and ends not in physical gratification, but in a future possibility for ethics. This is a curiously moral and law-abiding eros, which would in part explain its trenchant heterosexuality. Chanter speaks of the eclipse of eros in *Otherwise Than Being*,[32] but in a sense eros – perverse, unruly, amoral, mucky eros – was already banished from *Time and the Other*, for example, to make way for its better-behaved cousin.

It is possible, though, that a reference to this erotic eros is indicated in a parallel discourse on love in which two crucial aspects are emphasized: first, that the duality of the lover and the beloved is a closed couple, admitting no third party, and second, that love obeys its own laws, not those universal or logical laws that for Levinas make up the realm of political sociality. In 1953, in an essay entitled 'Freedom and Command', these characteristics explain Levinas's albeit fleeting reference to the *violence* of 'incantation, ecstasy and love.'[33] In the context of this essay, Levinas means to point out how in love I, the lover, or the violence of my freedom, is not called into question as I am or it is in the 'religious' situation of the face-to-face. 'The Ego and the Totality', published in 1954, elaborates on this theme, opening up the discussion with a consideration of guilt and pardon. Pardon, Levinas says,

> presupposes, above all, that the one wronged received all the evil of the wrong, and consequently disposes completely of the right to pardon . . . . But the conditions for legitimate pardon are only realized in a society of beings that are totally present to each other, in an *intimate society* . . . such a society is dual, a society of me and you. We are just among ourselves. Third parties are excluded.[34]

According to Levinas, it is in the nature of intentional acts to overspill my intention, to produce a range of meanings and consequences over which I have no control, thus affecting others, third parties, in unforeseen ways.[35] Your pardon absolves me only from a small part of this, but functions as if the pardon were all yours to give. Third parties are not taken into account and their pardon is not sought; their injuries go unnoticed and unatoned. One could legitimately accept pardon according to this structure, Levinas says, only if the other were God or a saint. No such legitimate relation of pardon actually exists, then, but in love one acts *as if* it does, as if the dual society were 'master of all its ins and outs': 'To love is to exist as though the lover and beloved were alone in the world. The intersubjective relationship of love is not the beginning, but the negation of society.' In love all my relation is exhausted in the other, and is hence love of one to the detriment of another, or all others. Third parties are excluded and so 'wounded', because the couple is a closed society.[36]

Love in the sense of eros is, then, presented as a degraded social relation, or even not, strictly speaking, as a *social* relation at all. In 'The Ego and the Totality' it is 'law' that is said to have priority (hence law becomes the site of pardon that takes all third parties into account – 'justice'), and 'politics', in its peculiarly Levinasian sense, is the proper of the human. Now of course it was possible for Levinas to have changed his mind, and if this account of eros seems to contradict those earlier, in *Existence and Existents* and *Time and the Other* and that later in *Totality and Infinity*, then such is his prerogative. But there is no contradiction when it is pointed out that what is missing from this 'negative' account of eros, and what transforms the others into 'positive' accounts, is precisely the phenomenon of fecundity. Eros, as intimacy and the shunning of sociality, is alien to ethics, politics, law and so on, because eros without fecundity is 'closed'; only fecundity 'opens' eros to social fraternity which, as will be shown, is the human of humanity: 'This is the primary sociality: the personal relation is in the rigour of the justice which judges me and not in the love that excuses me.'[37]

The discussion of love in 'The Ego and the Totality' already highlighted the exclusion of the third party as the basis of the violence of love, but the more significant discussion occurs in Section III of *Totality and Infinity*, in a subsection entitled 'The Other and the others' ('*Autrui et les autres*'). Here the relation between myself and the (face of) the Other, is said to take place 'in public', precisely in opposition to the intimacy of love:

> Language as the presence of the face does not invite complicity with the preferred being, the self-sufficient 'I-Thou' ['*je–tu*'] forgetful of the universe; in its frankness it refuses the clandestiny of love . . . . *The third party looks at me in the eyes of the Other* – language is justice . . . the epiphany of the face qua face opens humanity.

Twice more in the same paragraph the presence of the third party is equated with 'all humanity' and the 'human community' thus inaugurated is also described as fraternity, which itself is explained, as in Section IV, as related to paternity, or the 'community of the father'.[38] This community is the extension of the father–son relation; although the son is unique (in an ethical rather than a numerical sense), still '[p]aternity is produced as an innumerable future; the I engendered exists at the same time as unique in the world and as brother among brothers.' The son finds himself to be unique (or 'elected', Levinas also says) amongst other unique sons, his brothers, or his equals, in a relation of fraternity: 'The I as I hence remains turned ethically to the face of the other: fraternity is the very relation with the face in which at the same time my election and equality, that is, the mastery exercised over me by the other, are accomplished.'[39] The relation of fecundity in its elaboration as fraternity is thus the ground of ethics, and of sociality itself, where *le tiers* (the 'third', the 'third person') is always taken into account and where it is possible to say 'Us'. To this end fraternity and humanity become associated to the extent that Levinas refers, 'in a rather uncomplicated manner' as Critchley archly remarks,[40] to 'the human fraternity'.[41]

What is perhaps only implied here is made explicit in the Conclusions: 'To the extent that the face of the Other relates us with the third party, the metaphysical relation of the I with the Other moves into the form of the We, aspires to a State, institutions, laws, which are the source of universality.'[42] *Fraternity* is this ethical universality, where the particular nevertheless resists subsumption in the universal (the totality of the state) through the maintenance of ipseity in the uniqueness of the son, each son. At this point the significance of the masculine gendering of the account becomes clear. On the one hand, the sphere of universality, or 'universal justice' as Peperzak says,[43] is characterized in masculine terms because of the already available ideological association of the masculine with universality, as is most evident in the use, in languages from various different families, of the masculine pronoun to refer to an alleged neutral universality of the human. At the same time, what would normally be seen as the fateful refutation of its universality – the rather obvious fact that the masculine is unavoidably *masculine*, and hence particular – is here precisely what makes it work. If fraternity retains, simultaneously, the particularity of the uniqueness of each son and the generality of their relation in equality, this is conceptually possible partly because of the conventional ambiguity of the neutral universality/sexual specificity of the masculine. Thus even though one could, as Levinas suggests, speak without absurdity of mothers and daughters in the context of fecundity, the current ideological association of the feminine with sexual specificity would frustrate the desire for the universal signification intended with 'fraternity'; one does not speak, that is, of the 'human sorority', let alone *Liberté, Egalité, Sororité*.[44] The dissimulation of the sexual specificity of the masculine in fraternity often works, implicitly, surreptitiously, to exclude the feminine from the compass of the universal, both in terms of definition and more concretely in terms of rights, consideration, and so on. The effect of Levinas's unselfconscious employment of these gendered terms is unusual only in its transparency and ingenuousness. The association of the unmarked masculine with (sexual) neutrality and universality has its equally frank obverse in the conflation of the feminine with sexual difference, that is, with sexual particularity or specificity. Eros's opposition to universality ('I love *this one*', even if *this one* is one in a series of *this ones*[45]) is cemented precisely in its association with the feminine and its 'alterity-content', which is revealed as its 'peculiarity-content'.

It is difficult to characterize the status of the philosophical discourse in which fecundity and paternity are developed into the universality of fraternity. The thesis, such as it is, of the universal community of brothers is no longer an ontological one, although it is dependent on the prior ontological conclusion (the community of the father is said to be 'the establishment of a unicity with which the unicity of the father does and does not coincide. The non-coincidence consists, concretely, in my position as brother implying others at my side.'[46]) Fraternity, however, turns out to be not that which is to be deduced, but the ground from which a deduction takes place. In the preface to *Totality and Infinity* Levinas indicates that the argumentative mode of the book 'resembles what has come to be called the transcendental method'.[47] Accordingly, the working out of the analyses of fecundity does not end with fraternity; rather it implicitly asks, what must be true (what must be the case) if something like fraternity is possible? The introduction of *le tiers*, the third, is not therefore a movement forward from the closed community of intimacy towards the aim of fraternity, but a movement *backwards* enquiring into the conditions of possibility of fraternity. If this is not immediately obvious in *Totality and Infinity* (and I readily grant that it is not), the terms and the argument of 'The Trace of the Other' (1963) and later work allow the structure to be made clear.

The trace and 'illeity'

Although 'The Trace of the Other' seems to repeat, often in familiar phrases, much that was to be found in *Totality and Infinity*, it is only deceptively a simple reworking of old themes. Whereas in *Totality and Infinity* even the infinite time of fecundity – the absolute future opened in fecundity – was elaborated in terms of the transubstantiation of the ego, in 'The Trace of the Other', and arguably everything that follows, attention shifts elsewhere, or opens onto the thinking of an 'elsewhere'. This involves both the introduction of new terms and the metamorphosis of the meaning of old ones. The explanatory priority of the (Cartesian) idea of infinity, gives way to a greater focus on the Platonic Good beyond being, or the Platonic and Plotinian 'One' and – a fact which may seem incidental – the themes of the feminine, eros, paternity and fecundity are not explicitly mentioned at all.

In the second section, 'Movement without Return', Levinas's problem is a familiar one: the possibility of a relation with alterity which does not convert the other into the same. In 'Transcendence and Height', for example, this problem was described as one associated with the knowing ego. In 'The Trace of the Other', however, the task Levinas sets himself is not just that of postulating an alternative to the 'relation' of knowledge, but of explaining how any alternative resists *becoming like* the relation of knowledge: how is it that the face of the Other does not simply become a representation of the Other, in which the Other is known? Why, as the face appears in the world, it is not thereby compromised in its very appearing: 'How is such a production possible? How can the coming of the Other out of the absolute, in the visitation of a face, be in no way convertible into a revelation . . .? How is a face not simply a true *representation*, in which the other renounces his alterity?'[48] In part, the fear that the face will become simply a representation for the ego which faces that face fails to take into account that the very experience of the face is at once the putting into question of consciousness and the production of the ego. At the same time, however, *why* this should be the case, *how* the face 'does this', still needs to be explained. In a sense, the answer has already been given in the discussion of the idea of infinity, which is put in me from elsewhere, or as Levinas says, comes from 'beyond'. It cannot be assimilated in the context or 'horizon' of the world, into the world-order of concepts, because it is, in its very essence, (from) beyond the world. But not an *'arrière-monde'*, a world behind the scenes, which would in effect simply be to postulate worlds within worlds in never ending circles of the same: 'The *beyond* is precisely beyond the "world", that is, beyond every disclosure – like the One of the first hypothesis of the *Parmenides*, which transcends all cognition, be it symbolic or signified.'[49] This 'beyond' is said to be an absence which is radically withdrawn from disclosure and dissimulation, an absence that is signified in the face although not symbolically, as if the face were a mask. In another essay published two years later, 'Enigma and Phenomenon', Levinas explains that such a symbolic manifestation of absence would remain within the structure of correlation which defines thought as knowledge (*connaissance*).[50] But absence is also not simply revealed or indicated in an emptiness or blankness: 'The relationship which goes from a face to the absent is outside every revelation and dissimulation, a third way excluded by these contradictories.' Again, Levinas stresses the difficulty of thinking the possibility of the signification of an absence from beyond the order of the world, for any insertion into the order of the world is, for Levinas, inevitably absorption into the order of the same or, as is clearer in 'Enigma and Phenomenon', the order of Being. The absent beyond must, then, signify (or perhaps be signified in the face) without appearing, but must signify *itself*, that is, not let anything signify in its place symbolically: 'Such is the signifyingness of a trace. The beyond from which a face comes signifies as a trace.'[51]

This notion of 'trace', describing how transcendence can signify in the order of immanence without thereby being compromised, is by no means an easy one to understand. Levinas says that what is signified in the trace is the past, profoundly and absolutely past, a past which has never been present because it is inimical to revelation. This pastness refers not just to chronology, but to the impossibility of retrieving the past, bringing the past back into the present, through memory. This is elaborated in 'Enigma and Phenomenon' as a 'supreme anachronism'. Referring also to the 'anachronism' of my always-already being responsible (before any decision),[52] the trace is the trace of a past that has never been present: 'As transcendence, a pure passage, it shows itself as past. It is a trace.'[53] If this is a thought that is difficult to grasp, that is precisely the point. Levinas performatively demonstrates, in answer to his own question of whether any idea can escape compromising itself in the order of the same, an idea that enters into the order of discourse only in order to frustrate that discourse. This is why the trace, also called 'enigma' in 'Enigma and Phenomenon', is described, and in fact reveals itself here, as '*dérangement*', 'disturbance'.[54]

The 'third way', neither revelation nor dissimulation, that Levinas calls the trace is also said to be the 'personal order', and this personal order, which is beyond being, is more simply 'a third person [*une troisième personne*]'. The trace is the trace of the third person: 'Through a trace the irreversible past takes on the profile of a "He" ["*Il*"]. The *beyond* from which a face comes is in the third person. The pronoun *He* .... The *illeity* [*l'illéité*] of the third person is the condition for irreversibility.'[55]

With this neologism 'illeity', *le tiers*, the third person, who was *also* there in the face of the Other according to *Totality and Infinity*, who looked at me through the eyes of the Other, becomes that which *ensures* the very otherness of the Other. In a sense, *le tiers*, as illeity, has become more important than the Other, although the Other and illeity are not separable terms. It is no longer the Other who resists comprehension, but, as Levinas says in 'Enigma and Phenomenon', illeity:

> We hear this way to signify – which does not consist in being unveiled nor in being veiled, absolutely foreign to the hide-and-seek characteristic of cognition, this way of leaving the alternatives of being – under the third-person personal pronoun, under the word *He*. The enigma comes to us from Illeity.[56]

Manifested as face, appearing in the order of this world, what prevents the Other from becoming a mere phenomenon for me, a representation in a system of the same, is illeity. The aspect of immanence which ineluctably comprises the appearance of the face within the order of the world is not fatal because the trace of illeity in the face survives as pure transcendence:

> Only a being that transcends the world can leave a trace. A trace is a presence of that which properly speaking has never been there, of what is always past .... Illeity is the origin of the alterity of being in which the in itself of objectivity participates, while also betraying it.[57]

In *Totality and Infinity*, the discussion of fraternity and the role of the third person functions partly to undo the overly oppositional distinction between ethics and politics with which the book opens. In order that politics and the institutions of society more generally are thought as more than simply violence and totalization in their reduction of the Other to the same (in the notion of 'equality', for example), an ethically informed politics or sociality is mooted as fraternity. Before allowing Levinas to make this move, one might of course object to the initial (and discursively unjustified) characterization of politics as war (in many ways a reactionary and conventional designation, more suited to the theorists of society who begin with the innate depravity or selfishness of human nature), and to the implication that 'society' – that is, sociality in general – is somehow a secondary structure dependent on an original one-to-one relation. These objections are never explicitly addressed, but aspects of Levinas's later work could be construed as in some sense an acknowledgment of the problem.

In *Otherwise Than Being*, the erosion of the distinction between the ethical relation and the justice demanded by the third person – that is, the distinction between ethics and politics, in the earlier terminology – emerges strongly and takes the explicit form of the greater foregrounding of the third person and illeity. In this later work Levinas more often writes *'le prochain'*, the neighbour, instead of *'Autrui'*, and connects it with illeity thus:

> The illeity of the beyond-being is the fact that its coming toward me is a departure which lets me accomplish a movement toward the neighbour. The positive element of this departure, that which makes this departure, this diachrony, be more than a term of negative theology, is *my responsibility for the others*.[58]

This movement towards *le prochain* (the word indicating, etymologically, closeness), this 'proximity' is said to be a relation without mediation, but the trace of illeity still 'passes' through it: 'A third party is also approached; and the relationship between the neighbour and the third party cannot be indifferent to me when I approach. There must be justice among incomparables.'[59] That the approach of the third person is, otherwise said, illeity, is clear in Levinas's denial that this is, empirically, the interruption of us two people by another person, which would be dependent on a contingency. The relation with *le tiers* is said to be a correction of the asymmetry of proximity, but it is not thereby a degradation of the relation. On the contrary, '[c]onscience is born as the presence of a third party. It is the entry of the third party, a permanent entry, into the intimacy of the face to face.'[60] More importantly, however, the argument that the third person (illeity) is an essential constituent of the (ethical) approach to the neighbour is elaborated in terms of the notion of 'fraternity', familiar from *Totality and Infinity*, connecting the notions of fraternity, proximity, the neighbour and illeity across the various texts.[61]

According to this constellation of terms, the introduction of illeity in the later texts functions as a commentary on the notion of the third person in *Totality and Infinity*, elaborating it in such a way as to make its status as a philosophical category – rather than an empirical presence – clear. Illeity refers not to the actual third person but to that which signifies in the third person from 'beyond': transcendence. What is too rarely understood in the reception of Levinas's philosophy is that this 'beyond' is a category that *cannot* simply be glossed as the Other, or the face; this is the meaning of the title of Section IV of *Totality and Infinity*: 'Beyond the Face'. This crucial point marks one of Levinas's most deliberate philosophical stands against Heidegger. The face, for Levinas, appears in the world. The discussion of the notion of illeity unambiguously, asserts, however, that the aspect of transcendence – that which prevents the face (the Other) from becoming merely an entity within-the-world – is 'beyond' the world, in contradistinction to the transcendent world-horizon of Heidegger's *Being and Time*.[62]

The distinction between 'transcendence' and 'the face' or 'the Other' is a distinction of philosophical register – the difference between the meta-physical and the phenomenological in Levinas's work; a distinction, note, which it is still possible – indeed necessary – to make even if, as Section I of *Totality and Infinity* makes clear, the former is only ever 'enacted' in or through the latter. Accordingly, just as the relation of eros (romantic or sexual love) is said to exclude the third, there is also a sense in which this would be true of the ethical or religious relation *were it not for illeity*. This is clear in a late essay on Buber, where 'beyond' Buber and the I-Thou relation, Levinas says with all humility and due regard to his predecessor, 'we have been led to call [in the text] upon the third person, to that which we called *illeity*, in order to speak of the infinite and of divine transcendence, *other than the alterity of Autrui*. It is the illeity of God which sends me back to the service of the neighbour, to responsibility for him.'[63] Illeity is what makes the ethical relation ethical; it is a condition of possibility for ethics and in that sense metaphysically prior.

As a philosophical category, 'illeity' functions in much the same way as 'infinity', and its relation to the face is similarly that of a metaphysical cat-egory to its phenomenological pointer, both in terms of experience and its philosophical elaboration. In the preface to *Totality and Infinity* Levinas says that phenomenology 'is a method for philosophy, but phenomenology – the comprehension effected through a bringing to light – does not constitute the ultimate event of being itself.'[64] The mention of being may appear to be confusing, given the project of the disavowal of the primacy of ontology, but Levinas's own reference immediately afterwards to the section 'Beyond the Face' gives one to understand that this event is the ontological novelty approached through fecundity. In the broadened elaboration of paternity as the community of the father – fraternity – this ontological structure is cru-cial, but not because of any chronological (or indeed linear) relation of cause and effect or suchlike. In line with his claimed transcendental method, the condition of possibility for fraternity is revealed in the other direction, as it were – in illeity or transcendence. The relation between the transcendence of the ego in fecundity (transubstantiation of identity, the introduction of plur-ality into being – ultimately, fraternity) and the transcendence of the tran-scendence of the ego (illeity) is not therefore that the former makes the latter possible but that the former – being, to be blunt – is such that the latter (transcendence) may *appear* to us.

This might be construed as Levinas's reply to the tragic nature of Kantian ethics. The noumenal/phenomenal distinction, mapped onto the realms of freedom and natural causality respectively, mean that for Kant ethics is ultimately located in a kingdom of God to which empirical human being has no access, at least not in this life. The postulation of the two standpoints is not a philosophical resolution of this problem, more a way of making it psychologically palatable, justifying the continuation of something like the practice of ethics – praise and censure – in this world. For Kant the phenomenal world is such that the noumenal is radically and by definition incommensurable with it. For Levinas, on the other hand, the phenomenal world – being, the ontological continuity in discontinuity of fecundity – is such that, in the mark of a trace, transcendence (the beyond) may enter without being irredeemably compromised. 'Ethics' is the phenomenological account, the empirical possibility and/or actuality of transcendence in this world; as such, transcendence is presupposed.

The two theses animating the discussion of fecundity – the ontological thesis of the plurality in/of being and the metaphysical thesis of transcendence in/as illeity – dovetail in the brief, difficult remarks on the relation between fecundity, desire and goodness. Once again, the sense of the 'beyond the face' is demonstrated. The movement of desire, Levinas says, does not stop at the Other because the Other is not a limit ['*n'est pas terme*'] but the site of the engendering of desire:

> The other that Desire desires is again Desire; transcendence transcends toward him who transcends – this is the true adventure of paternity, of transubstantiation . . . . Transcendence, the for the Other, the goodness correlative of the face, founds a more profound relation: the goodness of goodness. Fecundity engendering fecundity accomplishes goodness.

These passages could perhaps be read as the assertion that metaphysical desire not only transcends need, but also transcends itself in a discontinuous but infinite renewal (without satisfaction) which outlives any desiring ego, but in which any desiring ego lives. One could say that desire incessantly gives birth to itself, and that this movement of desire is 'goodness', but paraphrase is always extremely difficult with assertions of this kind: 'In paternity desire maintained as insatiate desire, that is, as goodness, is accomplished. For desire to be accomplished is equivalent to engendering good being, to being goodness of goodness.'[65]

These passages are surely mystifying (not to say mystical) without the interpretative presupposition that the event of fecundity – the instantiation of the plurality of being – is the ontological 'accomplishment' or realization of the beyond, of transcendence, of what, previously, was referred to in Platonic terminology as the Good beyond being. References in 'The Trace of the Other' to the Platonic and Plotinian One would seem to confirm this. Being, then, in fecundity – or the fecundity *of* being – is such that transcendence may appear in the order of the world without being compromised, or being in fecundity/the fecundity of being *is* this appearing. The beyond being appears in being as the rupture of ontological unity, and as 'goodness' shares the transcendental/transcendent status of 'the Good' in Plato: 'superior to [being] in dignity and power.'[66] *This* is the conclusion to the discussion of fecundity, very far now from the this-worldly phenomenology of eros.

CHAPTER FOUR

A Maternal Alternative? Levinas and Plato on Love

If the worldly context and elaboration of the phenomenology of eros and fecundity, and indeed of ethics, is subordinated to the philosophical priority of transcendence as something akin to 'the Good' – something, definitively, not 'of' this world even if the ontological conclusion of fecundity lets it appear in this world as 'trace' – developments in *Otherwise Than Being* might be read as a re-worlding. In particular, a new insistence on the themes of *jouissance* and sensibility and the introduction of the trope of maternity might be read as the re-establishment of an ethics firmly grounded in the human – specifically the frailty and vulnerability of the human – whilst at the same time recognizing and in some sense making amends for the egregiously masculine tenor of the previous work.

In *Totality and Infinity* sensibility and *jouissance* are affective structures associated with the 'pre-ethical' or atheist ego of Section II. Insofar as the 'economy' of *jouissance* entails the incorporation of alterity, the linear sequence of the book leads from this to the unassimilable alterity of the Other. However, reading the argument – as Levinas suggests – according to a transcendental method, the movement is reversed: *jouissance* and sensibility are then not earlier structures to be overcome, but conditions of possibility to be discovered. The fact that what is thus conditioned – the ethical or religious relation – is described in Section III predominantly in terms of language/discourse and in opposition to certain institutional or universal structures tends to de-emphasize the role of *jouissance* and sensibility, but it does not thereby disappear. In *Otherwise Than Being*, on the other hand, *jouissance* and more particularly sensibility are foregrounded throughout. The main difference in the two texts is an easing apart, in *Otherwise Than Being*, of sensibility from *jouissance*, to produce a change of accent or tone. In *Totality and Infinity*, where sensibility *is* primarily *jouissance*, the emphasis falls on pleasure; in *Otherwise Than Being* the more dominant themes are pain and suffering.

As in *Totality and Infinity*, *Otherwise Than Being* recognizes human need as something other than a mere animal inconvenience. Need is dignified with a particular human and philosophical importance through an insistence on the fact that the human need to eat, for example, is the condition for the relation with the neighbour (*le prochain*) in which the humanity of the human is inscribed. In the earlier work this transcendental structure was signalled in the identification of other conditions. In *Totality and Infinity* the ethical rela- tion, the welcome of the Other, was said to be impossible with empty hands and closed doors,[1] hence the analysis of dwelling, work and possession. In 'The Trace of the Other' the word 'liturgy' in its non-religious sense was evoked in order to express the idea that in the ethical relation (or in the '*oeuvre*', the 'good work') one must have something to lose in order to have something to give.[2] In *Otherwise Than Being* these conditions are reduced to their most basic instance: 'To give, to-be-for-another, despite oneself, but in interrupting the for-oneself, is to tear the bread from one's own mouth, to nourish the hunger of another with one's own fasting.' Even more than this, 'one has first to *enjoy one's bread*, not in order to have the merit of giving it, but in order to give it with one's heart, to give oneself in giving it.'[3] In both *Totality and Infinity* and *Otherwise Than Being* nourishment is connected to *jouissance* in an essential way. In 1961, in characterizing all *jouissance* as 'ali- mentation', the transmutation of the other into the same/me, its non-ethical, egoistic nature was stressed. In *Otherwise Than Being* the nature of *jouissance* is fundamentally the same, but now 'ethics' is more explicitly thematized as the *foregoing* of nourishment. The literal ingestion of food is still the model of egoism, and now its reverse also – tearing the bread from my mouth – plays a significant role.

This is also expressed in terms of the viscerality of human being: 'Only a subject that eats can be for-the-other, or can signify. Signification, the-one- for-the-other, has meaning only among beings of flesh and blood.'[4] Con- ventionally, the reference to the composition of the human as 'flesh and blood' implies susceptibility, vulnerability even unto death, and this is just what Levinas intends. The vulnerability of sensibility is also, or makes possible, vulnerability to proximity, to the neighbour. Thus proximity will also be described as trauma,[5] and in *Otherwise Than Being* the themes of pain and suffering come to the fore. The epitome of sensibility is, however, character- ized as maternity,[6] and in a sense, the choice is an obvious one for Levinas. At one point, 'the knot of subjectivity' is described as 'the torsion of the Same and the Other . . . . Intrigue of the Other-in-the-Same', which is or which accomplishes itself in proximity.[7] It is not difficult to see, in a rather literal way, how prenatal maternity could become the paradigm case of 'the-Other- in-the-Same', or of passive (and perhaps unchosen) responsibility. References to the 'gestation' of the other in the same, used metaphorically but also as a description of 'maternity'[8] reinforce the case. 'Maternity', however, also signi- fies in other than these obviously 'spatial' terms. The Biblical association, for example, of maternity with suffering also refers the reader to that corporeality of the subject particularly insistent in prenatal maternity. Its specifically Levinasian association then situates maternity as archetypical of the idea of nourishment introduced through the theme of mouth and bread. Again, pre- and post-natal maternity provide literal examples of nourishing the other with food that one has enjoyed, but also carry the conventional symbolic signification attached, for example, to the figure of Demeter.[9]

The choice of the trope of maternity is an obvious one, then, because of the already established cultural signification of the maternal as paradigmatic of care (nourishment) and responsibility. However, there is also a sense in which maternity makes more sense than paternity in the context of Levinas's account of the philosophical significance of fecundity. Every discussion of fecundity, paternity and filiality, in which Levinas stresses the originality of the relation in which the son both is and is not the father, would seem to be applicable *a fortiori* to the mother-child relation. If in the son the father both remains himself and yet becomes other than himself, how much more true is this of the mother's relation to the child when there is, at one level, a sharing of subsistence if not substance such that the child is *of* the mother. How much more meaningful is the notion of transubstantiation in this gestation which has confused the distinction between the literal and the metaphorical almost beyond repair.[10] This presupposes, however, that the notion of the maternal is or may be slotted into the analyses of the familial terms in the earlier work. If, on the other hand, it is introduced as some sort of corrective to these latter, the relation between 'maternity' and 'paternity' will be more complex and problematic. Insofar as this relation apparently presents itself in terms of the shift from a patrilineal to a matrilineal 'fecundity', the earlier question of the feminine also resurfaces: is maternity an elaboration of the previous discussion of the feminine, or, as substitute paternity, something opposed to it?

Maternity and the feminine

For Catherine Chalier the ultimate meaning of the feminine as maternity in *Otherwise Than Being* has the virtue of admitting the feminine to the ethical realm from which it/she was excluded in *Totality and Infinity*, although the reduction of the feminine role in ethics to maternity is still restrictive.[11] If Chalier's reconstructive project tries to re-inscribe the non-maternal feminine as ethical against the grain of Levinas's analyses, her argument is still Levinasian in inspiration. In several key texts Levinas raises the idea of an 'effeminization' of the virility of being. The ontological function of the feminine is said, for example, to be tied to the surmounting of that 'alienation' which results from the masculinity of the universal conquering logos,[12] in such a way as to hint at a possible *feminization of the ethical*. Although this remains undeveloped in *Totality and Infinity*, Levinas does speak there of the effeminization of the virile ego in its relation with the feminine in eros.[13] The ethical relation, described as an end to the mastery of the subject, could also be read as *implying* a feminization, even if the word is not actually used in this regard. This entails the detachment of the notion of the feminine from the female (the woman) in order to articulate it as a more general concept. In *Ethics and Infinity* Levinas says of the notion of the feminine in *Time and the Other*: 'Perhaps . . . all these allusions to the ontological differences between the masculine and the feminine would appear less archaic if, instead of dividing humanity into two species (or into two genres), they would signify that the participation in the masculine and the feminine were the essence [*le propre*] of every human being.'[14] According, one imagines, to such hints, Chalier's reinscription of the feminine in ethics is what she calls 'the feminine as the disruption of being by goodness and beyond maternity . . . . Is this not the meaning of the feminine in the human being?'[15] Having made such a move, however, Chalier goes on to resist reading the maternal in precisely this way, that is, as a (feminine) model for the disruption of the virility of being, or a (feminine) model for responsibility/substitution, objecting to the too-conventional ascription of feminine excellence to maternity (and only to maternity).

Monique Schneider, on the other hand, reads in Levinas's later work a notable attempt to reverse or make good what she sees as the matricidal impulses of Western thought, visible already in Aeschylus's *Oresteia* where Athena avows her purely masculine parentage and the priority of the father in procreation.[16] Schneider points also to the ancient figure of Baubô as evidence of this denegation of maternal origins and of a corresponding uneasiness with the mouth as the opening on to '*les entrailles*', in French both the entrails and the space of gestation. In Greek mythology Baubô is the woman who made the unhappy Demeter laugh by exposing her genitals, an apparently coarse and vulgar act. The few extant sculptured representations of Baubô[17] are accordingly somewhat grotesque: headless and ugly, her face appears in/on her abdomen, conflating eyes with breasts and mouth with vulva.[18] Baubô is presented as both obscene and risible, her vulva both hidden and announced (in agreement with the Freudian explanation of the fetish) by the buccal analogue. Against the cultural background given expression in the figure of Baubô, Levinas's references to maternity and to the mouth constitute for Schneider a revaluation of both, an attempt to re-inscribe them in the human: that is, to rescue them from their pre-human or pre-cultural associations.[19]

Insofar as Schneider considers these themes in isolation from the overall project of *Otherwise Than Being* her thesis is persuasive. Even within the broader context of Levinas's work, the thesis holds as a possible description of Levinas's compensation for his earlier elision of maternity in favour of paternity. More generally, the introduction of the maternal may be figured as an almost expiatory gesture with regard to the earlier analyses of the feminine. Levinas says nothing explicit to that effect, and the most significant critique of the philosophical treatment of the feminine in Levinas's work – Chalier's *Figures du féminin* – was published some years after *Otherwise Than Being*, including the latter within its critical compass. It is not impossible, though, for Levinas to have been aware of the form such a critique would take. Later, in 1991, in the Preface he wrote for Chalier's *Les Matriarches*, Levinas acknowledged the legitimacy of the general feminist argument of Chalier's *Figures du féminin*, and although he makes no explicit reference to his own work the implicit message is *mea culpa*. Chalier's book is, after all, primarily about Levinas. *Figures du féminin*, he says,

> has much in common . . . with the objections levelled by contemporary feminism at all attempts – or all seeming attempts – to confine the feminine to a condition which, however dignified it may be, still separates woman from the highest human destiny reserved for masculinity. These protestations against the ideal of woman as no more than the guardian of the hearth – the 'homely' woman [*femme dite intérieur*] – are also implicit in this book, as is the opposition to those who would seek the fulfillment of the feminine within the limits of the intrigues of love, as celebrated by novelists and poets.[20]

Whether or not it is possible to read this retrospective admission into *Otherwise Than Being*, the introduction of the idea of the maternal may be construed as a re-presentation of the feminine in a guise that does not exclude it from the 'highest human destiny' and/or as a recognition of and corrective to the concomitant masculine-dominated theme of fecundity. For Bernard Forthomme, the analyses of the feminine in *Totality and Infinity* lead to an account of subjectivity that is essentially masculine, although this is not, he thinks, necessarily a criticism. While the virility of Levinas's philosophy does indeed speak against any pretensions to universality, 'this would simply be the logical consequence of the micro-logic within which the relation to the other is situated. This relation is revealed to be irreducible to any synoptic view or to any reading which goes indifferently from one to the other or *vice versa*.'[21] Later, however, Forthomme's comments would seem to show that the virility of *Totality and Infinity*, while perhaps bearing witness to a certain performative enactment of non-reciprocity, is nevertheless inferior to the femininity of the model of maternity. Maternity, he says, goes beyond the bipolarity of masculine and feminine, revealing the 'neutrality' of the subject and an ethics above sexual difference, a position which he believes to have superseded the restrictive masculine standpoint of *Totality and Infinity*.[22]

Forthomme's point would seem to be that while the schematism of *Totality and Infinity* – a schematism based on sexual difference – does allow Levinas to open up the phenomenological tradition to 'the forgotten horizons of sensibility',[23] the analysis remains trapped within this schematism. In the model of maternity, on the other hand, (ethical) responsibility, which was also called metaphysical desire, is neither masculine nor feminine, and this testifies to a more profound, one might also say more equitable, metaphysic. In this

Forthomme takes it for granted that the notion of maternity in this philo-sophical elaboration is not exclusive to the female. Levinas himself never explicitly signals the metaphorical nature of maternity, but there is much to suggest it. Although the model for ethical responsibility is in some sense feminine, this is a femininity that can (and ought) to be assumed by the male as well as the female. This is the possibility that Chalier seems not to accept, but which for Forthomme affirms the pre-eminence of maternity.

In a reading which might almost be a dialectical resolution of these two positions, John Llewelyn suggests that maternity functions effectively as a sort of corrective to the earlier discussion of the feminine, even if Levinas did not consciously intend this.[24] When Llewelyn says that the need to escape from the virile, heroic conception of subjectivity demands '[a]nother geneal-ogy, another *parenté* for man',[25] it is not therefore entirely clear whether he believes Levinas to have succeeded in answering this demand. To the extent that Levinas has not succeeded, Llewelyn 'fills in', as it were, but with insights and concepts gleaned from Levinas's own writings. Accordingly, if the use of a vocabulary of patrilinearity, for example, *seems* on the surface to affirm a patriarchy which would be wholly consonant with the virility of the domination of the Logos, of Being, or of the One, the analyses of fecundity, paternity and filiality *in fact* 'deconstruct' this, as is perhaps borne out by the introduction of the idea of maternity.[26] Llewelyn would then allow patrilineal filiation to signify in a non-patriarchal way under the influence of the sign of maternity. For Chalier such a possibility does not, and cannot arise. Chalier's argument is based on the assumption that the idea of paternity – biological or not – could not have performed the work that Levinas sets it in his text because of the fact of its already being inscribed within (or being the very enactment of) a system of the law, the (paternal) name, or 'the proper'.[27] Chalier, unlike Llewelyn thus insists on a certain deference to historical and material context, according to which wishing does not make it so. Law, name, logos, 'the proper', the implications of 'paternity', from which Levinas's text is not exempt, reinscribe a certain symbolic order at the same moment as Levinas's attempts to disrupt it.

Llewelyn's reading, however, is no mere apologia. According to a Nietzschean idea of genealogy, he winkles the conditions of possibility for the later works out of Levinas's earlier texts without implying any simple relation of origin or of cause and effect. At the same time, the readings of the earlier texts are informed by the demands of the later ones, bearing witness to a certain 'reading backwards' in which a hermeneutics of the past (texts) is sacrificed to the exigencies of the present. Reading backwards this also means that the ethical excellence of the maternal rubs off on the seemingly pre-ethical feminine. In essence, the trace of the perfection of maternity passes through the feminine as what Llewelyn calls 'elleity'. Llewelyn also coins the term 'illelleity' to signal the non-biological nature of the notion of a maternity that is not exclusively female: 'Neither simply active nor simply passive, if the middle voice of responsibility has a gender it is that of the middle sex. The middle sex is not neuter. It is chiasmically bisexual. But what we are talking about here is humanity prior to the sexual difference.'[28] This seems not unlike the, perhaps utopian, thought articulated by Derrida in an interview from 1981:

> what if we were to approach here (for one does not arrive at this as one would at a determined location) the area of a relationship to the other where the code of sexual marks would no longer be discriminating? The relationship would not be a-sexual, far from it, but would be sexual other-wise: beyond the binary difference that governs the decorum of all codes, beyond the opposition masculine/feminine, beyond bisexuality as well, beyond homosexuality and heterosexuality which come to the same thing.[29]

With this Derrida does not envision a discourse in which masculine and feminine would no longer exist, but one in which they would 'no longer be discriminating'. This is not a commentary on Levinas, but it seems to articulate Llewelyn's position on him well. In more conventional terms Llewelyn expresses the absence of such a discourse (or 'genealogy') as one in which 'the woman in the man is sacrificed to phallogocentrism. Because man's maternity is passed by, and therefore the closest, the Other in the mother.'[30] The other genealogy, the other *parenté*, is also described as another humanism, or a humanism of the other man[31], and thus Llewelyn's reading joins Chalier's too: 'Is this not the meaning of the feminine in the human being?'[32]

Two points arise from these various readings. Firstly, the maternal is not intended to designate something exclusively female; that is, it is intended to signify beyond any biological reference. It would thus appear to function much like the previous trope of paternal fecundity, the biological *origin* of which Levinas avows whilst also emphasizing its tendency to signify beyond this. It is only in later work, however, that the biological aspect of fecundity is decisively denied, as in the 1979 preface to *Time and the Other*, in *Ethics and Infinity*, and in *Otherwise Than Being* itself where, in a passage that leads on to a discussion of fraternity, Levinas speaks of the kinship relation [*relation de parenté*] *outside of all biology*.[33] This is a small but significant shift, signalled almost indirectly in the substitution of *parenté* for *paternité*. Its conjunction with the introduction of the notion of maternity is no coincidence. Biological origin and signification is played down – or indeed wholly dismissed – after the shift from the paternal to the maternal because maternity, as the apogean model for responsibility and substitution, must be a universal model. To say that nothing of the biological must remain in the maternal *parenté* is to say that its specifically *feminine* content – connoting particularity, peculiarity –

must be excised. In the later work, however, the explicit disavowal of biology is displaced analogously onto discussions of, or references to, paternity. Retrospectively, paternity signifies non-biologically in order that it might mirror and at the same time justify or explain the non-biological status of maternity.

The second point is accordingly paradoxical. Important differences notwithstanding, the various readings of maternity share a sense of the femininity of this notion, however problematic. Even when Llewelyn insists on the 'bisexuality' of maternity, this amounts to a de-biologizing of a notion which nevertheless remains feminine in origin and in its primary symbolic significations. For Llewelyn, as I have said, this explicitly amounts to a prioritizing of the feminine in the later work. It is perhaps worth considering, then, what relationship the bisexual but feminine notion of maternity could possibly have with the feminine, as at first glance they would seem to be fundamentally incommensurable. The feminine as it appears in Levinas's work up to and including *Totality and Infinity* is a term parasitic on, or even constitutive of, an idea of sexual difference. It is the very alterity or specificity of the feminine *qua* feminine that gives philosophical sense to the part it plays, making it ostensibly incompatible with the idea of bisexuality suggested by Llewelyn. If the maternal is to 'belong' to the feminine in this schema, it must belong wholly or not at all; Llewelyn's 'bisexuality' would simply mean a compromise in or of sexual difference.

This argument, however, makes a biologistic mistake. For while biologically it is true, so far at least, that gestation and birth in the human being are exclusive to the female, the philosophical elaboration of this fact takes place at the level of the symbolic. It is possible to fantasize a symbolic order based on a cultural elaboration of the biological experience (which is not only biological) of maternity, and it is this that Llewelyn spells out in his claim that '[a]nother genealogy, another *parenté* for man requires to be found.'[34] According to this 'other genealogy' the symbolic figure of the mother would signify, for both the male and the female, a relation or a value apart from biology; that is, it would play a symbolically important (privileged) part in founding myths and social structures of all kinds (not just within the family structure). For this there need not have been matriarchies in the historical past, and one does not necessarily need to postulate the Great Mother or the Goddess. At issue is not the reclamation of an archaic past but the immediate demands of the present and those of the future. For Llewelyn, for example, the requirement for another genealogy is articulated in the context of deep, ecological concerns.[35] Matriarchal utopias, either past or future, do not come into it. The idea of a maternal genealogy invokes instead the possibility for the restructuring of thought, which is what makes it a philosophical project. In the context of Levinas's philosophy, one could argue that the relationship between the feminine and maternity is in part precisely what allows the latter to play its philosophical role. As apogean responsibility, maternity as feminine signals, for Levinas, a particularity that expresses the uniqueness of one's responsibility for the Other, the impossibility of interchanging responsibilities with another of one's kind. The feminine maternal genealogy, if it worked, would emphasize this particularity, or revalue it. But to what extent does Levinas succeed in suggesting, if not effecting, this 'other genealogy' with his employment of the notion of maternity?

Reading generously, the claims made on behalf of Levinas's introduction of maternity work by presupposing or themselves aiming to effect a displacement of paternity. However, this overlooks (it *needs* to overlook) the fact that paternity, in its elaboration as filiality and fraternity, still plays a significant part in *Otherwise Than Being*. If, most obviously, maternity is not called upon to develop the ontological conclusion of the discussion of paternal fecundity this would not be surprising, given the more scrupulous attempt in *Otherwise Than Being* to avoid the language of ontology. This fact is, however, still significant in highlighting that to this extent maternity *is not* fecundity in this sense. Furthermore it is also not akin to the structure of paternity as the more elaborate generation of filiality or fraternity; these latter survive in *Otherwise Than Being* as something markedly different from maternity.

As in *Totality and Infinity*, the 'transition' to fraternity goes via the intervention or recognition of *le tiers*, the third (person). In *Totality and Infinity* the trace of *le tiers* in the eyes of the Other ensures that the intensity of the ethical relation does not become *injustice* with regard to all the others. The significance of this has been most fully elaborated by Simon Critchley in his claim that the ever-present presence of the *le tiers* attests to the ultimately political horizon of Levinasian ethics. The third does not come to join me in my relation with the Other, or does not follow on from an initial encounter with the Other: 'The ethical relation does not take place in an a-political space outside the public realm; rather, ethics is always already political, the relation to the face is always already a relation to humanity as a whole.'[36] It is this dimension of the ethical relation which distinguishes it from love understood as eros. The same move to *le tiers* is, if anything, even more important in *Otherwise Than Being*. It appears alongside the necessity to return, and not just in philosophical discourse, to the order of 'the Said'. This 'Said', however, is not one uninformed or uninterrupted by the trace of the Saying, not an unjustified but a *justified* Said, because of its relation to *le tiers*, the opening up of the order of truth and, what seems to be the most important word for Levinas, *justice*.[37] 'If proximity ordained me only to the other', Levinas says,

> there would not have been any problem . . . . It is troubled and becomes a problem when a third party enters . . . . What then are the other and the third party for-one-another? What have they done to one another? Which passes before the other? . . . It is of itself the limit of responsibility and the birth of the question (a question of conscience): What do I have to do with

justice? Justice is necessary, that is, comparison, coexistence, contemporaneousness, assembling, order, thematization.[38]

That Levinas then aligns this realm, these questions, with philosophy is perhaps not surprising. What might not have been anticipated, however, is the inversion of this love of wisdom into the wisdom of love: 'Philosophy is this measure brought to the infinity of the being-for-the-other of proximity, it is the wisdom of love.'[39] The love of wisdom by itself, even with the best of intentions, would court the danger of abstraction, and one thinks, for example, of the arid formalism of Kant's deontological morality or of Plato's ultimately parthenogenetic philosopher-lover in his solitary contemplation of the realm of Ideas. The love of love, on the other hand, would be the exclusivity of romantic or erotic love, ultimately not just privileging the beloved above all others, but also privileging the self – self-indulgent. When Levinas describes philosophy as 'the wisdom of love in the service of love' he thus describes the Said said in the service of the Saying, the 'justified Said', in which wisdom has learnt from love, or in which politics is not uninformed by ethics.[40] This is often translated into the familiar 'Levinasian' idea of the primacy of ethics. Less familiar, however, is Levinas's equal insistence on the need to understand 'justice' as the demand that ethics be similarly informed by politics, in the sense of a certain restriction, the 'measuring' of infinity, the comparison of incomparables, or 'equality'. Politics, justice, and even philosophy refer ethics to the public space of the gaze of the third party, to society, to institutions, to a community of which I am a citizen and in which I am entitled to call the Other to account.[41]

This community, however, as elaborated in *Otherwise Than Being*, is still the masculine community of brothers, that apparently neutral and universal community of the 'human fraternity' familiar from *Totality and Infinity*.[42] Once this community, and the wisdom of love that informs it, appear in *Otherwise Than Being*, the trope of maternity drops out, much as the feminine ceases to play a role in *Totality and Infinity* after the elaboration of fecundity as fraternity. Thus a familiar pattern is repeated. Proximity understood as maternity occupies a position in *Otherwise Than Being* not wholly dissimilar to that of eros in *Totality and Infinity*. By itself, as paradigmatically ethical, the proximity of maternity seems to harbour that same tendency to exclusivity previously located in eros. The intimacy of the ethical couple based on the mother and child, what Levinas calls 'the intimacy of the face-to-face',[43] the ethical substitution of the former for the latter, runs the same risk of the exclusion of the third party.

It may be objected that nothing like 'proximity by itself' is thinkable within the context of *Otherwise Than Being*, but it is Levinas who says that the relationship with the third party is 'an incessant *correction* of the asymmetry of proximity.'[44] That there is a need for correction would indicate the possibility of a certain *excessive* proximity, an excess or intensity which the language of the descriptions of proximity inevitably associate with eros. The intense physicality of the passages on sensibility and proximity, the almost sadistic/masochistic descriptions of the skin exposed to injury and wound, 'the pain [that] penetrates into the very heart of the for-oneself',[45] *jouissance*, and, of course, aspects of maternity itself (skin, breast, caress) are erotically charged images. If, then, nothing like 'proximity by itself' is thinkable within the Levinasian text, it is still the case that the very proximity of proximity invites certain erotic possibilities that stand in need of 'correction'; indeed, the fraternal community demands it, for one cannot be 'close' to all one's brothers, and one must look beyond the face of one's neighbour. At the very least, then, maternity does not function like the notion of paternity in the previous texts. Maternity does not *replace* paternity, and the latter survives, somewhat covertly, in the fraternal community which it founds. The necessity to overcome the duality of erotic coupling in *Totality and Infinity*, has become, in *Otherwise Than Being*, the necessity to overcome (to 'correct') the duality of the asymmetrical ethical relation, epitomized in maternity. Levinas's text has not been able to effect or install an alternative feminine *parenté* because ultimately maternity must and does give way to paternity, that is, to the law of the father. Maternity, indeed, as associated with the particularity of the feminine, is *outside* of any *parenté* when this is understood, as paternity is, as the institution of a *universal* order of the human, of sociality, community and philosophy.

Levinas and the Symposium: *what is love?*

The introduction of the idea of maternity is not an alternative to the masculine category of paternity because it is not the same sort of thing. It is not performing the same philosophical role. Maternity does not replace paternity. On the contrary, maternity gives way to paternity in philosophical importance because it is still through the transformation of the latter that transcendence is thought. Maternity, as ethics, is phenomenologically important, but phenomenology is not the ultimate philosophical goal. If in *Totality and Infinity* the elaboration of paternity as fraternity leads 'beyond the face' to transcendence, this movement is restaged in *Otherwise Than Being* as the affirmation of the 'wisdom of love'. The textual development of the wisdom of love also makes it clear that the philosophical problematic of transcendence is, even at this late stage in Levinas's work, still being played out in relation to the themes of eros and fecundity, and in particular through the opposition between eros and non-erotic love. The development of this opposition is often marked as the distinction between 'eros' (*l'éros*) and 'love' (*l'amour*), terms which appeared to be used synonymously in, for example, *Time and the Other*. In *Otherwise Than Being* no such confusion is possible as the remarks on eros

become progressively more and more negative. Granted that there are relatively few references to eros, much from the previous work is presupposed in
Otherwise Than Being. In Chapter III, in the context of a discussion of proximity and obsession, a footnote reminds the reader of the primacy of ethics over
eros; in the final chapter another reference suggests that the erotic relation
consists in an attachment to essence (not, therefore, a movement *au-delà de
l'essence*), that it belongs to a certain category of pleasures including intoxica-
tion and drunkenness where pleasure is separated from the responsibility for
another, from the law.[46] The opening of the subject to the *au-delà* is, then, a
non-erotic opening. Eros, however, more than just ethical privation, the privation of 'Good', is aligned with a certain 'positivity' of evil. Responsibility
for the neighbour is said to be:

> an assignation to a non-erotic proximity, to a desire of the non-desirable, to
> a desire of the stranger in the neighbour. It is outside of concupiscence,
> which for its part does not cease to seduce by the appearance of the Good.
> In a Luciferian way it takes on this appearance and thus claims to belong to
> the Good, gives itself out to be its equal, but in this very pretension which
> is an admission it remains subordinated.[47]

The reference to Lucifer is no doubt hyperbolic, but one takes the point.

If one has to search for these explicit references to eros in *Otherwise Than
Being*, in the essays that followed they are often prominent. In 'God and
Philosophy' (1975) the 'transcendence of the desirable' is said to be 'beyond
interestedness and eroticism'; responsibility for the other is 'the non-erotic
par excellence.'[48] In his Sorbonne lectures of 1975–6 published under the title
Dieu, la mort et le temps, non-erotic love is contrasted with the erotic (which,
confusingly, is called '*amour*'),[49] and in the conversations dating from 1986,
collected in *Autrement que savoir*, Levinas once again speaks of a response to the
face of the Other as love without concupiscence. Jean-Luc Marion (one of
Levinas's interlocutors) notes his surprise at Levinas's use of the word 'love'
when previously he had refused it as the most 'prostituted'. Levinas replies
that certainly he is wary of 'what one *usually* calls love', that is, primarily,
sexual love.[50] A passing mention here of the field of psychoanalysis also
reminds the reader *why* Levinas speaks out against eros in this way. It is not,
despite the earlier reference to Lucifer, that eros is *bad* in itself, but that it is
not primary. As Levinas says in 'And God Created Woman', the sexual is only
an accessory of the human; 'culture is not determined by the libido.' Furthermore, '[t]hese are not mere subtleties. What is challenged here is the
revolution which thinks it has achieved the ultimate by destroying the family
so as to liberate imprisoned sexuality.'[51] Levinas speaks therefore *against* the
contemporary claims made on behalf of eros, what he calls in the 1979 preface
to *Time and the Other* 'the simplicity of contemporary pan-eroticism.'[52]

In one sense, then, love supersedes eros in philosophical importance in Levinas's work in a fairly straightforward manner. At the same time, however, love remains *dependent* on eros in a much more complex relation. Love is defined and elaborated in opposition to eros in such a way that the latter is essential to love, albeit as negated. Love, indeed, is sublated or sublimated eros and, as such, a further elaboration of fecundity. That this is the case is startlingly evident in a comparison with Plato's *Symposium*. The parallel is so striking that Levinas's debt to Plato would be obvious even if he did not signal it explicitly.[53] In fact, the *Symposium* contains exactly that movement from eros to fecundity which is traced in Levinas's work, and indeed the same presumption and 'justification' of transcendence. The relationship is not, however, entirely straightforward, and the nature and location of its complexity is telling. Levinas's early references to the *Symposium* are predominantly negative: 'In Plato, Love, a child of need, retains the features of destitution. Its negativity is the simple "less" of need, and not the very movement unto alterity. . . .. [T]he Platonic interpretation . . . completely fails to recognize the role of the feminine.'[54] This does not mean that Platonic eros is elaborated in what one would now call homosexual terms, but that it is a misunderstanding of the relation to the Other as absolutely other, an alterity paradigmatically feminine in Levinas's *Existence and Existents*. In other words, Plato fails to see the positivity of the 'separation' from the Other in the erotic relation, characterizing it only as 'lack'. In *Time and the Other*, much the same point is made: 'Set against the cosmos that is Plato's world, is the world of the spirit where the implications of eros are not reduced to the logic of genus [*genre*], and where the ego takes the place of the same and the Other takes the place of the other.'[55] Again Plato misunderstands the specificity of the other as *autrui*, witnessed in the fact that for him the beloved is, ultimately, only significant as an example of the beautiful.

However, Levinas's later references to Platonic eros become more and more positive. Although the problem identified in *Existence and Existents* remains, it is *relocated* in the speech of Aristophanes, rather than that of Socrates. If for Levinas Aristophanes' bewildered and lost 'halves' come to signify eros as the simple negativity of lack, elements of Socrates' or Diotima's speech then seem, on the contrary, to provide something like the account of eros in *Totality and Infinity*. Specifically, Levinas draws attention to Diotima's story of the birth of Love as most consonant with his own account of eros:

> Can the Platonic myth of love, son of abundance and of poverty, be interpreted as bearing witness to the indigence of a wealth in desire, the insufficiency of that which is self-sufficient? Has not Plato, in the *Symposium*, in rejecting the myth of an androgynous being, affirmed the non-nostalgic nature of desire, the plenitude and the joy of being who experiences it?[56]

In Plato's dialogue the myth of the birth of Love is recounted to explain the origin of the nature of Love as Socrates has just disclosed it. Love of something, according to Socrates, is always *lack* of that thing and the desire to possess what one lacks in perpetuity. Love is also said to be love of beauty, in which case it follows that Love *lacks* beauty, and as 'what is good is the same as what is beautiful', Love lacks goodness.[57] As, according to Socrates, there is always a middle ground between extreme opposites (there is, for example, 'a state of mind half-way between wisdom and intelligence'), the fact that he lacks beauty and goodness makes Love not ugly and bad but 'something between the two'. As it could not possibly be thought that any god would be anything other than good and beautiful, this proves for Socrates that Love is not a god. But neither is he a mortal, 'he is half-way between mortal and immortal . . . half-god and half-man', his function being '[t]o interpret and convey messages to the gods from men and from men to the gods'. Love thus has 'an intermediate nature' and it is this nature that the myth of the birth of Love is meant to explain.

Feasting with the gods on the day Aphrodite was born, Contrivance, the son of Invention[58] fell into a drunken sleep and Poverty 'thinking to alleviate her wretched condition by bearing a child to Contrivance, lay with him and conceived Love.' Love, with an innate passion for beauty, became Aphrodite's follower and servant. Because of his maternal origin Love 'is always poor . . . hard and weather-beaten, shoeless and homeless', but being his father's son he is also 'bold and forward and strenuous'. Taken together his parentage means that he is neither mortal nor immortal, 'but on the same day he will live and flourish . . . and also meet his death; and then come to life again through the vigour that he inherits from his father. What he wins he always loses, and is neither rich nor poor, neither wise nor ignorant.' This latter quality assures Love a place as one of the class of lovers of wisdom: 'his father was wise and fertile in expedients, his mother devoid of wisdom and helpless.'

Levinas's explicit remarks on the *Symposium* indicate that it is the double and contradictory parentage of Love which provides the most fertile philosophical ground, because here one finds the positivity of negativity, riches within poverty (the erotic relation without relation), and poverty within riches (the disappointment of love become possession). The sense of this complimentary reading of Diotima's position depends, moreover, on an interpretative opposition to Aristophanes' speech, the crux of which is that 'love is simply the name for the desire and pursuit of the whole.'[59] Accordingly, the failure to achieve unity, the failure to fuse with the beloved, would be no more than the failure of love *tout court*. Love would be, in this version of Aristophanes' speech, the tragedy of humankind played out in comic form, whereas Diotima is able to read this failure in its true, positive sense.

Aristophanes' speech is, however, ill-served by Levinas's comments. The central motif of the speech – the original three sexes, quadripedic, double-headed, and so on, spinning round on their eight limbs in cartwheels until all cut in two – would be generically recognizable to Plato's contemporaries. Descriptions of composite and sundered beings would be well known from the works of Hesiod and Empedocles, for example, and would take on particular relevance given that these descriptions tended to appear in cosmogonical and theogonic contexts in which the appearance of Love was always an element. As in the following from Empedocles, Love unites what Hate has torn apart:

> There budded many a head without a neck,/And arms were roaming, shoulderless and bare,/And eyes that wanted foreheads drifted by . . . . In isolation wandered every limb,/Hither and thither seeking union meet . . . . But now as God with God was mingled more,/These members fell together where they met,/And many a birth besides was then begot/In a long line of ever varied life . . . . Creatures of countless hands and trailing feet. . . . Many were born with twofold brow and breast,/Some with the face of man on bovine stock,/Some with man's form beneath a bovine head,/Mixed shapes of being with shadowed secret parts,/Sometimes like men, and sometimes women-growths.[60]

This same sense of chaos and confusion, promiscuous mixing, adventitious and bizarre coupling is also more a feature of Aristophanes' tale than most readings now acknowledge. In modern times, although it is generally assumed that Socrates' speech forms the 'metaphysical core'[61] of the *Symposium*, many of Plato's readers have had the sense that there is nevertheless a grain of truth in Aristophanes' Empedoclean speech. Indeed, in common parlance it is not unusual (even if it is rather silly) for people to speak of their partners as their 'other half'. It is also interesting that in both the scholarly and the popular imagination, Aristophanes' heterosexual hermaphrodite has achieved a certain fame at the expense of his other two homosexes. Levinas himself refers to the myth of the androgyne as if this was the determining moment of the speech,[62] even though the reader of Plato is given to infer that the members of the symposium were not themselves originally hermaphroditic and that this is not the most significant of the three sexes. Fouillée well illustrates these two points together as he contemplates the 'profound thinking' in Aristophanes' speech: 'Is love not the union of two beings who complete each other, as if each found in the other that which they had previously lost? Does not each sex have the very qualities which its opposite lacks, if not entirely, at least in part?'[63] The illusion of the complimentarity of the two sexes seems to give credence to one particular version of the Aristophanesian myth with its homosexual elements elbowed out. But the ideal of love as ultimate union is not in principle incapable of recognizing homosexual love in equal measure, and its force remains visible in many Western discourses. In 'Beyond the

Pleasure Principle' Freud attributes his idea that the origin of a drive (in particular, the death drive) is the need to restore an earlier state of things to Aristophanes' speech in the *Symposium*.[64] Apparently amalgamating both Freud and Plato, Georges Bataille later wrote in his essay *Eroticism*: 'We are discontinuous beings, individuals who perish in isolation in the midst of an incomprehensible adventure, but we yearn for our lost continuity. My aim is to show that with all [three types of eroticism] the concern is to substitute for the individual isolated discontinuity a feeling of profound continuity.'[65]

Levinas's *opposition* to the Aristophanesian myth is also based on this read-ing – that is, love seeks to achieve union or fusion – and the counter-thesis that fusion or unity in love is impossible. For Levinas love desires not a nostalgic return to stasis but reaches out instead towards the other and ultim-ately towards a future: the impossibility or 'failure' of fusion is the very positivity of love. Levinas's rejection of the myth would thus seem to presup-pose that for Aristophanes love is only truly consummated if the lovers do actually find their other halves and live together in life-long union as one.[66] The implication of the speech itself, however, is more that this search is something akin to that for the needle in the haystack. Aristophanes' story is, precisely, *mythic*; it demands a more interpretative reading than Levinas's or than that based on the alleged complimentarity – the psychological and physical 'fit' – of the sexes. Aristophanes is more plausibly read as suggesting, mythically, that the man or woman in love acts *as if* they were trying to join together with their beloved, *as if* they sought union. And if even Aristophanes' lucky couples who do in fact meet their other half cannot achieve union without the divine intervention of Hephaestus, the blacksmith-god who will meld them together, what hope is there for the rest of us? As an ironic counsel of perfection, the real message would run contrary to the manifest content: union is unrealizable, but that does not stop us searching, like Empedocles' limbs adrift, for an end to our loneliness in love.[67] Accordingly, the speech is more 'Levinasian' than Levinas realizes. Consummation is the never-ending search not *for* a lover but *with* a lover, the impossibility of union is at once the guarantee of desire and – what Levinas's phenomenology of eros paradoxically avoids – the source of erotic pleasure. Lucretius illustrates this beautifully:

> They clasp bodies avidly and join the saliva of their mouths; /They breathe with mouth close-pressed to mouth/But to no avail, since they are able to rub off nothing,/Nor to penetrate and to pass into each other's bodies/With their whole bodies, for so they seem to wish/And to be striving to do. They are thus bound together/In the bonds of insatiable love while their very limbs melt,/Overcome with ecstasy.[68]

If Aristophanes' myth articulates, in a complex manner, the impossibility of fusion, it is left to others to elaborate its consequences or significance. In *The Philosophy of Love* (1535), Leone Ebreo, in dialogic form, interprets various Greek myths in terms of the Old Testament. In common with many Christian apologists (although Ebreo himself was a Jew), he teaches that Aristophanes' speech is Plato's bastardized version of a story told long before by Moses: the creation of Adam and Eve. At the creation of Adam on the sixth day he contained both male and female, hence the Platonic hermaphrodite. In taking one of Adam's ribs or sides, that is, 'the side or feminine person which was behind Adam's shoulder',[69] Eve was created as distinctively female, hence the split in the hermaphrodite. As Aristophanes gives the reason for this as over-weening human pride, some Christian commentators see it as an allegory for original sin.[70] Ebreo, however, does not. Man and woman, he says, 'being two divided halves of a single individual, come together again as one body and individual in the marriage and union of the flesh.'[71] In both Moses and Plato the basic split is the same, but, crucially, Ebreo believes each places a different interpretation on it: Moses, in opposition to Plato, holds the division to be for the better. The connection with Levinas's discussion of the creation in 'And God Created Woman' is obvious. Levinas speaks there of the original 'humanity' of the human, only afterwards to become sexed as masculine and feminine, in terms of a first hermaphroditic creature ('male and female created he them'). Like Ebreo, but in much greater detail, Levinas may be read as placing a different, positive, slant on the Aristophanesian split, which, in the early phenomenology of eros, becomes the very basis of the alterity of the Other, impossible to overcome.

Ambiguity and dialectic

Levinas's claim, however, is that any commonality with Plato rests on the description of the nature of Love according to his mixed parentage, an aspect of Socrates' or Diotima's speech. Neither mortal nor immortal, neither wise nor ignorant, Love is always described as 'something between the two'. In the actual description the 'both-and' relation is equally as prominent as the 'neither-nor' structure. In Levinasian terms, Love's nature is essentially *ambiguous*, an idea at least as old as the Orphic fragment which claims to have sung of 'the splendid and glorious Eros of a two-fold nature.'[72] In one sense it is, however, very odd – or at least profoundly un-Platonic – to locate 'ambiguity' as the virtue of this text. Platonic dialectic, that is, aims at the elimination of ambiguity, not its celebration. In the *Phaedrus* Socrates persuades Phaedrus that in listening to speeches we are most likely to be misled when the meanings of words are uncertain or ambiguous.[73] The reason Phaedrus was earlier misled by Lysias' speech – and what made it possible for Socrates to argue sophistically in his first speech – was precisely the ambiguity of the word 'love'. The dialectical method recommended there – the passage from genus to species – enables Socrates to distinguish between good (right hand) and bad (left hand) love.[74] Earlier the same method was used to break the generic 'madness' down into its four main species (the fourth being, of course, the divine madness of love). Now this method is ostensibly *opposed* to the trajectory of Diotima's speech in the *Symposium*: the passage from particulars to universals. In order to make the movement from particular beauties to universal beauty possible, however, Diotima first practises the same dialectical method of the *Phaedrus*. Immediately after the myth of the birth of Love, an ambiguity or confusion in the use of the word 'love' is discussed. If the aim of love is the possession of beauty or, what is the same thing, the good, and if it may be assumed that all men desire the good, why do we not speak of all men being in love, but say rather that some are in love and others are not?

The explanation, according to Diotima, is that 'we isolate a particular kind of love and appropriate for it the name of love, which really belongs to a wider whole, while we employ different names for the other kinds of love.'[75] The same is true of 'poetry', which originally meant 'creation' quite generally, but is now confined to that part of the field of poetry/creation which deals with music and metre. According to the same structure, in the *Phaedrus* the meaning of the word 'rhetoric' (previously confined to speeches in a court of law or similar) is broadened to the more general 'method of influencing men's minds by means of words.'[76] Similarly, in the *Symposium*: 'The generic concept [of love] embraces every desire for good and for happiness; that is precisely what almighty and all-ensnaring love is.' However, 'those whose passion runs in one particular channel usurp the name of lover, which belongs to them all, and are said to be lovers and in love.' This particular channel is sexual or romantic love.

All men, then, are 'in love', that is, all men desire the perpetual possession of 'the good'. In further explaining how love 'in perpetuity' is possible, Diotima then applies the same semantic expansion to the idea of procreation. By what 'method' or through which 'function', she asks, is love's eternal aim to be achieved? According to Diotima: 'The function is that of procreation in what is beautiful, and such procreation can be either physical or spiritual.' To procreate and bring forth in beauty is the function of love because 'procreation is the nearest thing to perpetuity and immortality that a mortal being can attain.' Love must desire immortality as well as the good, because only with immortality will the lover be able to enjoy the good in perpetuity. In the following passages the desire for immortality becomes the driving force of all love. Love of fame, the desire to beget children and the creative desire of the soul to beget spiritually are all aspects of the desire for immortality.

In attempting to explain to Socrates 'the perfect revelation' to which the mysteries of love may lead, Diotima then describes four stages – or four sorts of lover – and the various methods of 'procreation' appropriate to them. First, in the contemplation of physical beauty, the lover will 'fall in love with one particular beautiful person and beget noble sentiments in partnership with him.' Second, in observing the kinship between physical beauty in one person and in another, the lover will acknowledge 'that the beauty exhibited in all bodies is one and the same' and 'he will become a lover of all physical beauty, and will relax the intensity of his passion for one particular person.' Third, he will come to reckon beauty of soul more valuable than beauty of body; 'he will be compelled to contemplate beauty as it exists in activities and institutions, and to recognize that here too all beauty is akin, so that he will be led to consider physical beauty taken as a whole a poor thing in comparison.' Thus 'having his eyes fixed on beauty in the widest sense . . . by gazing upon the vast ocean of beauty to which his attention is now turned, [he] may bring forth in the abundance of his love and wisdom many beautiful and magnificent sentiments and ideas.'

The 'perfect revelation', the fourth stage, occurs when the lover 'catches sight of one unique science whose object is the beauty of which I am about to speak': eternal beauty, absolute beauty, that of which all other beautiful things partake – beauty in itself. This 'one unique science' is of course philosophy.[77] The lover of wisdom whose contemplation of beauty has elevated him to this plane has reached the only region in which it is possible for him

> to bring forth not mere reflected images of goodness but true goodness, because he will be in contact not with a reflection but with the truth[.] And having brought forth and nurtured true goodness he will have the privilege of being beloved of God, and becoming, if ever a man can, immortal himself.

Taking the various movements together, the dialectic of Diotima's speech is complex or multiple. She begins by moving from the specific (one type of love: sexual/romantic) to the generic (love in its expanded sense), a movement echoed in the trajectory from the particular beloved to the universal Idea. At the same time, however, in the same dialectical movement, Diotima practises the method of division which allowed Socrates, in the *Phaedrus*, to separate out the four different types of madness. This aspect of the dialectic – the division of love into its different types or stages – aims, like the divisions in the *Phaedrus*, at the decisive overcoming of ambiguity. In this sense, Levinas's location of the philosophical virtue of the *Symposium* in the ambiguity of love would be mistaken. Levinas's claim, however, is somewhat different. For whilst it is true that the aim of the dialectic is the overcoming of the *semantic* ambiguity of the word 'love', Levinas's philosophical interest in and commonality with Plato lies in the description of the *ontological* ambiguity of love itself, which emerges in the story of the birth of Love.

But in what does this ontological ambiguity really consist? It has been suggested that Socrates' speech in the *Symposium* stands out from the others in its attempt to hold together that which his friends all split apart; that is, only Socrates resists the temptation to see the ambiguity inherent *within* love as evidence of two separate types of love.[78] Pausanias, for example, holds that just as there are two Aphrodites (Heavenly and Common), so there are two Loves; Erixymachus agrees wholeheartedly with this distinction and tries to apply it more generally; Agathon and Aristophanes allegedly speak only of one type of love, the physical, thus splitting it off from its spiritual or 'transcendent' aspect. If this *is* the case with these others, however, Socrates is surely no different. For example, he makes a very clear distinction between physical and spiritual procreation, the characteristics of which tally point for point with the other speakers' descriptions of the two Loves, and most importantly in the gendering of them. According to Pausanias, Heavenly Aphrodite, daughter of Uranus, had no mother. Common Aphrodite, on the other hand, 'owes her birth to the conjunction of male and female', and she represents the sort of love that 'the baser sort of men feel', its two main characteristics being that 'it is directed towards women quite as much as young men', and that it is physical rather than spiritual. Heavenly Aphrodite, 'who has no female strain in her, but springs entirely from the male' is free from wantonness; lovers inspired by her 'are attracted towards the male sex, and value it as being naturally the stronger and more intelligent.'[79] When Socrates then distinguishes between different sorts of procreation he echoes Pausanias' distinction. Those, he says, 'whose creative instinct is physical have recourse to women', but there are others whose desire is of the soul. These others are not explicitly said to be lovers of men, but the elaboration of spiritual procreation in terms of the pederastic relationship clearly amounts to the same thing. The physical (also called the base) is associated with the feminine, and the spiritual, without a doubt the superior love for Socrates, is associated with the masculine.

Although the first step in the ladder of love begins with the contemplation of the *physical* beauty of the beloved it is immediately dissociated from the gratification of physical desires, as the 'function' of love at this stage is already to 'beget noble sentiments in partnership with him.' The reader of Plato knows from Socrates' jests in this and other dialogues that the latter was not immune to physical beauty. But Alcibiades' eulogy of Socrates which closes the *Symposium* establishes the proper attitude towards physical desire: renunciation; or what a modern reader might call 'sublimation'. As Socrates says, one must learn to make 'a right use of his feelings of love for boys', thus implying that there is also a 'wrong use'. That the physical origin of love is not forgotten is clear in the sexual imagery Socrates employs throughout. The passage at 206D is perhaps the most famous, even when, according to H.A. Mason,[80] translators of a sensitive (not to say homophobic) disposition tone it down (Percy Bysshe Shelley, for example, that well-known sexual radical of the early nineteenth century, found some passages in the *Symposium* so offensive – that is, so homosexual – that he simply left them out of his translation[81]). Hamilton translates as follows:

> when a person in a state of desire comes into contact with beauty, he has a feeling of serenity and happy relaxation which makes procreation possible. But, when ugliness is near, the effect is just the opposite; he frowns and withdraws gloomily into himself and recoils and contracts and cannot unite with it, but has painfully to retain what is teeming within him. So a person in whom desire is already active is violently attracted towards beauty, because beauty can deliver its possessor from the severity of his pangs.

As beauty is what makes *procreation* possible, the birth metaphor at the end cannot conceal that the dominant image is erection and ejaculation.[82] This image is also familiar from the *Phaedrus*. Describing the beginnings of the regrowth of the wings of the soul, Socrates tells how 'each embryo feather throbs like a pulse and presses against its proper outlet, so that the soul is driven mad by the pain of the pricks in every part.' (Hamilton presumably did not intend the comic *double entendre* in his translation, but it now appears felicitous.) On seeing the beloved, however, when the lover's 'soul is refreshed by the flood of emanations the closed passages are unstopped; he obtains a respite from his pains and pangs, and there is nothing to equal the sweetness of the pleasure which he enjoys for the moment.'[83]

The physical or the sexual is not disavowed, then, but it must be properly channeled. It remains, but as a constant threat, a threat which only the 'truly superhuman and wonderful'[84] Socrates is fully able to resist. In the *Phaedrus*, for example, Socrates speaks of the corrupted man who

> does not quickly make the transition from beauty on earth to absolute beauty; so when he sees its namesake here he feels no reverence for it, but surrenders himself to sensuality and is eager like a four-footed beast to mate and beget children, or in his addiction to wantonness feels no fear or shame in pursuing a pleasure which is unnatural.[85]

Sexual desire is the worm at the core of love and it is the purpose of Socrates' speech in the *Symposium* to eliminate it. The final stage of the ascent to absolute beauty leaves the earthly world behind entirely, the lover having turned his gaze away from the beloved, from beautiful objects in general, and even from the abstract beauty of institutions. The separating out of different types or forms of love – the overcoming of semantic ambiguity – is at the same time the overcoming of the ontological ambiguity of love, that is, the purification of the highest form of love, the isolation of an unambiguous spiritual form, or the resolution of ambiguity through sublimation.[86]

It is not the case, then, that Socrates manages to keep together what the other speech-makers split apart. On the contrary, there is evidence to suggest that it is precisely the others who refuse to separate out love in its physical and its spiritual aspects. Phaedrus, for example, speaks of the pederastic coupling in terms of the spiritual virtues of nobility and honour. Pausanias defends the love relationship in terms of right behaviour and worthy ends: 'There is, as I stated at first, no absolute right and wrong in love, but everything depends upon the circumstances; to yield to a bad man in a bad way is wrong, but to yield to a worthy man in a right way is right.'[87] These two speeches, along with that of Agathon, have often been interpreted as cynical 'noble' apologias for sexual gratification, the model of which is the speech of Lysias recited second hand in the *Phaedrus*. Mostly, however, this reading is no more than a prejudice, reinforced over the past 200 years or so by generations of moralizing and disapproval from homophobic commentators, as if the sexual expression of love between two men was, *a priori*, a base or perverse urge which they would try to veil in noble sentiment.[88] There is, of course, no reason to believe this. Even Aristophanes, whose speech is often represented as the most physically oriented, says that '[n]o one can suppose that it is mere physical enjoyment which causes the one [lover] to take such intense delight in the company of the other. It is clear that the soul of each has some other longing which it cannot express, but can only surmise and obscurely hint at.'[89] The sexual expression of love, physical interconnection, would then be seen as the doomed attempt, perhaps the only one possible, to satisfy rather than to replace the yearnings of *the soul*. This is why, in fact, fusion is impossible; bodies can be locked together, but not souls. Agathon's speech provides a final example. Love, he says, 'has established his dwelling in the characters and souls of men', and 'anyone whom Love touches becomes a poet'.[90] Of course, the juxtaposition of poetry and love is not merely adventitious in the speech of a poet, but it also allows Agathon to demonstrate one aspect of Socrates' speech even better than the philosopher himself. Agathon's lover, Pausanias, is present at the symposium, but his speech is addressed directly to Phaedrus, a young man renowned for his beauty, captured in the meaning of his name ('bright' or 'radiant'). Inspired, then, by either Pausanias or Phaedrus, perhaps both, Agathon is touched by love, his speech a poetic creation and a performative enactment of love in Socrates' sense; Agathon, that is, gives birth in beauty.

Levinas's phenomenology of eros and the later thought of a love devoid of eros is more congruent with the speech of Socrates and Diotima than any other because it follows the same pattern. The ambiguity of love, understood as a relation of contradictories (transcendence/immanence, spiritual/physical, divine/profane) gives way both in Socrates' speech and in Levinas's intellectual trajectory to a distinction between two different sorts of love: the physical (eros proper) and the spiritual (love proper).[91] What Levinas calls the ambiguity of love is also thematized as the threat of sexual infection. The tendency towards immanence in love – one side of its essential ambiguity – is not the grit that makes the pearl, but rather its fatal flaw. Perhaps the most forceful expression of this idea in *Totality and Infinity* is made with explicit reference to the *Symposium*:

> an essential aspect of love, which as transcendence goes unto the Other, throws us back this side of immanence itself . . . . Love as a relation with the Other can be reduced to this fundamental immanence, divested of all transcendence . . . . Aristophanes' myth in Plato's *Symposium*, in which love reunites the two halves of one sole being, interprets [love] as a return to self. Enjoyment justifies this interpretation. It brings into relief the ambiguity of an event situated at the limit of immanence and transcendence.[92]

The point is made again, in 1975, in 'God and Philosophy', this time with reference to Diotima's alleged insight that the dual parentage of love – its ambiguity – means that it is subject to the malignant vulgarity of concupiscence.[93] For Levinas concupiscence is bad insofar as it inevitably involves a return to self, insofar as it is compromised by a residual, and in the end determining, connection with (bodily) need; in *Totality and Infinity* need is actually described need as '*Vulgar Venus*'.[94]

The move in Diotima's speech from love of one particular beautiful person to love of all beauty is mirrored in Levinas's move from the closed circuit of the couple to more 'universal' structures. Furthermore, for Levinas and for Plato in all of the speeches of the *Symposium*, whether two different aspects or two different sorts of love, physical eros is consistently associated with the female or the feminine and spiritual love (which *is* philosophy: love of wisdom) with the male or the masculine. The decreasingly negative character of Levinas's references to Platonic eros, and the increasing tendency to identify Aristophanes' speech as illustrative of a degenerate understanding of eros may be explained as the Aristophanesian lovers coming to represent for Levinas eros proper (erotic eros), once the distinction has been made in Levinas's work between eros and love. They represent not just eros considered in its negative aspect but *eros itself*, insofar as eros has come to signify, for Levinas, an inferior relationship, and insofar as Levinas tacitly agrees with the dominant interpretation of Aristophanes' speech as concerned only with the physical, the sexual, aspect of love. For Levinas too, then, the resolution of the semantic ambiguity (the distinction between erotic and non-erotic love) is at the same time the resolution of the ontological ambiguity into two distinct and now unambiguously separate phenomena: eros and love.

The distinction between eros and love also explains the absence in Levinas's later work of such critical comments on Socrates'/Diotima's speech as were found in *Existence and Existents*. For whilst it is not explicitly acknowledged, Levinas's discussions of paternity and fecundity clearly owe a great deal to the *Symposium*, most obviously in the parallels with Plato's 'procreation'. Despite Levinas's apparent wish to distance himself from Plato's theme of immortality, he often speaks of paternity as the continued existence of the self in the other 'across the definitiveness of an inevitable death', of the way in which fecundity 'escapes the punctual instant of death', although keen also to emphasize that he is not talking about 'eternal life'.[95] But the idea of immortality in the *Symposium* is similarly complex. It is remarkable, as Cobb points out,[96] that the doctrine expounded by Socrates/Diotima in the *Symposium* rests partly on the assumption of the *mortality* of the soul, in contrast to what is taught in the *Phaedo*, for example. In a long explanation of the possible meaning of immortality through procreation, Diotima remarks that even during life any living being 'does not in fact retain the same attributes, although he is called the same person; he is always undergoing a process of loss and reparation, which affects his hair, his flesh, his bones, his blood, and his whole body.' Similarly, she says, a man's soul is undergoing constant change, not just with regard to character, habits, and so on, but also knowledge; what is called recollection of a piece of knowledge is in fact the implantation of a new impression to replace a lost one, which gives knowledge only a 'spurious appearance of uninterrupted identity.' It is this that ensures the 'immortality' of the mortal:

> It is in this way that everything mortal is preserved; not by remaining for ever the same, which is the prerogative of divinity, but by undergoing a process in which the losses caused by age are repaired by new acquisitions of a similar kind. This device, Socrates, enables the mortal to partake of immortality, physically as well as in other ways; but the immortal enjoys immortality after another manner.[97]

The similarity to Levinas is striking.

It is appropriate that 'immortality', however, will find its highest expression in a fecundity of the soul, procreation in the non-corporeal realm of Ideas. The fruits of the highest stage of love – the love of wisdom – are 'beautiful and magnificent sentiments and ideas',[98] children of the soul which, Plato says, everyone would prefer to children 'after the flesh'. Levinas's 'filiality' is similarly not restricted to children after the flesh. If, as he says, the fecundity which issues in the father-son relationship is not *only* to be understood biologically, it would refer also to the teacher-pupil relationship, for example, as in the ideal non-sexual Platonic presentation of pederasty. As Peperzak rather coyly puts it, Levinas's '"paternal Eros" reminds us of Plato's transformation of love into a passion for good education.'[99] In response to

Poirié, Levinas himself emphasizes not just the possibility of diverse interpretations of 'filiality', but that interpretation itself is a mode of filiality.[100]
For Plato the highest aim and end of love, 'to bring forth not mere reflected
images of goodness but true goodness', is possible only because the lover, in
the contemplation of the Idea of the Beautiful or the Good, is 'in contact not
with a reflection but with the truth'.[101] Or, as Levinas puts it: 'Transcendence,
the for the Other, the goodness correlative of the face, founds a more profound
relation: the goodness of goodness. Fecundity engendering fecundity accomplishes goodness'; 'For Desire to be accomplished is equivalent to engendering good being, to being goodness of goodness.'[102] Paternal fecundity, like
Platonic procreation, is the route to metaphysical transcendence. Levinas's
Aristophanesian phenomenology of eros gives way to a Platonic metaphysics
of love, a move mirrored in the Platonic sublimation of passionate sexual love
into the spiritual contemplation of the realm of Ideas, and ultimately the Idea
of the Good.

This Levinasian fecundity remains determinately paternal despite the
introduction of the idea of maternity in *Otherwise Than Being*. Platonic procreation is similarly masculine despite, as some commentators have pointed
out, the presence of a metaphorical maternity – images of pregnancy and
birth – in the *Symposium*. Much as the introduction of the notion of maternity
in Levinas's *Otherwise Than Being* has been interpreted as a move into a feminine or even feminist discourse, Arlene Saxonhouse, for example, has argued
that the metaphor of birth in the *Symposium* supplants those of impregnation
and ejaculation and constructs the female as the model for mankind, gendering the philosophic eros as feminine such that the female is no longer only
associated with the body.[103] As well as the metaphor of birth, there is the
attribution of the source of knowledge to Diotima, a woman. As there is no
evidence that allows the question of Diotima's actual historical existence to
be decided either way, Luce Irigaray, for example, concentrates on the fact of
Diotima's sex *within the fiction* and elaborates on this symbolically through the
metonymic substitution of 'Diotima's philosophy' for 'feminine philosophy'.
Socrates, she says, borrows Diotima's wisdom and power, and for the first part
of her speech at least, Diotima's 'dialectical' teaching on love presents the
reader with a model or a method of mediation which resists the dualistic
domination of the either/or, neither/nor structure of Socratic dialectic.[104] In
some ways, this is not unlike the ontologically ambiguous structure of the
feminine in Levinas's earlier work.

According to Adriana Cavarero, however, Plato's use of the Diotima character is 'a subtle and ambiguous strategy requiring that a female voice
expound the philosophical discourse of a patriarchal order that excludes
women, ultimately reinforcing the original matricide that disinvests them.'
Like Aeschylus' Athena, Diotima is a woman made to renounce or denounce
the female. The exquisite irony of Diotima is that she does so through the use

of a feminine vocabulary of pregnancy and parturition: 'In Diotima's speech maternal power is annihilated by offering its language and vocabulary to the power that will triumph over it, and will build its foundations on annihilation itself.'[105] As A.W. Price notes, there is, however, a confusion in or of the metaphors of begetting and bearing in the *Symposium*.[106] Plato says, for example, that the procreative impulse which all men have will fuel a natural desire to beget children (of the body and of the soul), and the relief afforded by contact with beauty is described according to the mechanism of orgasmic release. At the same time, however, the lover is said to '[bring] to birth the children he has long desired to have'. The English translations of Hamilton and Lamb attest to this difficulty in their different renderings of key passages, for example, 206C: 'All men, Socrates, have a procreative impulse, both spiritual and physical' (Hamilton); 'All men are pregnant, Socrates, both in body and in soul' (Lamb). The well-known metaphor of midwifery, used by Socrates in the *Theaetetus*, for example, cannot but add to the confusion.[107] Against the background of Cavarero's analysis, however, this 'confusion' could be seen as deliberate. In interweaving the metaphors of begetting and birthing the passage for the attribution of the latter to the male is perhaps eased and the metaphor seems less 'unnatural'. If begetting is, conventionally, associated with the male, and birthing, more obviously, with the female, the mixed metaphors further serve what Cavarero calls 'the mimetic effect of confusing or commingling the male and the female voice.'[108]

In the *Symposium* any actual references to women as participants in the procreative process are limited to the biological, the inferior realm of the physical which the philosopher will have decisively overcome. Spiritual procreation, that is, falls under the auspices of Heavenly Aphrodite whom Pausanias did not just describe but *defined* as motherless. Socrates does not disagree; indeed, his argument is an elaboration of this very thought; any procreation associated with the woman (actual maternity) is soon dispatched along with the physical itself. Far from being an introduction of the maternal into philosophical discourse, then, the *Symposium* effectively dismisses it, and not through any simple disavowal, but through a complex appropriation of linguistic images and the puppet character of Diotima. In the *Theaetetus* Socrates says that the function of actual midwives is less important than his, and that his 'differs from theirs in being practised upon men, not women, and in tending their souls in labour, not their bodies.'[109] Philosophers beget, they become pregnant, they give birth and they assist at birth; it is then a small step to the idea that the philosopher assists at the *rebirth* of his beloved, or even that he is reborn himself, with a purely masculine parentage. The only 'maternity' which concerns Plato in the *Symposium* is that which can be appropriated for the male, and for one very obvious reason: the dialogue is about *philosophy*, and as Cavarero says, '[t]he pregnant birth-giving male, like the male who practices midwifery, stands as the emblematic figure of true philosophy.'[110]

The comparison with Plato also shows that even the move beyond the biological makes little or no difference to the gendered configuration of Levinas's philosophy, when the biological or the sexual-physical (eros) is structurally associated with the feminine. The move beyond eros (in the narrower sense) does not involve a move beyond the sexually differentiated into the realm of universality or 'humanity' when eros is associated with the feminine. It involves a move beyond the feminine into a realm of masculine exclusivity. In Plato's era, the time of the gynaeceum, the characterization of the intellectual, the political – even the ethical – as masculine was perhaps more obvious. In part, for example, Diotima's speech in the *Symposium* is reported by Socrates because the actual presence of a female participant at such a gathering would not have been permissible. The ideology of the make-up of the all-male symposium is then mirrored in the intellectual content of the speeches, especially that of Socrates, where the ascent of the ladder of love is an overcoming of the physical associated with the feminine into a purer masculine realm. The case is not much different with Levinas. Insisting on the non-biological nature of paternity, for example, reinforces rather than diminishes its masculine signification when the biological (the physical, eros) has been decisively aligned with the feminine. For both Plato and Levinas the feminine aspects of their descriptive phenomenologies of eros give way to the masculine metaphysics of love as transcendence. The apparent privileging of maternity in both philosophies is also superficial when for both the maternal as feminine – compromised by its association with the erotic and the physical – must be transcended in paternity/fecundity/procreation; that is, in philosophy, the (spiritual) love of wisdom or the wisdom of love: goodness.

In the Platonic dialogues, the moment of contact between the lover of wisdom and the transcendent 'Good' is always expressed indirectly in mythic or poetic terms. In the *Phaedrus* the immortal souls (pre-lapsarian, not ever having been incarnated) go outside of the vault of heaven to stand on the back of the universe (Hamilton), pass outside and take their place on the outer surface of heaven (Fowler), to view that of which no mortal poet (Plato included) has or will have ever adequately sung, 'reality without colour or shape, intangible but utterly real, apprehensible only by intellect'.[111] 'The Good', like the sun with which it is compared, begets in its own likeness and reveals itself in its offspring – hence Socrates denies that he can speak of it directly or 'in itself'.[112] According to Levinas, in thus conceiving the Good as beyond being, and in identifying love as the movement towards the Good, 'Plato catches sight also of aspirations . . . in which we recognize the pattern of Desire . . . . The place of the Good above every essence is the most profound teaching, the definitive teaching, not of theology, but of philosophy.' This transcendence of the Good with respect to being should, Levinas says, 'have served as a foundation for a pluralist philosophy in which the plurality of being would not disappear into the unity of number nor be integrated into a totality.'[113] With Levinas, it did. The transcendence of the Good – accomplished in/as fecundity – is the foundation for the philosophy of the ethical or religious relation. Furthermore, the elaboration of this in the terms of a basically Platonic movement through eros to procreation in/of the Good reveals transcendence as, in some sense, masculine – transcendence *of* the feminine – and not merely in outward expression but structurally, fundamentally. The introduction of maternity in *Otherwise Than Being* operates *within* this structure, not against it. However, if this is how Levinas's philosophy works, it is also, as the next chapter shows, in another sense, precisely how it does *not* work.[114]

CHAPTER FIVE

Affectivity and Meaning: the Intelligibility of Transcendence

The naming of transcendence as 'Goodness' is probably the most opaque moment in Levinas's philosophy. The appeal to Plato's brief references to the 'Good beyond being' helps little in clarifying what it actually means, as these are equally gnomic, and Levinas did not intend the appeal to be explanatory anyway. The problem is, of course, that of which *Otherwise Than Being* is a performative enactment: the attempt to say what cannot be said without betraying the saying, the attempt to articulate conceptually that which resists and is presupposed by the concept, the attempt to speak of the 'beyond being' when the language of being is the only one available. In the *Republic* Socrates' attempt to express the Good in the similes of the sun and the cave are not merely expressions of his own inability to explain it adequately, they are also meant to convey that it is in the nature of the Good to present these difficulties. Without understanding the character of goodness, however, nothing can be known of the value of anything else, as all things are dependent on it. One must try to speak, therefore, of the unspeakable; one must go on. Socrates will say, then, that the Good is something like a transcendent transcendental, surpassing but conferring reality on being, allowing things not just to be known but also to *be*. Imagine for a moment, as the neo-Platonists did, that this is the highest point of the Platonic philosophy; everything that Plato has ever wanted to say is expressed in this almost fumbled description of the Good beyond being. If there is a sense in which Plato gets 'carried away' with his thought of the Good beyond being this does not mean that he goes too far; it is consonant with the divine madness of philosophy, the soaring of the winged soul, philosophical 'enthusiasm' (which means, etymologically, to be possessed or inspired by a god), ecstasy. It seems, to his listeners, excessive. In reply to Socrates' attempt to define the Good, Glaucon makes a joke, causing great laughter: 'It really must be miraculously transcendent!' (Lee); 'It's way beyond human comprehension, all right' (Waterfield); 'Heaven save us, hyperbole can go no further' (Shorey).[1] As the second translation in particular captures, the joke rests on the *double entendre*: both the Good and Socrates' explanation of it are incomprehensible. Socrates takes it to refer to his own explanation, and blames the others for forcing him to speak about what he has already admitted is beyond him. It may be the only genuine moment of humility in the admission of ignorance in all the Socratic dialogues. It is hard not to admire Plato for piercing his own seriousness with this joke, for admitting the apparent implausibility of the metaphysical claim and his own inability to justify it. But Glaucon's reply is not mere ridicule; there is a certain embarrassment in his inability to understand. He and the others want Socrates to go on, and the sun and cave similes follow.

Levinas does not, to my knowledge, make jokes about transcendence as 'Goodness', but like Socrates he does insist – in almost exactly the same words – that the articulation of something like the Good, even if this takes place in 'hyperbole, in the superlative', is necessary in order that we may 'catch sight of and conceive of value.'[2] Playing Glaucon to his Socrates, then, one may at once admit one's scepticism and yet try to find a way to understand. If it is not possible to define what 'Goodness' or 'transcendence' (the beyond being) *is*, one may at least try to understand what it *does*, philosophically, and what 'justification' Levinas offers in the spirit of the Socratic simile. In fact, Levinas is actually quite clear about the necessity to presuppose the transcendence of 'Goodness' (although it can, and will, be called other things), and its philosophical justification lies in phenomenological attestation. More specifically, it is in the region of *affectivity*, phenomenologically uncovered, that an attempt is made to point to an 'experience' of transcendence which, like Socrates' 'Good', cannot be translated into the propositional structure of cognition (which for Levinas means 'knowledge') but which nevertheless has an intelligibility of its own: affective intelligibility. In the philosophical genealogy of this idea in Levinas's work, however, the relations between the ideas of eros, *jouissance*, affectivity, and ethics are extremely problematic. One finds, that is, that both eros and ethics emerge as paradigmatically affective, and that the description of their essential characteristics reveals a kinship bordering on identity. At the same time, the familiar insistence on the distinction between eros and ethics becomes ever more emphatic. What, then, is the purpose of this distinction. What philosophical role is it called upon to play in the 'justification' of transcendence, and what are the consequences of its collapse? At the same time this discussion affords an opportunity to question what has been implicitly criticized in earlier chapters: the adequacy of Levinas's phenomenology of eros. My suggestion is that to the extent that the phenomenology of eros succeeds, it is in the demonstration of its *affective* structure. This is a structure which eros shares with ethics, when the latter is understood as the face-to-face relation with the Other. It is because of Levinas's apparent need to separate these two out that his phenomenology of eros ultimately suffers.

Eros: enjoy

If the significance of eros lies in its *affective* nature, 'affectivity' would, in one sense, refer quite simply to the capacity to affect and to be affected, a condition of experience in which clear-cut distinctions between intellection and physical states, between subject and object, are inappropriate and inapplicable. In Levinas's early work, where the importance of the erotic relation is based on the formal structure of sexual difference, the characteristic affectivity of eros has yet to emerge. This amounts, in fact, to the absence of any specifically phenomenological account of eros; when this is remedied in *Totality and Infinity*, eros emerges as saturated/saturating affectivity. In Platonic terms, the erotic relation as a 'formal structure' was not 'manic' eros, and only the latter can properly be the object of a phenomenology.

Having made the move to manic eros, it might have made sense, from the beginning, to understand the alleged 'ambiguity' of love in terms of its affective structure. Eros, that is, constitutes an affect in which it is difficult to separate out whether it is the loving subject or the beloved object that is responsible, as it were, for 'generating' the affect. In the *Phaedrus* Plato may be read as revealing something of this structure. The lover is 'possessed' by the divine madness of love when the sight of the beloved (the beloved's beauty) reminds him of the Idea of beauty; the lover is transfixed or affected by the beloved because of an idea of his own. In the description of how the young beloved falls in love with his older (and thus, for Plato less attractive) lover Plato focuses on how the 'stream of longing' (that is, 'desire' (Fowler)) overflows the lover's heart, is bounced back to its origin in the beloved and hence enters and affects the latter with the same love. The beloved, then, in experiencing the 'counter-love which is the reflection of the love he inspires',[3] is in some sense the origin of the affect he undergoes. Another word for this is, of course, 'narcissism', although this is a narcissism dependent on the mediation of the other for its affective intensity. The *Phaedrus* would also appear to demonstrate the more strictly psychological and psychoanalytic meanings of an 'affect': the emotion or the somatic 'expression' associated with an idea (for Plato, an Idea). The *Phaedrus* – especially in its later discussion of rhetoric – almost theorizes the power of images, narratives, ideas, situations and so on to produce erotic affects. Erotic affect is, then, a phenomenon which problematizes, among other things, the physical/intellectual distinction to which Plato is otherwise so committed.

For Levinas this constitutive ambiguity – that erotic desire begins 'in' neither the subject nor the object exclusively, and that it is simultaneously psychic/somatic – becomes separated out into its narcissistic and Other-regarding components, the former the aspect of immanence, the latter of transcendence. The immanent aspect which comes from and returns to the lover is associated with need; in its transcendent aspect – that which comes from and goes to the Other – it is associated with metaphysical desire. The ambiguity which gives rise to eros then becomes the 'problem' of the tendency of metaphysical desire to turn into selfish sensual concupiscence (or need). Eros, to perform its philosophical role, needs to find a resolution in fecundity. To the extent that this constructs the ambiguity of the affective structure as a problem to be overcome it moves from a phenomenological to a moral or evaluative register. This discourse was already predisposed, it would seem, to pass judgement on eros, having already presupposed that the properly erotic was to be associated with the domain of need. Eros *as* eros, eros in its properly sensual aspect, remains essentially 'voluptuosity' which aims not at the Other but at the other's voluptuosity: 'it is voluptuosity of voluptuosity, love of the love of the other',[4] or love of the other's love. But in interpreting this as a return to self – love of the self – Levinas fails to keep the tension or ambiguity of eros alive, reducing it to an auto-erotic solipsism (which is, of course, impossible).

It is interesting, however, that this does *not* mean that Levinas is unable to convey anything of the nature of the erotic relation. In the first few pages of the 'Phenomenology of Eros', Levinas manages to describe, for example, the maddening yet exquisite frustration of a caress which could never possess nor satisfy its object; 'It *searches*', he says, 'it forages . . . a movement unto the invisible . . . . The desire that animates it is reborn in its satisfaction . . . . Voluptuosity does not come to gratify desire; it is this desire itself . . . [it] is impatience itself, breathes impatience and chokes with impatience.'[5] Perhaps the most significant word, however, is *attendrissement*, literally 'tenderizing', more poetically, softening, melting, yielding, dissolving, or in Alphonso Lingis's apt translation simply 'being moved'; in short, affectivity. But, to repeat, this 'being moved,' this melting, is not transcendence. Transcendence, or metaphysical desire, would be a ceaseless movement towards exteriority, towards the Other, while eros, for Levinas, completes a circular movement back to the self in its seemingly inevitable transformation into the satisfaction of a need. The Other exists only for the satisfaction of my desires; I, ultimately am only concerned with myself. Thus the character of eros – eros without fecundity – is essentially unethical, or perhaps non-ethical. This is the judgment on eros when eros is described – and described very well – as the affective state of voluptuosity, very different from the 'formal structure' outlined in the earlier work. This eros, affective eros, manic eros, must be overcome in the name of both transcendence and ethics.

But given that there is no necessity to understand eros in these terms, and no explanation – only a presumption – of the compromising association of the properly erotic with need, why does Levinas think of eros in this way? What is it about eros that slides it into the unethical or into immanence? An answer may lie in the fraught relationship between eros and *jouissance*. According to the analyses of Section II of *Totality and Infinity*, *jouissance*, or enjoyment, is a non-theoretical relation to the world:

We live from 'good soup,' air, light, spectacles, work, ideas, sleep, etc . . . . These are not objects of representations. We live from them . . . . The things we live from are not tools, nor even implements, in the Heideg-gerian sense of the term. Their existence is not exhausted by the utilitarian schematism that delineates them as having the existence of hammers, needles, or machines. They are always in a certain measure – and even the hammers, needles and machines are – objects of enjoyment.[6]

Jouissance, Levinas, says, 'does not belong to the order of thought but to that of sentiment, that is, the affectivity wherein the egoism of the I pulsates.'[7] The 'I' does not enjoy, the 'I' *is* enjoyment: 'Life is affectivity and sentiment; to live is to enjoy life.'[8] *Jouissance* is thus not one affective state amongst others but the very state of affectivity itself. As a relation to the world it could only be described in terms of intentionality if that word were to lose the intel-lectualist bias which Levinas, rightly or wrongly, discerns in Husserlian phe-nomenology. In enjoyment the things are not the contents of an intentional aiming towards, but the very nourishment of life: 'Life's relation with the very conditions of its life becomes the nourishment and content of that life. Life is *love of life*, a relation with contents that are not my being but more dear than my being: thinking, eating, sleeping, reading, working, warming oneself in the sun.'[9]

Thinking, eating, sleeping, reading, working, warming oneself in the sun, but not *loving*, much as one might expect *jouissance* to imply such a thing. According to Levinas: 'What is termed an affective state does not have the dull monotony of a state, but is a vibrant exaltation in which dawns the self.'[10] Strange, then, that thinking, eating, sleeping, reading, working, warming oneself in the sun, should be 'vibrant exaltations' when eros is not. But of course eros is; eros cannot not be evoked in the word *jouissance*:[11] 'Life does not consist in seeking and using up [*consumer*] the fuel furnished by breathing and nourishment, but, if we may so speak, in consummating [*con-sommer*] terrestrial and celestial nourishments.'[12] Here, then, as elsewhere, if eros is not mentioned by name, its presence still hangs heavy over the whole account of enjoyment.

If the description of enjoyment bears witness to an irresistible being-affected, it is not the outcome of a choice. In its connection with the needs of the body, according to which I do not represent things to myself or constitute things for myself in intentional thought but devour or soak them up, it is tempting to read Levinas's account as, in part, an attempt to relieve human need of its purely biological signification, to show that what is human about human need is its character as always already meaningful. The satisfaction of human needs is in itself in excess of the demands of need insofar as satisfaction is also enjoyment. This is what Levinas means when he says that the human is happy to have needs. To be sure one eats to satisfy a hunger but one also enjoys one's food, and the aspect of enjoyment turns the act into something else besides: 'To enjoy without utility, in pure loss, gratuitously, without referring to anything else, in pure expenditure – this is the human.'[13] In short, enjoyment is the human; the satisfaction of human needs is not lived as utilitarian means-end behaviour but is enjoyed, almost decadently. And although Levinas himself does not draw this conclusion, the being-human of human needs amounts to the impossibility, finally, of separating out need from desire. I both need and desire the food I consume, which is why Levinas can speak of enjoyment and life as the 'consummation' of (my relationship with) terrestrial and celestial nourishments.

Levinas himself, however, resists this implication and depends in the analysis of enjoyment and eros on a distinction between need and (metaphysical) desire. Insofar as eros is implicated in this account of *jouissance*, it enjoys both its positive and its negative characteristics. Eros delights as joyful affectivity, it carries within it the specifically human element of desire, but reverts, ultimately, into need. The raptures of consummation notwithstanding, the food *is* consumed, the lover *is* used up. And yet earlier, in making a distinction between eating and loving, precisely this connection was being challenged. In *Existence and Existents* loving is distinguished from eating in being essentially unsatisfiable. Love is not a need that can be satisfied through the consumption of an object, even if in the pursuit of our desires we sometimes act as if it could, hence 'the ridiculous and tragic simulation of devouring in kissing and biting.'[14] The nature of desire is mistakenly confounded with the nature of a need that seeks some thing, but desire is, in a sense, a hunger for nothing. Desire has no object, strictly speaking. Desire as affect, is void of representational content; it is, as a friend once remarked, 'empty excitement.' Accordingly, one might also remark the ridiculous and tragic simulation of loving in the devouring of food; the pathetic attempt to sate an unspecified, objectless desire with bread and potatoes.

This means that while one crucial aspect of the description of eros does correspond to the account of enjoyment in *Totality and Infinity*, another is significantly absent. Sensibility, Levinas says, 'is not a fumbling objectification. Enjoyment, *by essence satisfied*, characterizes all sensations whose representational content dissolves into their affective content.'[15] Like enjoyment, then, eros would be identified by its affective content, but *contrary to enjoyment*, would be by essence *unsatisfied*. In that case, what compromises enjoyment – its ultimate transformation into the satisfaction of my need – *would not* be true of eros, an incessant movement of desire. Levinas himself notes that this inability to be satisfied by an object (or an act, one might add), also called the 'pathos' of eros, is not its failure but its essence: '*The very positivity of love lies in its negativity*.'[16] It would appear, then, that the negative judgment on eros in *Totality and Infinity* is the result of its implication in the account of unethical or pre-ethical enjoyment, when, in fact, eros is not the same sort of thing as enjoyment as Levinas defines it. Enjoyment, by essence satisfied, would be, as Levinas says, the consummation of one's relation with the world through the self-satisfaction of breathing and nourishment. Eros, by contrast, would be the *interruption* of enjoyment thus defined; the affectivity of eros manifests itself not as easy-breathing enjoyment, but in the inability to breathe easy, through the *disruption* of breathing and even of nourishment, through the disturbance, then, of 'thinking, eating, sleeping, reading, working, warming oneself in the sun.'

And yet, undeniably, eros is there in the account of *jouissance*, and legitimately so. It is there in the word and it is there in the stress on affective, rather than representational, content. So how can it both have and not have a place in the description of *jouissance*? The answer lies in the presentation and function of affectivity. The realm of affect, that is, is not limited to *jouissance* and eros but also characterizes the face-to-face relation of ethics, and as such affectivity itself emerges as an even more ambiguous phenomenon.

Ethics as affect

Section III of *Totality and Infinity* begins with a subsection entitled 'Sensibility and the Face', in which Levinas outlines a critique of 'sensationalist' theories of perception: theories which posit for analysis subjective experiences or sensations without reference to the object that produces or provokes them. This critique is made under the influence of the idea of intentionality, which ties subjective experience to its object in an essential way. But, Levinas says, this critique of sensation – that is, the idea of intentionality – must itself be subject to critique for its failure to 'recognize the plane on which the sensible life is lived as enjoyment.'[17] According to this second critique, the notion of sensation is somewhat rehabilitated 'when we see in it not the subjective counterpart of objective qualities, but an enjoyment "anterior" to the crystallization of consciousness, I and non-I, into subject and object . . . . The senses have a meaning [*Les sens ont un sens*] that is not predetermined as objectification',[18] that is, the senses have an *affective*, not a representational meaning, and this meaning is explicitly linked with the subject/object ambiguity of affectivity. What is contentious about this, however, is not the implicit distinction Levinas makes between the senses and cognition, but the explicit ascription to the former of an affective *meaning* that is somehow different to the meaning associated with cognition. This is no small claim, and it plays a role of the utmost importance in the justification of the later metaphysical claims.

Levinas goes on to say that the relation with alterity – the relation with the Other – is *outside* of enjoyment. It is 'different from experience in the sensible sense of the term, relative and egoist.'[19] Nevertheless, the encounter with the Other is still an encounter in the domain of the sensible as the title 'Sensibility and the Face' suggests, and it is also dominated by its affective rather than representational content. What distinguishes it from enjoyment, also affective, is the fact that, uniquely, the encounter with the Other is one in which the sensible 'resists.'[20] The Other is not assimilable, not available for alimentation or transmutation into the same; one cannot 'enjoy' the Other, indeed the Other puts an end to all enjoyment. The Other reveals, in the midst of self-satisfaction

> an insufficiency . . . without possible satisfaction – not only unsatisfied *in fact*, but outside of every perspective of satisfaction or unsatisfaction. The exteriority foreign to needs would then reveal an insufficiency full of this very insufficiency and not of hopes, a distance more precious than contact, a non-possession more precious than possession, a hunger that nourishes itself not with bread but with hunger itself. This is not some romantic dream, but what, from the beginning of this research imposed itself as Desire. Desire does not coincide with an unsatisfied need; it is situated beyond satisfaction and nonsatisfaction.[21]

'Desire' here is of course metaphysical desire – ethics – but its descriptive proximity to eros is quite obvious. What ethics and eros have in common, then, – what separates them both out from enjoyment – is the affective hollowing out of a space in which they each breed and feed upon and magnify their own hunger.[22] That the discussion of this ethical relation in *Totality and Infinity* is subsequently played out in terms of language or discourse perhaps serves to cover over the underlying emphasis on ethics as affectivity, ethics as sensibility. If the encounter with the Other interrupts enjoyment with an appeal which 'arouses my goodness'[23] it is nevertheless the case that this appeal consists not so much – perhaps not even at all – in *what* is said but in the affective fact of the saying of it, and my being open to this appeal is my capacity to be affected. Very briefly, this emphasis might constitute a reply to Derrida's deconstructive critique of Levinas in 'Violence and Metaphysics', in the sense that Derrida perhaps failed to take the dimension of affectivity sufficiently into account, or subordinated affectivity to conceptualization according to some apparent logocentric necessity.

On the other hand, one strong objection to this could be based on a counter-reading of some of the essays published soon after *Totality and Infinity*, especially 'Enigma and Phenomenon', construed as a response to Derrida's criticisms. In an attempt to demonstrate that the event of the encounter with the Other is beyond or outside of or irreducible to the terms of a traditional phenomenology, Levinas repeatedly uses the word 'disturb-ance', '*dérangement*'. His argument is that in the speech of the Other there is an excess of signification which is not only irreducible to the rational content of what is said in the speech, but is also irreducible to the rational order of discourse as such, when this order is understood as the limited conceptual apparatus of Western philosophy and the discourses which are dependent on it. He says:

> Everything depends on the possibility of vibrating with a meaning that is not synchronized with the speech that captures it and cannot be fitted into its order; everything depends on the possibility of a signification that would signify in an irreducible disturbance. If a formal description of such a disturbance could be attempted, it would have to speak to us of a time, a plot, and norms that are not reducible to the understanding of being, which is allegedly the alpha and the omega of philosophy.[24]

Levinas is clear, however, that this is not to be understood as the disturbance of the irrational or the absurd. It is, he says, 'possible only as the entry into a given order of *another order* which does not accommodate itself with the first.'[25] Making the same point in 'Meaning and Sense' Levinas approvingly cites Sartre's description of the experience of the possibility of another perspective – the perspective of the Other – as the haemorrhaging of my order: 'And Sartre will say that the Other is a pure hole in the world – a most noteworthy insight, but he stops his analysis too soon.'[26] In all of this the point would seem to be the possibility of another order of *intelligibility*, rather than a region of affectivity which would stand over and against an intelligible order. It is the possibility of being intelligible otherwise, rather than recalcitrant to intelligibility, that concerns Levinas here, thus seemingly undermining the idea that it is affectivity that is doing the work.

This objection, however, is based on the (as yet unjustified) presumption of a distinction between intelligibility and affectivity. According to such a presumption, affective disturbance can only be understood as an interruptive unintelligibility or as signifying *beyond* intelligibility in the manner, perhaps, of a negative theology signifying an ineffable 'beyond'. But whether or not this presumption could be further argued and justified is beside the point, when it is Levinas's avowed intention to question it precisely *as presumption*. He does this with the counter-presumption of an *affective intelligibility* or an *intelligibility of affect*, although what that might mean is not at this stage clear. The position is more fully worked out in *Otherwise Than Being*, where the argument for the affective nature of ethics and for the distinctive intelligibility of this affectivity is, once again, played out within the framework of an operative distinction between ethics and eros. If, in this later text, this distinction is even quicker to collapse than in the earlier work, the problem of trying to understand Levinas's insistence on it now appears as related to the presumption of the idea of an affective, non-cognitive intelligibility.

Pleasure/pain

As remarked in the previous chapter, the return in *Otherwise Than Being* to the themes of sensibility and *jouissance* is in one sense unexpected, both because of their association with the egoistic, non-ethical 'I' in *Totality and Infinity*, and because of their historic association with eros, increasingly opposed to or contrasted with ethics in an explicit way.[27] If, however, in *Otherwise Than Being*, one finds sensibility and enjoyment integral to the elaboration of ethical proximity, the way has already been paved by the emphasis on affectivity. In both the earlier and the later texts, it is the non- or pre-intentional (non- or pre-thematizing) nature of sensibility that is stressed; the difference between the texts is one of accent. Both stress the corporeality of the subject as sensibility, but in *Totality and Infinity* the emphasis falls on pleasure, while in *Otherwise Than Being* the keynote is suffering.

In the later text it becomes clear that sensibility – the subject as incarnate, fleshy and vulnerable, the subject as 'entrails in a skin' – is the precondition for ethics. According to this fleshy vulnerability the affectivity of ethics – the being affected by the Other – is described in strikingly visceral terms. Ethics always was an end to enjoyment, but now, called proximity, it is described in terms of psychic and physical suffering. Proximity is not a state of rest or repose but restlessness and disquietude; more, it is physical discomfort, the 'groaning of the entrails,' for example.[28] Over and over, Levinas asserts in *Otherwise Than Being* that this intensely affective ethics is not eros. This is a responsibility before eros, he says; I can only enjoy the other and suffer by the other if I am already for-the-other.[29] This is a non-erotic proximity he says, at one point three times in as many paragraphs.[30] And yet, despite these disclaimers, it is remarkable that the descriptions of ethical proximity – or the *symptoms* of ethical proximity, one might say – are clearly and powerfully erotic in nature. One of the very few direct references to eros, specifically to the caress and sexuality, describes it as 'the overexaggeration of tangency, as if tangency admitted of gradation, right up to contact with the entrails, one skin going underneath another skin.'[31] This is eros. At the same time, the most insistent descriptions of ethical proximity then speak of the skin exposed to injury and wound, the pain that penetrates into the very heart of the for-oneself, the almost unbearable hypersensitivity of the skin responding to the merest brush, untranslatably, *'sensibilité à fleur de peau, à fleur de nerfs'*.[32] It is the respiration of the skin prior to any intention, a being turned to the other as a being turned inside out, a going beyond the skin, to the underside of the skin, a getting underneath the skin, being obsessed by the Other despite oneself, a nakedness more naked than any excoriation (*dépouillement*), a being exposed or open to the possibility of pain, grief, distress [*douleur*] or exploitation.[33] This proximity, Levinas says, as a modality not of knowledge but of obsession, is, affectively, a 'shuddering', noting that his use of this last term (*frémissement*) is a translation of Plato's φρικη in the *Phaedrus*, the uncontrollable shuddering or shivering that comes over the lover at the sight of the beloved.[34]

And yet, Levinas insists, ethics is not eros; eros is not ethical proximity. Accordingly, the introduction of the idea of maternity – and in particular the condition of prenatal bearing – may now be understood as an attempt to emphasize at once the visceral affectivity of ethics *and* its non-erotic status, presuming, as he does, that maternity is not erotic. 'Ethically', maternity signals the excess of proximity as the other *in* the same:

> sensibility is being affected by a non-phenomenon . . . it is a pre-original not resting on oneself, the restlessness of someone persecuted . . . . It is a writhing in the tight dimensions of pain, the unsuspected dimensions of the hither side. It is being torn up from oneself, being less than nothing, a rejection into the negative, behind nothingness; it is maternity, gestation of the other in the same. Is not the restlessness of someone persecuted but a modification of maternity, the groaning of the entrails, wounded by those it will bear or has borne?[35]

Levinas has said that the meaning proper to the sensible has to be described in terms of enjoyment and wounding;[36] the very terms of proximity. The emphasis on maternal *suffering* would then seem to be an attempt to demarcate an ethical domain of sensibility or affectivity from a non-ethical domain, that is from sensibility or affectivity as *jouissance*. Affectivity is rehabilitated, separated out from its over-identification with enjoyment, through its allegedly non-erotic ethical signification as suffering, the contortions of the original being-exposed to the proximity of the other. In order to do this, however, Levinas has to pass over without mention the *jouissance* of maternity, the erotic – even orgasmic – aspects of pregnancy, parturition and post-natal feeding as well as the erotic potential in or of *suffering* itself. And if suffering is only eroticized through its stylization and as symbolic of other possibilities, this is no less true of the trope of maternity in *Otherwise Than Being*. Levinas tries to separate out the affective domain of ethics (persecution) from eros (*jouissance*), but even in maternity, with all this restless groaning and writhing, with these 'unsuspected dimensions of the hither side', eros is never far away. In fact, the descriptive symptomatology of ethics borders that of eros so closely that there are times when even the subtlest diagnostician would be unable to decide between them. At whatever level of consciousness, Levinas recognizes this when, in speaking of the (ethical) obsession with and possession by the Other he refers the reader to the Song of Songs, to the lover's ecstatic lament: 'I am sick with love'.[37]

This line betrays the fact that what it is about eros that accounts for its insistent return in this discussion is precisely the ambiguity that Levinas himself ascribed to it, although here with a different content: neither pure enjoyment nor pure suffering, eros is both enjoyment *and* suffering, it encompasses within itself both of the two poles of affectivity that Levinas had identified, and in this sense could lay claim to a certain pre-eminence in the order of affectivity, one which is affirmed in the language of *Otherwise Than*

Being against the apparent authorial *vouloir dire*. Furthermore, resisting the Levinasian impulse to separate eros from ethics also means refusing the value judgment passed on eros because of its alienation from 'the Good'. Without subscribing to the naive pan-eroticism which Levinas disparages, this would at least indicate a further ambiguity in/of eros; if not beyond good and evil then at least between them and both.

Affectivity and intelligibility

If in the work after *Otherwise Than Being* Levinas's overt commitment to the distinction between ethics and eros becomes even more insistent, the structure of denial and negation is obvious. Evidence of psychoanalytic formations, however, ought not to obscure the function that this distinction actually plays in the elaboration of the speculative philosophical position that is the main preoccupation of Levinas's late work. Given that the distinction *is* maintained with ever-greater explicitness, despite (more likely, because of) its continual collapse within the phenomenological discourse that is meant to sustain it, the question is, why? What is it that this distinction itself is called upon to support? The question returns us to Levinas's presumption of an affective intelligibility, or an intelligibility of affect: the claim, otherwise stated, that 'the senses have a meaning that is not predetermined as objectification',[38] an affective, rather than a representational meaning.

At times Levinas writes of the affective sensibility of ethics as an empirical phenomenon.[39] I have argued, however, that the phenomenological descriptions of the experience of the encounter with the Other have a functional importance, indicators, in another idiom, for that which, paradoxically, surpasses phenomenology. In a footnote to the essay 'God and Philosophy' Levinas makes this particularly clear: 'It is the meaning of the beyond [being], of transcendence, *and not ethics*, that our study is pursuing. It finds this meaning in ethics.'[40] It is in ethics, then, that affectivity allegedly delineates the way to another order of intelligibility, or that affectivity itself is delineated *as* another order of intelligibility. In *Otherwise Than Being* this is most explicit in the section 'Sensibility and Cognition', where the former is distinguished from the latter and, indeed, affirmed as its ground. The critique of the primacy of cognition (of thematization, conceptualization, the identification of *this* as *that*, ideation – in general, 'knowing') is familiar from much of Levinas's previous work. He adds here that even sensible intuition, a reference to the meaning-giving, constituting intentionality of Husserlian phenomenology, is already a movement beyond the 'being affected' of sensibility to the activity of identification. The 'exposedness to affection, [that is,] vulnerability' is not, he says, reducible to 'knowing' or to sensible intuition in this sense:

sensation, which is at the basis of sensible experience and intuition, is not reducible to 'clarity' or to the 'idea' which one draws out of it. Not because it would comprise an opaque element resistant to the luminousness of the intelligible [but because] It is vulnerability – *jouissance* and suffering – whose status is not reducible to the fact of being put before a spectator subject. The intentionality of disclosure, and the symbolization of a totality which comprehends the opening of being aimed at by intentionality, would not constitute the sole or even the dominant meaning of the sensible. . . . The dominant meaning of sensibility, already caught sight of in vulnerability, and which will be shown in the responsibility characteristic of proximity – in its restlessness and its insomnia – contains the motivation for its cognitive function.[41]

To admit this, Levinas says, is to recognize that there is a sense, a meaning, other than that given to us by ontology, by which he means a sense, a meaning, other than that of the resourceful conceptuality of the Greek logos.[42] As ground and motivation of knowledge, sensibility, this 'immediacy on the surface of the skin – its vulnerability – is to be found anaesthetized in the process of knowing. But also, no doubt, repressed or suspended.'[43] The original scratch on the surface of the skin, then, arouses one to the Other – that is, to ethics – before this arousal is anaesthetized and/or repressed in the process of knowing. This in fact passes no judgment on knowing – if affectivity is first and foremost eros and suffering there is, obviously, a need for respite – Levinas only wants to insist on the recognition of the ground and motivation of knowing in sensibility and/or affectivity.

But there are in fact two very different claims being made here, or at least one could read Levinas as asserting two very different positions. There is, firstly, the position that sensibility (the realm of affect) is the ground or the condition for the order of meaning associated with cognition, representation, and so on (everything that is for Levinas encompassed with the umbrella term 'knowledge'). If this is reminiscent of both the Kantian transcendental aesthetic and Heidegger's discussion of mood in *Being and Time* this is no coincidence.[44] More generally, though, according to whatever philosophical preference one construes the role of sensibility as ground or condition of cognition, it is not contentious that there *is* some such role for it, at least so long as the words 'sensibility' and 'cognition' continue to be used in the conventional manner. The second position, however, is a different kettle of fish. This is the claim that sensibility (the realm of affect) has itself a *meaning* that is different and irreducible to the order of meaning associated with 'knowledge'. This claim is asserted against the assumption that the order of 'knowledge', defined in terms of the subject-object structure and an intentional aiming of the former towards the latter, defines the limits of intelligibility. Although significantly different in both motivation and conclusion, this is clearly a continuation of the Heideggerian critique of the philosophical primacy of epistemology. Now, though, Heideggerian philosophy itself is also contained within the compass of that which is to be dethroned, with Levinas's claim that the meaning of sensibility, the meaning of (or, rather, revealed through) ethics as effect, is a meaning beyond being, otherwise than being, or beyond essence.

It must be stressed that this 'beyond' (beyond epistemology, beyond ontology) is precisely *not* beyond intelligibility for Levinas. This is the whole point: 'The adventure of knowledge which is characteristic of being, ontological from the first, is not the only mode, nor the preliminary mode, of intelligibility or meaning. Experience as the source of meaning qua knowing has its motivation in a meaning that at the start is not a knowing at all.'[45] If this appears to be counter-intuitive this would only be, for Levinas, because prevailing philosophical orthodoxy is such that 'meaningful thought, and thought about being, would be pleonasms and equivalent pleonasms.'[46] It would, similarly, only be according to the same set of assumptions that affective (or non-cognitive) meaning, affective intelligibility, would appear to be an oxymoron. The problem, Levinas says in 'God and Philosophy', 'is whether the meaning that is equivalent to the *esse* of being, that is, the meaning which is meaning in philosophy, is not already a restriction of meaning . . . . Over and beyond being does not a meaning whose priority, translated into ontological language, would have to be called *antecedent* to being, show itself?'[47]

The ambiguity of the conflation of these two claims remains unremarked by Levinas and hence, unsurprisingly, unresolved. It does however become clear that it is the second, stronger and more contentious, claim that is the important one for the 'justification' of the metaphysics of transcendence. Indeed, it is the assertion of the priority of this claim, over and against the first, that actually constitutes his philosophical position, when this assertion has become, at its speculative height, the assertion of the priority of the intelligibility of *transcendence* over that of the *transcendental*. The words 'infinity,' 'God' and 'Good,' the gesture towards the Platonic 'One', are, for Levinas, the necessarily inadequate indicators of a transcendent intelligibility, intelligible, that is, outwith the bounds of conceptual mediation which are, for him, the bounds of 'being'. Furthermore, the intelligibility of the transcendent is not just different to conceptual thought but must be presupposed, according to Levinas, as its motivation and its ultimate justification, if signification, rationality, consciousness, 'the meaning which is meaning in philosophy' – in sum, 'being' – is not to collapse under the weight of its own sheer contingency and want of foundation. Spirit, if you like, in a spiritless world, the Good beyond being or what Levinas once elaborated as the transcendent 'sense' ('*sens*') that gives direction to the 'meaning' ('*signification*')[48] which arises in a transcendental field. The French '*sens*' means both 'sense' (as in 'meaning') and 'direction', allowing Levinas to imply 'sense' as transcendent-transcendental *orientation* much more easily than in the English. With the phrase '*le sens unique*' (which also means 'one way street') he also manages to suggest a univocity of meaning which, for him, it is necessary to think if plurality is to be more than simply relativism: 'Do not meanings require a unique sense from which they derive their very signifyingness?'[49] Loss of this unique sense, he says, is otherwise known as the death of God. Transcendence, then, is a necessary presupposition if there is to be any meaning with a relation to 'Truth' (Levinas's word). To have reasserted this in a philosophical climate of 'contemporary anti-Platonism' more attached to notions of finitude and semantic pluralism – explicitly, for example, against Merleau-Ponty's location of the origin of meaning in culture[50] – is what it means for Levinas to have '*retrouvé le platonisme*'.

Immanent and transcendent affectivities

It is of course in the nature of these speculative claims that they cannot be proved in any straightforward sense. Levinas's philosophical method therefore consists in a series of metaphysical declarations apparently extrapolated from and further supported by phenomenological evidences. Metaphysical truths are revealed through phenomenology, both in the sense that phenomenology allows one to encounter them and that it functions verificationally after the event of disclosure. In this way, the strong claim for the intelligibility of transcendence is apparently based on, revealed through or justified by the appeal to the phenomenology of the ethics of affect. Without this, it is no more than an assertion, and one which looks increasingly like theological compensation. In understanding Levinas's claim it is therefore crucial that the appeal to this base be properly examined. This reveals, however, that Levinas invokes a phenomenology of affectivity and borrows its persuasive findings to lend weight to a claim which is, at the same time, possible only as a complete *revocation* of the importance of the affective realm. This duplicity only really becomes clear in the later essays, but, in retrospect, it continually manifests itself throughout Levinas's work, symptomatically, as the breakdown of the distinction between ethics and eros, a distinction on which those texts nevertheless insist.

The associative process of thought which leads from affectivity to the intelligibility of transcendence goes via the claim that the senses have an affective *meaning* which is not reducible to the representational meaning structure of knowledge. This claim about the affective *meaning* of the senses – the distinct *intelligibility* of affectivity – is paradoxically based on a surreptitious separation of the realm of affectivity into two distinct genres. This is most explicit in 'God and Philosophy'. There Levinas explains that philosophies with transcendental consciousness as their starting point 'are not disturbed by the phenomenological interpretation of affective states' precisely because this transcendentalism always interprets affectivity as founded on representation. This interpretation succeeds, Levinas says, 'in the measure that affectivity is taken at the level of a tendency, or concupiscence, as Pascal would say – at the level of an aspiration which can be satisfied in pleasure or, when unsatisfied, remains a pure lack which causes suffering.'[51] In the terminology of Levinas's earlier work, this means that, insofar as affectivity is related to the domain of *need*, where, broadly speaking, satisfaction depends on the availability of an object corresponding to the subject's need, the being-meaningful of affectivity *is* best understood according to the subject-object structure of knowledge. The reference to Pascal gives us to understand that eros would belong to this region of affectivity – a suspicion fully confirmed in a later reference to Plato's *Symposium*[52] – even though this would sharply contradict the definition of eros as distinct from the satisfiable need to eat.

At the same time, the identification of a region of affectivity associated with need does not exclude, Levinas says, 'the possibility that, in another direction besides that of a tendency going to its term, there break out an affectivity which breaks with the form and the purpose of consciousness, and leaves immanence, is a transcendence.'[53] This other affectivity, this 'desire', 'is of another order than the desires involved in hedonist or eudaemonist affectivity and activity, where the desirable is invested, reached, and identified as an object of need.' This desire is 'Love without Eros', transcendence, ethics.[54] This twofold characterization of affectivity – the resolution of its ambiguity into two distinct genres – replicates, and attempts to strengthen further, the familiar distinction between eros and ethics, need and desire. But once again the distinction undoes itself in the moment of being spoken. Ethical, non-erotic affectivity is described as 'a dazzling, where the eye takes more than it can hold, an igniting of the skin which touches and does not touch what is beyond the graspable, and burns.'[55] In the next paragraph, exactly that imagery used in *Existence and Existents* to identify the particularity of love is now used to mark out an alleged non-erotic affectivity which 'hollows out a desire which cannot be filled, nourishes itself with its very augmentation, and is exalted as a desire, withdraws from its satisfaction in the measure that it approaches the desirable.'[56]

Why, then, insist on a distinction between ethics and eros, when every instance of this insistence only works to contrary effect? In fact, the separation of ethics from eros masks a more fundamental distinction between the intellectual and the sensible, a distinction which must remain hidden if the claim for the intelligibility of transcendence is to be left with defence. Recall that the claim is allegedly based on or revealed through the phenomenology of affectivity. This phenomenology is indeed persuasive. It appeals to the reader's sense that there is certainly some truth in the idea that affective experience is not reducible to the structures of propositional logic. Erotic desire is meaningful to the human being other than as an intentional aiming towards an object; the existential meaning of declarations of love are not exhausted by an examination of their propositional content. We know this. But to then conclude that affective phenomena thus indicate that the senses have a *meaning* other than that associated with cognition is wrong. It is accomplished only by falsely restricting the meaning of 'meaning' in intellection to the structures of propositional logic, noting that there is more to meaning than this, and then locating this excess in the senses, falsely confining knowledge/cognition to a strict subject-object structure (a structure which the idea of intentionality, for example, had already done much to problematize in its absolute formulation). Levinas accuses the philosophical tradition of restricting the meaning of 'meaning', but his own argument rests on a concurrence with this point. It is true that love is a relation of greater complexity and meaning than a grammatical analysis of 'I love you' is capable of expressing, and that epistemology may not have much to say about it, but to leap from this to the necessity to propose a unique sensuous meaning is wholly unjustified, and one which, moreover, the very originality of the idea of affectivity would challenge.

The claim that the senses have a meaning proper to themselves borrows its plausibility from an account of affectivity which quite rightly points to experiences and structures that may confound the logic of identity or the subject-object dualism, for example, and which suggests a transcendental role for affective structures in the achievement of meaning. This latter is the weaker of the two claims identified earlier: the position that sensibility (the realm of affect) is the ground or the condition for the order of meaning associated with representation, cognition, and so on. It is the conflation of this claim with the claim that sensibility has a meaning *of its own* that lends the latter a spurious credibility. That the latter cannot be defended is revealed in the necessity which imposes itself on Levinas of separating out the domain of affectivity into its immanent and transcendent aspects, a distinction flagged as that between eros and ethics. In effect this is a distinction between a sensible affectivity and an intelligible affectivity, where only the second (affective infinity, for example[57]) is transcendent, the first being a tendency in the domain of need.

The perverse upshot of this textual manipulation of 'affectivity' is the reassertion of the distinction between the sensible (need) and the intellectual (desire), when it is precisely the disruption of this distinction which is the achievement of philosophical descriptions and interpretations of affectivity. What is, in terms of traditional conceptual categories, the ambiguity of affectivity, is artificially separated out into opposing lots for which 'eros' and 'ethics' are, respectively, metonyms. The latter (ethics) then purportedly discloses the truth of the claim for the intelligibility of transcendence, drawing support from the phenomenology of affectivity when *in fact* the possibility of transcendence thus understood (opposed to 'eros' and all that it represents) is only achieved by separating off an intelligible affectivity from the domain of the sensible. The claim is parasitical on the phenomenological content of sensible affectivity whilst at the same time denying it. In being forced to divorce intelligible affectivity from any sensible component, which is to divorce it from anything which would justify its characterization *as affective*, the argument becomes the claim that the senses have a meaning of their own which is wholly non-sensual, and the phenomenological ground on which rest the claims for the intelligibility of transcendence collapses in contradiction. The impossibility of separating affectivity out into its sensible and intellectual components is revealed through the ceaseless collapse of the distinction between eros and ethics, its manifest presentation. Seeping relentlessly back into the places from which Levinas would banish it, eros, fittingly, reintroduces the constitutive ambiguity at the heart of affectivity, muddying the clear pool in which is reflected only a ghostly figure of a transcendent intelligibility.

The critical questions which Derrida puts to Levinas in 'Violence and Metaphysics' are, Derrida says, questions of language. This is perhaps most obvious in the charge that the Levinasian discourse against ontology 'must ceaselessly suppose and practice the thought of precomprehension of Being .... There is no speech without the thought and statement *of* Being.'[58] In imagining that the thought of Being is nothing other than a violence otherwise avoidable, in imagining a non-violent language which could do without the verb 'to be', Levinas imagines (although of course this is only implicit) an impossibility: the separation of thought and language (attested in Levinas's apparent proximity to the Platonic valorization – in the *Phaedrus* – of speech over writing). Speech as immediacy – the nudity of the face of the Other – would be language without rhetoric, a purely heterological thought (thought 'to the Other', renouncing the concept) as the source of meaning and language: according to Derrida a *dream* which 'must vanish *at daybreak*, as soon as language awakens'.[59] Perhaps trying to avoid these 'questions of language', the main theme in *Otherwise Than Being* – responsibility before all choice, the being already substituted for the Other, obedience before any voluntary decision – points, Levinas says, to an antinomy (or a series of antinomies) which bears witness to 'the Good' as this beyond being, the anteriority of responsibility is the Goodness of the Good, the Good assigns the subject to approach the Other.[60] But still, in thus separating the source and the possibility of sense from what Derrida calls 'the violence necessary in historical actuality' (or the violence of the concept) Levinas 'prop[s] up thought by means of transhistoricity .... For Levinas, the origin of meaning is non-history, is "beyond history"', which is doubly strange for the Jewgreek-Greekjew inhabiting and ranging across – coupling – two histories.[61]

History, system, the order of Being, rhetoric, phenomenology, ontology and the order of language itself insofar as it is inextricably complicit with these – in short, the symbolic order – are secondary structures for Levinas, dependent on and 'after' (in terms of both metaphysical and ethical priority), the transcendent orientation of meaning from 'beyond'. This beyond as the Good would 'assign' the subject to the Other, give the subject its meaning and subjectivity through this assignation otherwise known as 'ethics'. As 'proof' – albeit the proof akin to a mythic idiom, which is not to be despised or dismissed as 'rhetoric' – the this-wordly phenomenology of ethics and eros would allegedly demonstrate, in a way one would be tempted to call gnostic were it not for the association of the latter with 'knowledge', the possibility of and necessity for transcendence and, therefore, its intelligibility. In fact, however, the phenomenology of this-worldly structures can do nothing of the sort. It can point to structures of transcendence within, that is, immanent to, consciousness (which, in a nutshell, is what Husserl thought he had done in engaging with the problem of epistemology), and it can reveal alternative conceptions of being other than those based on the identity of the whole or of the subject – as with the ontological conclusion of the analyses of fecundity which, *contra* Levinas, there is no necessity to think as a filiation or a paternity akin to monotheism[62] (many brothers, one father, one authority).

It is more difficult, and more exigent, to locate 'the Good' in this world than 'beyond' it, or to locate 'the Good' without the aid of a beyond. To this end the development of the phenomenological analyses begun by Levinas would always, in fact, point inexorably back to language, sociality and history as *conditioning*, not just conditioned, or to the world itself as transcendent orientation, albeit one with no 'ethical' guarantee. Phenomenology, that is, works *against* the metaphysics of infinite transcendence, not for it; this is what the immanent critique of Levinas reveals.

Coda: Metaphysics and Feminism

I have argued that Levinas's claim to have retrieved a certain Platonism is the expression of a metaphysical project to reassert the meaning of and necessity for a thinking of transcendence, the orientation of a 'beyond' as the necessary presupposition of meaning itself. 'Ethics', I have argued, names the experience of a relation, a human event, that operates as the phenomenological attestation – 'proof' in the widest sense – of transcendence. My contention is, therefore, that the moment of metaphysics has priority in Levinas's philosophy, a point that the emphasis on ethics in the reception of Levinas's work has tended to obscure.

The evidence for this reading has come from a consideration of Levinas's discussions of eros, the feminine, sexual difference, fecundity, paternity, filiality and fraternity; the moment of Platonism has been most fully elaborated in relation to Plato's celebrated discussions of love. From this, two main results have emerged. The first is an insistence on the importance of these often marginalized – sometimes ignored – themes in Levinas's work. Relocating them to the centre of Levinas's philosophy effects a change of perspective which enables a new view of the whole, a reading of the basic project which might otherwise have remained unarticulated. The second takes the form of a feminist critique, one which begins with the details of certain themes and broadens out to encompass the role of these themes in the overall philosophical scheme; a critque, then, not just of 'the feminine', but also of the philosophy of transcendence within which it figures.

Accordingly, two main objections immediately suggest themselves, objections which may, for the moment, be considered as addressing two different issues: the question of the priority of metaphysics and the matter of the feminist critique. First, does not Levinas himself affirm the priority of ethics? Does he himself not insist that metaphysics and ethics are co-extensive? Second, what of the alternative readings that have seized on the notion of the feminine and claimed it for radical feminist ends?

The priority of the metaphysical idea

In *Totality and Infinity* Levinas writes that one of his objectives is '[t]he establishing of this primacy of the ethical, that is, of the relationship of man to man – signification, teaching and justice – a primacy of an irreducible structure upon which all the other structures rest'.[1] One could, no doubt, find many more passages like this, especially in the work of this period. They appear, superficially, to refute the thesis of the primacy of metaphysical transcendence. This is, however, to misunderstand both what 'ethics' is and the context in which such remarks are made. Quite generally, the primacy of ethics is affirmed *not* in relation to metaphysics but to phenomenology and/or ontology and what Levinas takes to be their refusal of transcendence, a refusal also referred to as contemporary anti-Platonism. The affirmation of the primacy of ethics is, then, not opposed to but *constitutive of* the primacy of transcendence.

In the specific case above, Levinas's remarks appear in a discussion of man's (sic) relation with God. Theological concepts, he says, remain empty so long as they draw no signification from human relationships – man's relation with God cannot be conducted in ignorance of the world of men and things: 'There can be no "knowledge" of God separated from the relationship with men. The Other is the very locus of metaphysical truth, and is indispensable for my relation with God.'[2] Metaphysics is enacted, he says, where the social relation is enacted, implying that the metaphysical relation is with God. Furthermore: 'The role Kant attributed to sensible experience in the domain of the understanding belongs in metaphysics to interhuman relations.'[3] Metaphysics without ethics is empty, but correlatively ethics without metaphysics is blind. Levinas's position – most notably in the Preface and Section I of *Totality and Infinity* – thus *seems to* attest most profoundly to the equiprimordiality of ethics and metaphysics, or the impossibility of thinking one without the other.

In his most recent work on Levinas, Derrida considers a similar problem of priority. In 'A Word of Welcome', a meditation on the idea of 'welcoming' in *Totality and Infinity* leads Derrida to a description of that book as 'an immense treatise *of hospitality*.'[4] Presupposing for the moment that the ethics of hospitality is foundational – that is, that ethics comes first – the question is: can this ethics of hospitality found a law or a politics? More specifically, in the precise context of the welcome of the immigrant or asylum seeker, can this ethics found a law or a politics of hospitality? Derrida raises the question in this form, however, only to point out that it is precisely the structure of foundation, 'a hierarchy of founding and founded, of principial originarity and derivation'[5] that Levinas's work calls into question with the discussion of the welcome and of the role of the third. Welcoming, briefly, is already conceived as a response to the call of the Other, and yet for the call to be, precisely, a call, it must function in anticipation of that response.[6] Similarly, the role of the third cannot be understood as something that 'comes after' the ethical relation both because it (he?) is said to be always already there in the eyes of the Other, and to be the guarantee of 'justice', which prevents the immediacy of the face-to-face becoming ethical violence.[7] Transpose the first point about welcome and response into the idiom of the relation between self-consciousnesses and it appears familiar and uncontentious. Transpose the second into a point about language or the symbolic order and it too looks familiar. Derrida's point, however, may be extrapolated as follows. Given that these structures may be elaborated in a variety of philosophical idioms, the temptation with the Levinasian idiom is to arrange its elements in orders of priority when, in fact, the relations of conditionality in Levinas's work are impossible to straighten out: 'They defy chronology as much as logic.'[8] What, then, of the alleged priority of metaphysics?

A few pages later in Derrida's text, there is something of a volte-face. Referring to the problem of the relations of conditionality he says: 'These infinite complications do not change anything about the general structure from which they are, in truth, derived: discourse, justice, ethical uprightness have to do first of all with *welcoming.*' That is, one might say, granted that there is a real problem with the relations of conditionality, is it not also the case that Levinas *nevertheless* insists on a certain prioritizing? Is it not the case that *despite* the avowed co-conditionality of metaphysics and ethics, Levinas *in fact* presupposes the priority of the former? As a question of authorial intention this is unanswerable and philosophically uninteresting, but with regard to what is contained in the work itself, it is important.

Derrida's question to Levinas in 'Violence and Metaphysics' may be glossed as 'what lets the Other appear? What precomprehension allows the Other to appear in their being?' If Derrida's answer reasserted the need for ethics to 'go through' phenomenology and ontology, that is, it reasserted a necessary structure of mediation which we may understand as conceptual, Levinas could not accept this (despite the fact that Derrida's 'phenomenology' and 'ontology' were no longer the agents of neutralization that Levinas had taken them to be). Within these terms there can be, however, no Levinasian answer. Instead, the reply would have to be phrased in terms of the equiprimordiality of metaphysics and ethics. These two are most closely conjoined in the thinking of the idea of infinity. Levinas writes, for example, that '[t]he rigorously developed concept of . . . transcendence is expressed by the term infinity' and in the welcome of the Other 'the idea of infinity is consummated'. In other words, 'metaphysics is enacted [*se joue*] where the social relation is enacted';[9] transcendence appears as a gleam in the face of the Other. The ethical relation is *ethical* because of this gleam, and this gleam only gleams because there *is* a relation. What can this mean? If it affirms, finally, the co-conditionality and equi-primordiality of metaphysics and ethics, the necessity of the relation between transcendence and its appearing – the necessity of their simultaneity – the transcendence, to be intelligible, would be *finite*. If it is impossible to think the one without the other it is impossible to think transcendence except as *limited*. With this we approach the familiar problem which exercised the metaphysicians of the nineteenth century: the necessarily compromising nature of any relation with the Absolute, which, once in relation becomes 'relative to'. Far from being unaware of this problem, Levinas's whole project is conceived in response to it, precisely to refute the conclusion of the limitation or the finitude of the Absolute and to reaffirm the simultaneous possibility and necessity of the idea of *true* transcendence as radically ungrounded, unconditioned and unlimited. While the most important of Levinas's close philosophical predecessors, and also his contemporaries, sought the solution to the problem in an attempt to think transcendence in immanent or finite terms – Husserl for example, thinking the former through epistemology and Heidegger thinking the latter existentially – Levinas never ceased to conceive these projects as a betrayal of transcendence. All the same, it is difficult to see how Levinas's philosophy does not *in fact* endorse this kind of position, if transcendence comes about or arises in the context of the this-wordly finitude of the social relation, that is, if metaphysics and ethics are coeval. The only way, then, to hold on to the idea of a truly infinite transcendence – the first principle of Levinas's metaphysics – is precisely to *affirm* the priority of metaphysics and the 'independence' as it were, of the metaphysical idea. It is Levinas himself who must affirm the priority of metaphysics if the idea of infinite transcendence is to be maintained. If it is Levinas's own suggestion of co-conditionality that puts this priority in question, so much the worse for the metaphysics.

Feminism and the feminine

A second objection concerns the feminist critique of Levinas. In stark contrast to the analysis offered in this book, some feminist readers have claimed that the category of the feminine may be appropriated as a theoretical resource for various feminist philosophical or political projects. Recently, for example, one finds Bracha Lichtenberg-Ettinger in a series of conversations with Levinas trying to revive and rehabilitate the question of the feminine, despite Levinas's obvious reticence. Levinas warns Lichtenberg-Ettinger that it is

> [b]est to make only a few allusions to the subject of the difference of the feminine .... Above all do not commit yourself too much and do not exhaust this theme too far; you will be attacked, they will say that you have said too much or not enough. It would be better for you not to become entirely involved, stay on the edge. You see, the feminists have often attacked me .... [10]

Lichtenberg-Ettinger, however, insists that 'your [Levinas's] philosophy will be more and more central for talking about difference and the alterity of the feminine, and that we have not really measured its potential in this matter.'[11] Throughout these conversations Levinas maintains the position that sexual difference is to be subordinated to the properly human – to that which men and women allegedly share in equal measure and with equal responsibility – but if Lichtenberg-Ettinger persists, in spite of Levinas's unwillingness and even embarrassment in speaking of the feminine, this is because she sees in the alterity of the feminine a possibility for a radical reconsideration of its place in the history of Western philosophy and in the theoretical discourses (particularly, psychoanalysis) which the latter has spawned.

To illustrate, it is instructive to turn to the work of Luce Irigaray, whose position *vis-à-vis* Levinas is interestingly ambiguous. Viewed from the standpoint of Irigaray's history of Western philosophy, there is a sense in which the foregounding of the alterity of the feminine in Levinas's early work is an extraordinary move. Using Levinas's own terminology, Irigaray claims that it is precisely the alterity – or, alternatively, the specificity – of the feminine that has been the victim of philosophy's most systematic enterprise of the reduction to sameness:

> Now this domination of the philosophic logos stems in large part from its power *to reduce all others to the economy of the Same*. The teleologically constructive project it takes on is always also a project of diversion, deflection, reduction of the other in the same. And, in its greatest generality perhaps, *of eradication of the difference between the sexes* in systems that are self-representative of a 'masculine subject'.[12]

For Irigaray, the reduction of *sexual* difference to a 'neutral' economy of the same has been the most persistent crime of Western philosophy, and 'it is precisely philosophical discourse that we have to challenge, and *disrupt*, inasmuch as this discourse sets forth the law for all others, inasmuch as it constitutes the discourse on discourse.'[13] The way in which this demand is articulated situates Irigaray within the tradition to be disrupted. If for Heidegger the most pressing question was the question of the meaning of Being, Levinas, in opposition, appears to raise the question of the Other and declare it the most urgent. For Irigaray the question of the Other remains paramount, but not untransformed: 'Sexual difference represents one of the questions, or the question, which is to be thought in our time. Each epoch – according to Heidegger – has one thing to think. Only one. Sexual difference is probably that of our times.'[14] The question of the Other becomes primarily the question of sexual difference, as it is the difference of sexual difference that has, historically, suffered maximum erasure. The neutralization of sexual difference in/by philosophy has, however, taken a peculiar form. At first sight, the subsumption of the individual sexed subject in the mediating concept of the universal Subject or Individual appears to be an act of neutralization like any other. The reduction of sexual difference to 'the same' would seem to be the reduction of masculine and feminine to a neutral third term, maybe the neuter, which means, etymologically, 'not either', therefore 'neither of the two'. But it is not. Historically, the reduction of sexual difference has been the reduction of the feminine other to what Irigaray calls the 'masculine' economy of the same. This economy of the same is not mediated through a neutral term but through the criterion of the masculine itself. Within this economy the feminine other is not thought in her alterity *qua* feminine but only as the dialectical opposite of the masculine, the not-masculine. In effect, 'the feminine' translates as the inferior of the masculine, the copy of the original masculine, the pathologized masculine, the castrated masculine, and so on.

The use of gendered pronouns in many languages bears witness to this in a way that is more than simply a contingency of vocabulary, according to Adriana Cavarero. The work of conceptualization (the subsumption of particulars beneath a general concept) is always an *abstraction*, in English a word derived from the Latin meaning 'something drawn off or removed from (something specific)'. The abstraction necessary to reach the Platonic Idea, for example, involves a drawing away not just from the particularity of the things of this world, but from this world itself. Conceiving the abstract idea of Man involves a conceptual separation of soul from body, such that the essence of Man is said to reside in the immortal soul and the body becomes a mere accident of this world. The point is well illustrated in the Myth of Er in Plato's *Republic*. Er's account of the souls he saw in the underworld tells how each picked their 'lot' and thus chose a new life and a new body:

> he saw the soul that had once been Orpheus choose the life of a swan . . . . The soul of Thamyris chose the life of a nightingale, and he saw a swan and other singing birds choose the life of a man . . . . When [Atlanta] saw the great honours of an athlete's life she could not resist them and chose it. After her he saw Epeius son of Panopeus, taking on the role of a skilled craftswoman, and right among the last the buffoon Thersites putting on the form of an ape.[15]

As Cavarero says, 'the significance of the body is so slight [with respect to the soul] that it [the soul] might belong either to an animal or to an human, or, within the human species, either to the female or to the male gender.'[16] Having thus disembodied the Idea of Man Plato can with impunity abstract away from sex and/or gender and the Idea of Man (that is 'Man, as in the Greek singular noun *anthropos*'[17]) can more easily claim to represent both male and female, to be both neutral and universal. Cavarero reveals, then, the deep complicity between the word ('man') and idea/Idea: 'In the idea of "man" it is precisely the human male that is referred to, the male universalized to stand for the human species as a whole, and women are thus categorized as one of his inferior specifications. Women do not constitute the "other sex" of the human species, but rather a subspecies.'[18] The woman, who has her true essence in the idea of man, is logically a man, assigned by chance to a female body,[19] which is a mark of inferiority, for as Plato says in the *Timaeus*, 'men of the first generation who lived cowardly or immoral lives were, it is reasonable to suppose, reborn in the second generation as women.'[20]

For Irigaray, then, the 'masculine' refers to that which represents, in the eclipsed field of sexual difference, a specious universality, that which dissimulates, or does not name, its own specificity.[21] It is that which represents, therefore, a universal value against which everything is to be judged, and under whose banner every (feminine) other is to be subsumed. However, the feminine also bears a double signification. Which aspect of this double signification is stressed depends on which direction, or from which position, one chooses to look. The feminine is both (a) the traditional representation of the (inferior) dialectical opposite of the masculine, subordinated to it and its standard, and (b) something posited as incommensurable with the masculine philosophy of the same, something other than the masculine. Irigaray's contention is that, with very few exceptions, the feminine has only been thought within the history of Western philosophy as (a). Put in this way, the point of intersection with Levinas is obvious. Levinas's most fundamental assertion that the other has not been thought *as* other, but only as the not-same (like otherness as 'not-being' in Plato's *Sophist*), becomes Irigaray's fundamental assertion that the *feminine* other has not been thought *as* feminine other, but only as the not-masculine. It is thus clear why Levinas's insistence, in *Existence and Existents* for example, on the dimension of sexual difference in eros might be so important. In saying that it is in eros that the possibility of a radical thinking of transcendence arises, he says that it is in eros that the other is revealed *as* other. Furthermore, he claims that eros reveals the other *par excellence* to be the feminine, or that eros reveals the structure of sexual difference in its radicality. Levinas would seem, therefore, in accordance with Irigaray's feminist demands, to have introduced the thought of the feminine other *as feminine other*, in her specificity, or to have attempted to think 'the question of our times' – that of sexual difference – in its radicality.[22]

Such a reading is not necessarily troubled by the more problematic descriptive account of the feminine in *Time and the Other* and *Totality and Infinity*. In the earlier text Levinas stresses that '[w]hat matters to me in this notion of the feminine is not merely the unknowable, but a mode of being that consists in slipping away from the light.'[23] In both texts the feminine is characterized as a *mystery*, and in *Totality and Infinity* an absence, something evanescent which cannot be grasped or possessed in the caress, something that changes or reverts into its opposite as soon as one tries to pin it down: for example, modesty becomes immodesty, 'decent' discourse becomes indecency and ridicule, the inviolate becomes violated, the sacred becomes profane. On first impression these are, no doubt, tired clichés, otherwise familiar as the assertion of the inconstancy and caprice of 'woman', who is said to be so difficult to understand. But when the terms of understanding itself and the criteria for what will count as 'constant' (for example, according to certain notions of substance) are articulated within – or themselves constitute – what Irigaray calls the 'masculine economy of the same', Levinas's descriptions of the feminine, read as recalcitrant to these terms, take on a different hue. They could mean, for example, that the feminine (other) is radically and by definition – ontologically even – incapable of being 'known' according to these terms precisely insofar as it/she conserves its/her character *as* feminine. In Irigarayan terms, this is the definition of the feminine as that which is posited as fundamentally incommensurable with the masculine economy of the same. As a relation between incommensurables, the positivity of eros would be accomplished in this 'negativity'. The absence of the feminine other in eros is precisely the presence of the other *as* other, and could only be construed as a failure were it to be judged according to the aims of another project: possession, knowledge, seizure. In other words, the 'failure' of the (masculine) subject to 'account for' the feminine constitutes the positivity of sexual difference, or the positivity of the feminine as absolutely other.[24]

However, despite the fact that these feminist defences of Levinas can be articulated in an 'Irigarayan' language, they bear an only tangential relation to Irigaray's actual views on Levinas. In 'The Fecundity of the Caress', Irigaray reads Levinas's phenomenology of eros as suggestive of various possibilities which remain undeveloped or are immediately closed off, textually. In particular, Irigaray admires the descriptions of the erotic caress for their privileging of touch over vision, and, implicitly, for the emphasis on incarnation or bodily subjectivity ('they love each other like the bodies they are'[25]). The erotic relation also suggests, for Irigaray, a relation between subjects in which the other 'give[s] me back the borders of my body and call[s] me back to the rememberance of the most profound intimacy.' This 'intimacy' is apparently that of the mother-child relation, one which Irigaray holds to have been under- or badly-theorized in Western discourse. The erotic caress would then be something like a 'licking into shape', in the original (i.e. non-violent) signification of the phrase, a mutual 'fecundation' in which each brings the other to birth ('[b]ringing me back to life') through the caress.[26] This is asserted, however, *against* the Levinasian insistence that the erotic relation would be '[s]terile, if it were not for the child.'[27] Irigaray objects to the teleological imperative of Levinasian eros both in itself, as it were, and also because the elaboration of fecundity as paternity reduces the feminine to a means to an end, to the condition of *another's* possibilities (not her own), and ultimately to the status of object, or at least a non-subject reduced to infancy and/or animality. Insofar as she speaks explicitly of the feminine in Levinas (explicitness is not Irigaray's style), she places Levinas pretty firmly within the 'masculine economy of the same' which his defenders would read him as rejecting.

The same is also true in 'Questions to Emmanuel Levinas': 'The feminine, as it is characterized by Levinas, is not other than himself . . . . The feminine is apprehended not in relation to itself, but from the point of view of man'.[28] The most Irigaray is prepared to concede is that the texts open up a *possibility*, but one which they themselves nevertheless reject: 'After having been so far – or so close – in the approach to the other sex, in my view to the other, to the mystery of the other, Levinas clings on once more to this rock of patriarchy in the very place of carnal love.'[29] Irigaray identifies two levels in Levinas's discourse: the phenomenological and the metaphysical. Any positivity in the thinking of the (sexed) other, according to Irigaray, occurs in the phenomenological-descriptive approach which somehow avoids the order of metaphysics – where 'metaphysics' ('this rock of patriarchy') refers to the totality of a tradition based on the presumption of certain philosophical categories and logical structures which for Irigaray (moving beyond the Heideggerianism which named this 'metaphysics') excludes the feminine from, whilst making 'her' the condition for, representation. But the phenomenology of eros – specifically the phenomenology of the caress – falls back within the boundaries marked out by this metaphysics when Levinas subordinates the erotic relation to the imperative of paternal fecundity, which is to say, for Irigaray, that it 'falls back within the boundaries staked out by the philosophical constitution of the masculine subject.'[30]

Although these criticisms are immanent to the terms of Levinas's philosophy, they are important for the claim that Levinas's philosophy offers theoretical resources for feminism. The more pertinent critique, however – and one which would also have to be levelled at both his defenders *and* his critics here – would be one which questioned the presumption of the category of 'the feminine' in the first place. To what, exactly, does 'the feminine' refer? Irigaray's critique, for example, seems to presuppose that it is an actually existing something – an ontological kind – that is the legitimate subject of a phenomenology and may thus be well or badly described (or, to put it another way, the description of which may be more or less distorted by the presumptions of 'metaphysics'). If for Levinas the philosophical status of the feminine becomes less and less clear – hence his unwillingness, in part, to discuss it with Lichtenberg-Ettinger – he at least seems to want to insist on it as a *philosophical category* rather than simply an empirical content. His problem, however – textually and conceptually – has always been the impossibility of separating these two positions out. If the feminine is to function meaningfully at all, at no matter what level of abstraction, some reference, albeit implicit, to women or to the female – that is, some reference to an empirical content – is inevitable. And although Levinas himself strove (unsuccessfully) to avoid this, the connection between the philosophical category and its empirical content is the only possible ground for any claim that Levinas's philosophy has something to offer feminism, insofar as the latter is ultimately concerned with empirical men and women; that is, insofar as it is a political project. Derrida, for example, misses this point in *Adieu to Emmanuel Levinas*, when he claims that while the description of the feminine in Section II of *Totality and Infinity* means that the text may be read as 'a sort of feminist manifesto', the feminine must nevertheless be distinguished from 'the *fact* of empirical women'.[31] In this context, the rather obvious point that the feminine is meant to function as a philosophical category – that it is not meant to refer directly to an empirical content – fudges the issue entirely. It neither acknowledges that there *is* still some connection, nor gives any attempt to explain what it might be, whilst also failing to consider what the relation *needs to be* in order for there to be any positive feminist implication.

The acknowledgement – or presupposition – of the connection between the philosophical category and an empirical content is also the basis of the position from which Irigaray *criticizes* Levinas. But insofar as this position also fails to make the nature of the connection clear, it is itself extremely problematic. It carries within it the danger that the philosophical category – one which one might want to call, in Irigaray's sense, 'metaphysical' or ideological – becomes falsely substantialized in the body of women. To the extent that this is true of Irigaray she draws the accusation of 'essentialism' which, though seemingly crude, is not groundless.

Any attempt to claim that there might be some positive relation between feminism and the feminine in Levinas needs to show not only how this claim survives the clarification of the status and the role of the feminine within the broad sweep of Levinas's project, but also what 'the feminine' *is* exactly, and what the relation is between this category and the social context in which it acquires its meaning. Of course it is not impossible – indeed it is necessary – that the term be redefined and rearticulated as part of a project of social transformation, but there is nothing to suggest that this is what the champions of Levinas's 'feminine' are trying to do. Furthermore, a failure to distinguish between the different meanings of 'the feminine' in various discourses leads to a misidentification of the concept in Levinas's work. Lichtenberg-Ettinger, for example, seems to assume that Levinas's 'feminine' can slip between the specific context of his philosophical work and her own psychoanalytic framework, when the word has for Levinas *none* of the modern psychoanalytic meaning which – with acknowledged differences between authors – refers primarily to a subject position within the symbolic order. Irigaray is on surer ground in attaching Levinas's use of the word to a descriptive phenomenology, but still does not satisfactorily answer the question: a descriptive phenomenology of *what*, exactly?

In Anglo-American feminist discourses in particular, the distinction between 'sex' and 'gender' has functioned as an attempt to separate out some of the meanings attached to 'the feminine'. Translation difficulties between the English and the French often occur because of the lack of any exactly corresponding terms in the French (the French '*genre*' refers primarily to a type, a kind or a grouping, not to a *sexed* type) and – a closely connected point – because *le féminin* connotes *both* the English 'female' and 'feminine'.[32] English-speaking readers need to be particularly clear, therefore, in any appropriation of 'the feminine', what precisely it *is* that they are appropriating from Levinas. The noun form of 'the feminine' does not even appear in most English dictionaries (or if it does it refers to a grammatical form found in other languages). Its introduction into English is as a translation of its different and *specific* uses in the elaboration of various discourses in French. Of course, as different uses of the same word there *are* connections, and it is often precisely these connections that make any use of it difficult and dangerous; again, a point that Derrida seems unwilling to acknowledge.

In *Adieu to Emmanuel Levinas*, Derrida suggests two possible readings of the account of the feminine in *Totality and Infinity*. One approach, he says, 'would be to acknowledge, so as then to question, as I once did in a text to which I do not wish to return here ['At This Very Moment'], the traditional and androcentric attribution of certain characteristics to woman', which is Derrida's way of saying 'a feminist critique'. Another, however, that would not necessarily oppose this first reading, 'would no longer raise concerns about a classical androcentrism. It might even, on the contrary, make of this text a sort of feminist manifesto.' Instances of both types of reading have been discussed in this book, and the latter has been rejected. But, Derrida goes on: 'Need one choose here between two incompatible readings, between an androcentric hyperbole and a feminist one? Is there any place for such a choice in ethics? And in justice? In law? In politics? Nothing is less certain.'[33]

Well, actually, for the sake of a *feminist* politics, nothing is *more* certain than that we must choose; in this instance feminism *consists in* this choice. And if, finally, Levinas's discussion of the feminine has nothing to offer feminism today, this is also because of the impossibility of separating it out from the context of Levinas's philosophy as a whole. (The word itself may be so separated, but then it has nothing to do any longer with the specifically Levinasian treatment of it.) The feminine plays a role – particularly in its association with eros – in a metaphysics of transcendence, the various elements of which are consistently gendered in such a way that one may speak of a masculine transcendence *of* the feminine which it is impossible to reconcile with any feminist position. This point is internal to the working-out of Levinas's philosophy. From an external viewpoint, however, and one which would point frankly to the strong stream of Judaic patriarchalism bearing Levinas's philosophical reflection along, the more basic point is that the future of a twenty-first century feminist politics never was going to be found in a metaphysics of transcendence. Such a metaphysics remains fundamentally incompatible with a feminist theoretical project which aims to help transform society through the location of the origin of meanings – including that of 'the feminine' – in the finite structures of the world.

Notes

Introduction

1 One recent collection of essays on Levinas takes this phrase as its title: Adriaan T. Peperzak (ed.), *Ethics as First Philosophy: The Significance of Emmanuel Levinas for Philosophy, Literature and Religion*, Routledge, New York, 1995.
2 See, for example, Levinas, *Totality and Infinity: an Essay on Exteriority*, trans. Alphonso Lingis, Duquesne University Press, Pittsburgh, PA, 1992, p 52; *Totalité et infini: Essai sur l'extériorité*, Kluwer, Paris, 1971 (first published 1961), p 44.
3 Ibid., pp 35, 39, 43, 109; pp 24, 29, 33, 111.
4 See, for example, Jacques Derrida's funeral oration for Levinas, *Adieu to Emmanuel Levinas*, trans. Pascale-Anne Brault and Michael Naas, Stanford University Press, Stanford, 1999; *Adieu à Emmanuel Levinas*, Editions Galilée, Paris, 1997.

Chapter One The Metaphysics of Transcendence

1 In his 'Résumé de *Totalité et infini*', *Annales de l'université de Paris {Sorbonne, Paris V}* 31 (1961), n 3, p 386.
2 P. Shorey, *What Plato Said*, University of Chicago Press, Chicago, 1933.
3 Levinas, 'Meaning and Sense', Adriaan T. Peperzak, Simon Critchley and Robert Bernasconi (eds), *Basic Philosophical Writings*, Indiana University Press, Bloomington, 1996, p 42ff; 'La signification et le sens', *Humanisme de l'autre homme*, Fata Morgana, Montpellier, 1972, p 30ff.
4 Levinas, *The Theory of Intuition in Husserl's Phenomenology*, trans. André Orianne, Northwestern University Press, Evanston, 1989; *La théorie de l'intuituion dans la phénoménologie de Husserl*, Vrin, Paris, 1970.
5 Ibid., p 29; p 31.
6 Ibid., p 150/1; p 214/5.
7 Levinas 'Martin Heidegger et l'ontologie', *En découvrant l'existence avec Husserl et Heidegger*, Vrin, Paris, 1994, pp 53–76. First published in *Révue Philosophique* (mai–juin, 1932).
8 In Heidegger's words (*Being and Time,* trans. John Macquarrie and Edward Robinson, Blackwell, Oxford, 1990, section 1, p 21): 'a dogma has been developed which not only declares the question about the meaning of Being to be superfluous, but sanctions its complete neglect. It is said that "Being" is the most universal and the emptiest of concepts. As such it resists every attempt at definition.'
9 'Martin Heidegger et l'ontologie', p 57.

10 Levinas, *Existence and Existents*, trans. A. Lingis, Kluwer Academic, Dordrecht, 1988; *De l'existence à l'existant*, Vrin, Paris, 1993.

11 Ibid., p 19; p 19.

12 See Levinas, 'Reflections on the Philosophy of Hitlerism', trans. Seán Hand, *Critical Enquiry* (Autumn 1990); 'Quelques réflexions sur la philosophie de l'hitlérisme', Catherine Chalier and Miguel Abensour (eds) *Emmanuel Levinas*, Les cahiers de l'Herne, Paris, 1991.

13 Levinas, 'Signature', trans. A. Peperzak, in *Research in Phenomenology* VIII, 1978, 177; '*Signature*', *Difficile Liberté*, Albin Michel, Paris, 1976, p 406 (the title of the French is italicized throughout to distinguish it from the English translation).

14 See, for example, *Existence and Existents*, p 18; *De l'existence à l'existant*, p 17.

15 Ibid., p 19; p 19.

16 Levinas's phrase '*l'existence humaine*' ('Martin Heidegger et l'ontologie', p 57) is his more humanistic rendering of Heidegger's '*Dasein*'.

17 *Existence and Existents*, p 58; *De l'existence à l'existant*, p 95.

18 Ibid., p 61; p 99/100. The 'night' is not always to be taken literally: 'Thus one could also speak of the night in the full light of the day' 'Aussi peut-on parler de nuits en plein jour'. Ibid., p 59 (t.m.); p 97.

19 See Ibid., pp 45, 82, 83; pp 69, 140, 141.

20 'Signature', p 181; '*Signature*', p 407.

21 Levinas, 'Is Ontology Fundamental?', trans. Simon Critchley, *Basic Philosophical Writings*; 'L'Ontologie est-elle fondamentale?', *Entre Nous: Essais sur le penser-à-l'autre*, Paris, Bernard Grasset, 1991. An English translation of *Entre Nous: On Thinking-of-the-Other* is also now available, trans. Michael B. Smith and Barbara Harshav, Athlone Press, London, 1998.

22 Ibid., p 5/6; p 17/18.

23 See for example *Totality and Infinity*, p 65; *Totalité et infini*, p 60.

24 'Is Ontology Fundamental?', p 5/6; 'L'ontologie est-elle fondamentale?', p 18.

25 Ibid., p 6; p 18.

26 Ibid. (t.m.).

27 Ibid., p 7; p 19.

28 Jacques Derrida, 'Violence and Metaphysics', trans. Alan Bass, *Writing and Difference*, Routledge, London, 1990; 'Violence et métaphysique', *L'écriture et la différence*, Editions de Seuil, Paris, 1967.

29 See 'Preface to the German Edition of *Totality and Infinity*', *Entre Nous: Thinking-of-the-Other*, p 197/8; 'Preface à l'édition allemande' *Totalité et infini*, p I/II. (This preface does not appear in the English translation of *Totality and Infinity*.)

30 Levinas, 'Philosophy and the Idea of Infinity', trans. A. Lingis, *Collected Philosophical Papers*, Nijhoff, Dordrecht, 1987; 'La philosophie et l'idée de l'infini', *En découvrant l'existence avec Husserl et Heidegger*. Levinas, 'Transcendence and Height', trans. Simon Critchley, *Basic Philosophical Writings*; 'Transendance et hauteur', Catherine Chalier and Miguel Abensour (eds), *Emmanuel Levinas*, Les cahiers de l'Herne, Paris, 1991. Adriaan Peperzak devotes more than half of his book, *To the Other* (Purdue University Press, Indiana, 1993) to discussions of 'Philosophy and the Idea of Infinity' and *Totality and Infinity*, saying (p 38) that the former

probably affords the best introduction to the latter and to Levinas's last book-length study, *Otherwise Than Being*.

31 With Levinas prepared to single out so few examples, Plato in fact figures most significantly. Peperzak, *To the Other*, p 43, has amply demonstrated this with extensive referencing to the *Republic*, the *Phaedo*, and the *Symposium*.

32 Levinas, 'Philosophy and the Idea of Infinity', p 47; 'La philosophie et l'idée de l'infini', p 165.

33 Ibid., p 48 (t.m.); p 166.

34 Ibid.

35 'Transcendence and Height', p 14; 'Transcendance et hauteur', p 99.

36 'Philosophy and the Idea of Infinity', p 48; 'La philosophie et l'idée de l'infini', p 166.

37 A reference to Plato's *Theaetetus*, trans. H. N. Fowler, Loeb Classical Library, London, 1987, 189E.

38 'Philosophy and the Idea of Infinity', p 49; 'La philosophie et l'idée de l'infini', p 167. See also *Totality and Infinity*, p 43; *Totalité et infini*, p 34.

39 'Philosophy and the Idea of Infinity', p 49/50; 'La philosophie et l'idé de l'infini', p 167/8. See also *Totality and Inifnity*, p 44; *Totalité et infini*, p 35: 'The ideal of Socratic truth thus rests on the essential self-sufficiency of the same, its identification in ipseity, its egoism. Philosophy is an egology.' As a note to this discussion, it might be possible for an anglophone philosopher to ask whether this view of philosophy as egology and/or ontology is not one which has failed to cast its eyes across the channel. Is this history of philosophy not a peculiarly Franco-German account? The case of John Locke, for example, might seem to contradict many of the premises of egology. Locke denied that there could be such a thing as innate ideas, asserting instead that all the ideas in our minds could be accounted for by experience. Even simple ideas, he argued, are *put in us*, not self-generated, and this could be read as much as an argument against anamnesis as against rationalism. (See in particular Book I, ' No innate notions', of Locke's *An Essay Concerning Human Understanding*, Everyman, London, 1988.) Locke could thus be seen as part of a philosophical tradition, and not just in Britain, whose aim has been to demonstrate not the primacy of the ego in knowledge but the limits of the knowing consciousness, implying that there is always something 'outside', unassimilable. However, Locke's explanation of the acquisition of ideas rests on the presumption of an adequation between noesis and noemata: 'The senses at first let in particular *ideas* and furnish the yet empty cabinet; and the mind by degrees growing familiar with some of them, they are lodged in the memory, and names got to them' (Ibid., p 11). The stuff of the world was already predisposed to fit with 'ideas', waiting to take up their slot in consciousness or memory, and there is no suggestion that there might be an idea which does not 'fit' in the cabinet. On the contrary, 'ideas' are the common measure of man and the world, a thesis which is as much an egology as is the severest idealism. To be fair, Locke did recognize the difficulties of fitting the ideas of power and substance into his explanation, but this did not suggest to him that his explanation might be wrong or inadequate.

40 Edmund Husserl, *Cartesian Meditations*, trans. Dorion Cairns, Nijhoff, Dordrecht, 1988, pp 21, 18 (First Meditation).

41 'Transcendence and Height', p 13; 'Transcendance et hauteur', p 99.

42 Husserl, *Cartesian Meditations*, Second Meditation, p 33.

43 *Totality and Infinity*, p 87; *Totalité et infini*, p 86. See also 'L'oeuvre d'Edmund Husserl' in *En découvrant l'existence avec Husserl et Heidegger*. In the conclusion to this essay Levinas writes (p 49): 'Husserl's phenomenology is, in the end, a philosophy of freedom, of a freedom which is accomplished as and defined by consciousness; a freedom which does not only characterise the activity of a being but which posits itself before being and in relation to which being is constituted.' On the critique of Husserl see also Levinas's 1982 essay 'Beyond Intentionality', trans. Kathleen McLaughlin, Alan Montefiore (ed.) *Philosophy in France Today*, Cambridge University Press, Cambridge, 1983.

44 See for example 'Transcendence and Height', p 14 ('Transcendence et hauteur', p 99) where Levinas says that 'idealism is an egoism', and *Totality and Infinity*, p 169 (*Totalité et infini*, p.183), where idealism is said to be 'an eternal temptation' for any transcendental philosophy.

45 Husserl, *Cartesian Meditations*, Second Meditation, p 37.

46 Ibid., First Meditation, p 18.

47 *Totality and Infinity*, p 45; *Totalité et infini*, p 36.

48 See for example *Being and Time*, section 2, p 25.

49 *Being and Time*, section 1, p 22.

50 See, for example, *Being and Time*, section 43 (a). The parallelism between Heidegger's insistence on the primacy of Being and the generality of the concept makes more sense (that is, Levinas's reading is more plausible) when 'concept' is understood in what is perhaps its more originary sense – a taking together, a synthesis – corresponding to what Heidegger calls 'understanding'. However, Levinas's general point – his historical generalization – would be in danger of being shaken by this (and other) more nuanced accounts of conceptualization. In a sense, his criticisms of Heidegger (in this instance exemplifying a whole tradition) take what force they have precisely from the cruder reading.

51 Immanuel Kant, *Critique of Pure Reason*, trans. Norman Kemp Smith, Macmillan, Hampshire, 1990, especially the Transcendental Deduction (A and B).

52 'Philosophy and the Idea of Infinity', p 51; 'La philosophie et l'idée de l'infini', p 16. See also, for example, *Totality and Infinity*, p 42; *Totalité et infini*, p 33: 'Ontology, which reduces the other to the same, promotes freedom – the freedom that is the identification of the same, not allowing itself to be alienated by the other.'

53 'Philosophy and the Idea of Infinity', p 50; 'La philosophie et l'idée de l'infini', p 168.

54 Heidegger, 'On the Essence of Truth', trans. John Sallis, *Basic Writings* (ed. David Farrell Krell), Routledge, London, 1993.

55 Ibid., pp 120, 122.

56 Ibid., p 123.

57 Ibid., pp 124, 127.

58 'Philosophy and the Idea of Infinity', p 51; 'La philosophie et l'idée de l'infini', p 169.

59 Ibid., p 50 (t.m.); p 168.

60 *Totality and Infinity*, p 43/4 (t.m.); *Totalité et infini*, p 34.

61 Ibid., pp 44, 46; pp 35, 36/7. Emphasis in first quotation added.

62 'Philosophy and the Idea of Infinity', p 51; 'La philosophie et l'idée de l'infini', p 169.

63 Ibid., p 47 (t.m.); p 165: 'Le penseur entretient dans la vérité un rapport avec une réalité distincte de lui, *autre* que lui.' The verb *entretenir* also means 'to speak/converse with'. Levinas's sentence — not one of his clearest — thus also implies something like the keeping open of a dialogue with truth or with alterity.

64 See, for example, *Being and Time*, section 10, p 74.

65 Versions of Levinas's own account of his insistence on 'infinite transcendence' in relation to his philosophical predecessors may be found in the first three essays collected together in *Alterity and Transcendence*, trans. Michael B. Smith, Athlone Press, London, 1999; *Altérité et transcendance*, Fata Morgana, Montpellier, 1995.

66 Levinas's early (1947) *Time and the Other*, trans. Richard A. Cohen, Duquesne University Press, Pittsburgh, PA, 1987 (*Le temps et l'autre*, Quadrige/Presses Universitaires de France, Paris, 1994) which, as the title suggests, foregrounds the role of the Other in the very 'opening' of time, is both a more convincing engagement with Heidegger than that which emphasizes the role of freedom, and also one which is explicitly concerned with the question of transcendence.

67 Jean Wahl, *Existence humaine et transcendance*, Editions de la Baconnière, Neuchâtel, 1944, p 24. In *Totality and Infinity*, p 35 (*Totalité et infini*, p 24) Levinas refers to this text by Wahl and says '[w]e have drawn much inspiration from the themes evoked in that study.'

68 David Hume, *Enquiries Concerning Human Understanding and Concerning the Principles of Morals*, Clarendon Press, Oxford, 1988, p 165.

69 Auguste Comte, *Introduction to Positive Philosophy*, trans. Frederick Ferré, Bobbs-Merrill, Indianapolis, IN, 1970. In Comte's 'law of three stages' positive philosophy was to replace metaphysics, which latter was only a transitional stage from theological explanations.

70 Wahl, *Existence humaine et transcendance*, p 14/5.

71 Ibid., p 22.

72 René Descartes, *Discourse on Method and the Meditations*, trans. F.E. Sutcliffe, Penguin, London, 1988, Third Mediation, p 119.

73 That Levinas's scepticism with regard to Descartes' 'proofs' is no obstacle to the appreciation of the structure highlighted by Descartes is evident in *Totality and Infinity*, p 49 (*Totalité et infini*, p 41): 'Without deciding anything for the moment as to the veritable significance of the presence of the ideas of things in us, without holding to the Cartesian argumentation that *proves* the separated existence of the Infinite by the finitude of the being having an idea of infinity (for there perhaps is not much sense to proving an existence by describing a situation prior to proof and to the problems of existence), it is of importance to emphasize that the transcendence of the Infinite with respect to the I that is separated from it and which thinks it, measures (so to speak) its very infinitude.'

74 See, for example, 'Philosophy and the Idea of Infinity', p 53; 'La philosophie et l'idée de l'infini', p 171: 'what we find most distinctive is the Cartesian analysis of the idea of infinity, although we shall retain only the *formal design* [*le dessein formel*] of the structure it outlines.' See also *Totality and Infinity*, p 79; *Totalité et infini*, p 78: 'Our analyses are guided by a formal structure: the idea of Infinity in us.'

75 'Philosophy and the Idea of Infinity', p 54 (t.m.); 'La philosophie et l'idée de l'infini', p 172.

76 Irigaray, for example, seems to be criticizing Levinas on this score in 'Questions to Emmanuel Levinas: On the Divinity of Love', trans. Margaret Whitford, in Robert Bernasconi and Simon Critchley (eds.), *Re-Reading Levinas*, Athlone Press, London, 1991, p 113. Colin Davis, in *Levinas: An Introduction*, Polity Press, Cambridge, 1996, both criticizes and justifies Levinas's 'difficulty' (see especially Chapter 3, 'Ethical Language').

77 Jacques Derrida, 'Violence and Metaphysics', p 312, footnote to p 81; 'Violence et métaphysique', p 124.

78 Because there is no parallel English word for *autrui*, it has become conventional in English translations of Levinas to render it as 'Other' (capitalized), and *autre* as 'other'.

79 'Transcendence and Height', p 17; 'Transcendance et hauteur', p 101.

80 See 'The Other and the others' *Totality and Infinity*, p 212ff. (Lingis has 'The Other and the Others, in which the distinction is lost.) 'Autrui et les autres', *Totalité et infini*, p 233ff.

81 'Philosophy and the Idea of Infinity', p 55; 'La philosophie et l'idée de l'infini', p 173. The same language is often used in *Totality and Infinity*, for example, p 66; *Totalité et infini*, p 62: 'The eyes break through the mask – the language of the eyes, impossible to dissemble.'

82 See *Totality and infinity*, pp 50/1, 66, 69, 75; *Totalité et infini*, pp 43, 61, 65, 73. 'Philosophy and the Idea of Infinity', p 55; 'La philosophie et l'idée de l'infini', p 173.

83 On asymmetry see 'The Asymmetry of the Interpersonal' *Totality and Infinity*, p 215ff; 'L'Asymétrie de l'interpersonel', *Totalité et infini*, p 236ff.

84 See, for example, *Totality and Infinity*, pp 43, 82ff, 'Freedom called into question', p 171/2; *Totalité et infini*, pp 33, 80 ff. Wahl (*Existence humaine et transcendance*, p 22/3) also describes the 'movement of transcendence' in terms of a 'rupture' of consciousness which is also its accomplishment.

85 *Totality and Infinity*, p 84; *Totalité et infini*, p 82.

86 Ibid., p 203/4; p 223. See also p 301 ff. ('Freedom invested'); p 337ff.

87 In explicitly naming the relation in *Totality and Infinity* Levinas in fact seems to prefer the word 'religion', as, for example, at pp 40, 80; *Totalité et infini*, pp 30, 79.

88 'Philosophy and the Idea of Infinity', pp 54, 59; 'La philosophie et l'idée de l'infini', pp 172, 177. *Totality and Infinity*, p 25; *Totalité et infini*, p 10. See also Wahl, *Existence humaine et transcendance*, p 22: 'all relation must be broken, founded in this transrelational experience which is true experience, non-empirical experience.'

89 *Totality and Infinity*, p 47; *Totalité et infini*, p 38.

90 Levinas, 'Violence of the Face' (an interview with Angelo Bianchi), in *Alterity and Transcendence*, p 180; *Altérité et transcendance*, Fata Morgana, Montpellier, 1995.

91 'God and Philosophy', trans A. Lingis (revised by Robert Bernasconi and Simon Critchley), *Basic Philosophical Writings*, p 190 (footnote), emphasis added; 'Dieu et la philosophie', *Le nouveau commerce*, Printemps, Paris, 1975, Cahier 30–31, p 117.

92 See, for example, *Totality and Infinity*, pp 29, 78, 79; *Totalité et infini*, pp 15,76, 77.

93 For a few recent examples see Simon Critchley, *The Ethics of Deconstruction*, Blackwell, Oxford, 1992, pp 4/5; Adriaan Peperzak, *To the Other*, pp 46, 91 (footnotes 12, 14); Colin Davis, *Levinas: an Introduction*, pp 3, 40 (footnote 10).

94 For a more detailed discussion of the relation between Parmenides, Plato and Levinas, see Stella Sandford, 'Plato and Levinas: the Same and the Other', *Journal of the British Society for Phenomenology*, 30, No 2, May 1999.

95 Parmenides, Fragment 8, approx. lines 2–8 and 29–34, translated in A.H. Coxon, *The Fragments of Parmenides*, Van Gorcum, Assen, 1986, pp 60–4 and 68–70: 'being is ungenerated and imperishable, entire, unique, unmoved and perfect; it never was nor will be, since it is now all together, one, indivisible. For what parentage of it will you look for? How and whence grown? I shall not let you say or conceive, 'from Not-being', for it cannot be said or conceived that anything is not . . . remaining the same and in the same state, it [Being] lies by itself and remains thus where it is perpetually, for strong necessity holds it in the bondage of a limit, which keeps it apart, because it is not lawful that Being should be incomplete, for it is not defective, whereas Not-being would lack everything'.

96 All quotations are from the *Sophist*, trans. H.N. Fowler, Loeb Classical Library, London, 1987, pp 241–58, unless otherwise stated.

97 It seems that these 'kinds' or 'classes' ('*genos*') are simply alternative words for the Form or Idea ('*eidos*') and indeed are later used interchangeably. See Richard S. Bluck, *Plato's 'Sophist': a Commentary*, Manchester University Press, Manchester, 1975, p 133. Perhaps the new words signal the fact that the notion of com-mingling is a radical new departure in the theory of Ideas which announces that some things will commingle (being and rest), while others will not (rest and motion), rather like the letters of the alphabet, in which some 'elements' will perform a function, much like the vowels of the alphabet.

98 'We must place the nature of "the other" as a fifth among the classes in which we select our examples', and each class is said to partake of 'the Idea of the other'. On the other as an Idea see, for example, Stanley Rosen, *Plato's 'Sophist': the Drama of Original and Image*, Yale University Press, New Haven, CT, 1983, p 272; Auguste Diès, *Le définition de l'être et la nature des Idées dans le 'Sophiste' de Platon*, Vrin, Paris, 1932, p 10; Bluck, *Plato's 'Sophist'*, p 148; Victor Brochard, *Etudes de philosophie ancienne et de philosophie moderne*, Librarie Felix Alcan, Paris, 1912, pp 142, 143; F. M. Cornford, *Plato's Theory of Knowledge*, Kegan Paul, Trench & Trubner, London, 1935, p 279.

99 See *Sophist*, 255E: 'each [Idea] is other than the rest; not by reason of its own nature, but because it partakes of the idea of the other.'

100 See also Gilles Deleuze, *Difference and Repetition*, trans. Paul Patton, Columbia University Press, New York, 1994, p 32: 'here we find the principle which lies behind a confusion disastrous for the entire philosophy of difference: assigning a distinctive concept of difference is confused with the inscription of difference within concepts in general . . . . Difference then can be no more than a predicate in the comprehension of a concept.' See also p 51, for example. Deleuze thus *seems* to make a Levinasian critique of Plato and others but what Deleuze means by 'difference' is not at all what Levinas means by 'other'. Jacques Rolland de

Renéville, *L'un multiple et l'attribution chez Platon et les sophistes*, Vrin, Paris, 1962, points out that despite the fact that the intention of the *Sophist* is in part to prove that the other is an Idea distinct from the other Ideas, the definition of the other as not-being, as the principle of differentiation, in fact gives no more than instances of the Idea, not the Idea itself, or the Idea in-itself. What are in fact described are *ontic* occurences which partake of the Idea of otherness. How is it, Rolland asks (p 199), that 'the celebrated notion of [the other] posited first of all as a part of the totality of being . . . and thus called upon to play the role of a radical rebeginning for ontology, does not however help, in the last analysis, to explain any other alterity than that which holds sway between things, that [the meaning of] which is exhausted each time in the fact that any given being gives itself as other than the Others, without having brought to light the first, originary alterity, of which this other is, in some way, but the secondary manifestation? Would not one only be able to conceive that there was a multiplicity of things or ideas (of which each was other than the others), above all according to good Platonic logic, if there was not beforehand an Other in itself, by participating in which things or ideas precisely define themselves against which they are not? Without an idea of the Other in itself to which was imputable all that each recognized being retained of alterity?' He concludes (p 200): 'It does not . . . seem that this relation between the participant and that in which it participates helps us to understand the nature of the other.'

101 Catherine Chalier, *Figures du féminin: lecture d'Emmanuel Levinas*, La nuit surveillée, Paris, 1982, pp 16/7, 18, 141 (footnote 10).
102 Levinas, 'Au-delà de l'essence', *Revue de métaphysique et de morale*, juillet–septembre, No. 3, 1970, pp 265, 270.
103 See for example Aristotle, *Metaphysics*, trans. Hugh Tredennick, Loeb Classical Library, London, 1933, Vol II, 10 1054b p 14ff. and Plotinus, *Enneads*, trans. Stephen Mackenna, Penguin, London, 1991, II, p 4.
104 Diès, *La définition de l'être*, p 8, my emphasis. See also Bluck, *Plato's 'Sophist'*, p 161.
105 Plotinus, *Ennead* I, 8, p 58, emphasis added.
106 On the irreducibility and the positivity of otherness see Paul Seligman, *Being and Not-Being: an Introduction to Plato's 'Sophist'*, Nijhoff, The Hague, 1974, p 65; Diès, *La définition de l'être*, p 127; Brochard, *Études*, p 143.
107 Paul Ricouer, *Etre, essence et substance chez Platon et Aristote*, Société d'éditions d'enseignement supérieur, Paris, 1982, p 99.
108 Wahl, *Existence humaine et transcendance*, p 146.
109 Plato, *Republic*, trans. Desmond Lee, Penguin, London, 1988, 509B.
110 Which might be more properly translated as 'that the one is', since the Greeks did not have a word corresponding to the sense of the English 'exists'.
111 Plato, *Parmenides*, trans. H. N. Fowler, Loeb Clasical Library, London, 1992, 142A.
112 Levinas, 'The Trace of the Other', trans. A. Lingis, Mark C. Taylor (ed.) *Deconstruction in Context*, University of Chicago Press, Chicago, 1986, p 347; 'La trace de l'autre', *En découvrant l'existence avec Husserl et Heidegger*, p 189/90. See also pp 197, 201; pp 354, 358.
113 *Totality and Infinity*, p 103; *Totalité et infini*, p 106. See also pp 80, 102, 218, 292;

pp 79, 105, 241, 325. Also 'Philosophy and the Idea of Infinity', p 153; 'La philosophie et l'idée de l'infini', p 171.

Chapter Two *Feminine/Female/Femme: Sexual Difference and the Human*

1 Levinas *De l'évasion, Recherches philosophiques* 5, 1935–6, pp 377, 391, 392 (emphasis added).
2 On pleasure and shame see ibid., pp 381–5.
3 Ibid., p 384: 'The timid man who doesn't know what to do with his arms and legs is incapable, in the end, of covering the nudity of his physical presence with his moral personality.'
4 *Existence and Existents*, p 43; *De l'existence à l'existant*, p 66.
5 *Existence and Existents*, pp 95–6; *De l'existence à l'existant*, pp 162–4. An enigmatic reference to 'the father' also appears, signalling future themes. For the time being Levinas simply states that the asymmetrical *moi–toi* relation is the necessary presupposition for being or postulating 'the father': 'Asymmetrical intersubjectivity is the locus of transcendence in which the subject, while preserving its structure, has the possibility of not inevitably returning to itself, the possibility of being fecund and (to anticipate what we shall examine later) having a son.' (t.m.)
6 *Existence and Existents*, p 96 (t.m., emphasis added); *De l'existence à l'existant*, p 164.
7 Ibid.
8 Ibid., p 85; p 145.
9 *Time and the Other*, p 39; *Le temps et l'autre*, p 17.
10 Ibid., pp 40–42; pp 18–20.
11 Ibid., pp 54, 55; pp 34, 35 (all emphases added).
12 Ibid., pp 70–74; pp 56–63.
13 Ibid., p 77; p 65.
14 Ibid., p 79; p 69. In one sense the identification of the relation with *autrui* and the subject's relation to the future is a metaphorical identification based on the absolute alterity of the future and its essentially unknowable nature. Another sense, the more complex relation between the Other and the future which will emerge in the later discussions of fecundity, will be addressed in the next chapter.
15 Ibid., pp 85–6, 87–8; pp 77, 80.
16 Ibid., p 85; p 77/8. See also *Existence and Existents*, pp 85, 96; *De l'existence à l'existant*, pp 145, 164.
17 *Time and the Other*, p 36; *Le temps et l'autre*, p 14.
18 For attempts to argue along these lines see, for example, Robert John Scheffler Manning, 'Thinking the Other Without Violence? An Analysis of the Relation Between the Philosophy of Emmanuel Lévinas and Feminism', *Journal of Speculative Philosophy*, V, No 2, 1991, 135/6; Tina Chanter, 'Feminism and the Other', Robert Bernasconi and David Wood (eds), *The Provocation of Levinas*, Routledge, London, 1988, p 46.
19 Levinas, *Ethics and Infinity*, trans. Richard A. Cohen, Duquesne University Press, Pittsburgh, PA, 1985, p 66; *Ethique et infini: Entretiens avec Philippe Nemo*, Fayard, Paris, 1982, p 68. Levinas is referring back at this point to *Time and the Other*.

20 *Totality and Infinity*, pp 103, 110, 114, 144, 146; *Totalité et infini*, pp 105, 112, 118, 154, 156.
21 Ibid., p 111; p 113.
22 Ibid., p 54; p 46.
23 Ibid., pp 115, 131, 153; pp 119, 138, 152. Lingis translates 'La joie et ses lendemains' as 'Joy and its Morrows'; an archaic but happy translation.
24 Ibid., p 149; p 160.
25 Ibid., p 150; p 160–1.
26 Ibid., pp 151, 155; pp 161, 165.
27 Ibid., p 171; p 185.
28 Ibid., p 155; p 166.
29 See, for example, ibid., pp 68–9, 213; pp 64–5, 234. See also Chalier, *Figures du féminin*, pp 65–7.
30 See Chalier, *Figures du féminin*, p 100. Levinas also seems to confirm this in his conversation with Raoul Mortley (R. Mortley ed., *French Philosophers in Conversation*, Routledge, London, 1991, p 18): 'Sex itself is otherness of genre, but within a relation: so in a relationship with the feminine, a breaking of genre has already taken place. This is a very important *moment* in the accession to the total otherness of the face.' (Emphasis added.) But it is a moment *on the way* to total otherness, not total otherness itself.
31 *Totality and Infinity*, p 155; *Totalité et infini*, p 166. The picture is more or less the same in 'Judaism and the Feminine Element' (1960), trans. Edith Wyschogrod, *Judaism*, 18, No 1, 1969, 34; 'Le judaïsme et le féminin', *Difficile liberté*, Albin Michel, Paris, 1976, p 56: ' "without woman man knows neither good, nor succor, nor joy, nor blessing, nor pardon." Nothing of what would be required for a soul! Rabbi Joshua ben Levi added: "neither peace nor life." Nothing which transforms his natural life into ethics.' She makes his very soul possible.
32 *Totality and Infinity*, pp 170–71; *Totalité et infini*, p 185.
33 See Chalier, *Figures du féminin*, p 93.
34 Silvano Petrosino and Jacques Rolland, *La vérité nomade: Introduction à Emmanuel Levinas*, La Découverte, Paris, 1984, p 27 ff.
35 See, for example, Edith Wyschogrod, *Emmanuel Levinas: the Problem of Ethical Metaphysics*, Nijhoff, The Hague,1974, pp 66/7, 98, 116; Steven G. Smith, *The Argument to the Other: Reason Beyond Reason in the Thought of Karl Barth and Emmanuel Levinas*, California Scholars Press, Chico, CA, 1993, p 71; Gérard Bailhache, *Le sujet chez Emmanuel Levinas: fragilité et subjectivité*, Presses Universitaires de France, Paris, 1994, pp 23, 111, 141.
36 *Totality and Infinity*, p 157–8; *Totalité et infini*, p 169.
37 *Ethics and Infinity*, p 41; *Ethique et infini*, p 38.
38 Peperzak, *To the Other*, p 158.
39 Ibid., p 195.
40 As Chalier says (*Figures du féminin*, p 68), Levinas may indeed deny any reference to a being of the feminine sex, but, '{c}e qui ne laisse pas d'inquiéter', one does not therefore stop worrying. Davis, in *Levinas: An Introduction*, p 61, similarly points out that 'gendered vocabulary retains its connotations of gender even if we are told that it does not. . . . [Levinas's] language never escapes its socially conditioned context.'

41 John Llewelyn, *Emmanuel Levinas: The Genealogy of Ethics*, Routledge, London, 1995, p 87. See also John Llewelyn *The Middle Voice of Ecological Conscience* (hereafter referred to as *Middle Voice*), Macmillan, Hampshire, 1991, pp 22, 203, 213; *Emmanuel Levinas*, pp 87, 98, 99, 117, 119, 122, 137, 139, 146.

42 Jacques Derrida, 'White Mythology: Metaphor in the Text of Philosophy', *Margins of Philosophy*, trans. Alan Bass, Harvester Wheatsheaf, Hertfordshire, 1982; *Marges de la philosophie*, Editions de Minuit, Paris, 1972.

43 Llewelyn, *Emmanuel Levinas*, p 88.

44 Levinas, 'Meaning and Sense', *Basic Philosophical Writings*, p 37; 'La signification et le sens', *Humanisme de l'autre homme*, Fata Morgana, Montpellier, 1972, p 22.

45 Subsection A, section IV of *Totality and Infinity*, p 254ff, is called 'The Ambiguity of Love'; *Totalité et infini*, pp 284ff.

46 Ibid., p 254; pp 284, 285.

47 Ibid., pp 254 (t.m.), 255, 266; pp 285, 286, 298.

48 In this discussion of eros Levinas's designation of the beloved as feminine also bears witness to a certain heterosexuality; whether this is essential or simply expedient bears also on the question of the possibility of reversal. Tina Chanter's early suggestion that 'Levinas' account of femininity can apply to gays, just as . . . it can apply to heterosexuals of either sex'(Chanter, 'Feminism and the Other', p 46), presupposes that a simple reversal (or reversals) will suffice to make this philosophy universally applicable, rather than descriptive of only a masculine, heterosexual, subjectivity. Alphonso Lingis actually performs such a reversal, without explicitly signalling how his account differs from the Levinasian text on which he is commenting: 'Erotic voluptuousness would then be the moment and erotic intimacy the place where contact with the other in his or her vulnerability, mortality, insecurity in the world, in his or her agitation without projects and expressivity irremediably equivocal, in his or her gratuity . . . becomes voluptuous enjoyment.' Alphonso Lingis, *Libido: the French Existential Theories*, Indiana University Press, Bloomington, IN, 1985, p 68.

49 *Totality and Infinity*, p 256; *Totalité et infini*, p 286.

50 Ibid., p 150; p 161.

51 See, for example, ibid., p 258; p 289.

52 Ibid., p 256–57; p 287.

53 Ibid., p 258/9; p 289.

54 *Time and the Other*, p 86; *Le temps et l'autre*, p 78–79.

55 Léon Bloy, *Lettres à sa fiancée*, Delamain, Boutelleau, Paris, 1922, pp 80, 82.

56 'All things corruptible / Are but a parable; / Earth's insufficiency / Here finds fulfilment; / Here the ineffable / Wins life through love; / Eternal Womanhood / Leads us above.' Johann Wolfgang Von Goethe, *Faust*, Part Two, trans. Philip Wayne, Penguin, London, 1959. These are the final lines of the final act, p 288.

57 Bloy, *Lettres à sa fiancée*, p 21.

58 Ibid., p 27.

59 Goethe has Doctor Martinus cry ('in prostrate adoration'): 'O contrite hearts, seek with your eyes / The visage of salvation; / Blissful in that gaze, arise, / Through glad regeneration. / Now may every pulse of good / Seek to serve before thy face, / Virgin, Queen of Motherhood, / Keep us, Goddess, in thy grace.' *Faust*, Part Two, p 288. See also Bloy, *Lettres à sa fiancée*, p 85.

60 'Judaism and the Feminine Element', p 37 (emphasis added); 'Le judaïsme et le féminin', p 61. See also Bloy, *Lettres à sa fiancée*, pp 79, 81: 'The central concept of this book [the one Bloy plans to write] is woman's physiological sex, around which her whole psychology implacably coils and unwinds. To be blunt, woman is ruled by her sex, as man is ruled by his brain. The idea is not new, but it is possible to give it new life .... Every woman, *whether she knows it or not*, is convinced that her sex is Paradise .... From which comes the estimation of what she gives when she gives herself, and the measure of her sacrilege when she sells herself. To be sure, this is tremendously absurd. By here is my most unexpected conclusion. Woman IS RIGHT to believe and to absurdly claim all that. She is infinitely right, since that part of her body has been the tabernacle of the living God and the *solidarity* [between woman's sex and God] cannot be exagerrated in this troubling mystery.'

61 Sigmund Freud, 'On the Universal Tendency to Debasement in the Sphere of Love' (1912) in *On Sexuality*, trans. J. Strachey *et al*. Freud Pelican Library vol 7, Penguin, London, 1977, p 247ff.

62 'Judaism and the Feminine Element', p 37; 'Le judaïsme et le féminin', p 61.

63 *Totality and Infinity*, pp 260, 262; *Totalité et infini*, pp 291, 294.

64 Ibid., p 263 (t.m.); p 295.

65 Bloy, *Lettres à sa fiancée*, pp 21, 144. The reduction of the feminine to infancy and animality is one of the repeated critical refrains in Luce Irigaray, 'The Fecundity of the Caress', trans. Carolyn Burke, in Richard A. Cohen (ed.), *Face to Face with Levinas*, State University of New York Press, Albany, NY, 1986 (Also in *An Ethics of Sexual Difference*, trans. Carolyn Burke and Gillian C. Gill, Athlone Press, London, 1993); 'La fecondité de la caresse' *Ethique de la différence sexuelle*, Editions de Minuit, Paris, 1984.

66 See Chalier, *Figures du féminin*, p 93.

67 'Judaism and the Feminine Element', pp 34, 35; 'Le judaïsme et le féminin', pp 57, 58.

68 'And God Created Woman', trans. Annette Aronowicz, *Nine Talmudic Readings*, Indiana Universiy Press, Bloomington, IN, 1990, p 167–8 (t.m.); 'Et Dieu créa la femme', *Du sacré au saint: cinq nouvelles lectures talmudiques*, Editions de Minuit, Paris 1977, p 132. See also ibid., pp 164, 169; pp 126, 134.

69 Chanter, 'Feminism and the Other', p 46; Wyschogrod, *Emmanuel Levinas*, p 120.

70 'And God Created Woman', pp 172–3; 'Et Dieu créa la femme', p 141.

71 As indeed it did in the more ancient creation myth involving Lilith, who refused to be subordinated to Adam and who flew away.

72 'Il fallait procéder non pas en stricte justice, qui, elle, exige en effet, qu'il les eût surbordonnés l'un à l'autre.'

73 'And God Created Woman', p 173; 'Et Dieu créa la femme', p 142.

74 Ibid., p 174; p 144.

75 Ibid., pp 174, 177; pp 144, 148.

76 Simone de Beauvoir, *The Second Sex*, trans. H.M. Parshley, Picador, London, 1988; *Le deuxième sexe*, Gallimard, Paris, 1949.

77 Ibid., p 16; p 15.

78 Tina Chanter, 'Feminism and the Other', p 53.

79 See ibid., pp 36, 52. Richard A. Cohen makes a similar point in a footnote to his

translation of the offending passage in *Time and the Other*, p 85 (footnote 69), as does Susan A. Handelman in *Fragments of Redemption*, Indiana University Press, Indianapolis, IN, 1991, p 206.

80 Chanter, 'Feminism and the Other', p 35.
81 Manning, 'Thinking the Other Without Violence?', p 136.
82 *Time and the Other*, p 88; *Le temps et l'autre*, p 81.
83 De Beauvoir, *The Second Sex*, p 15; p 14; see also Chalier, *Figures du féminin*, p 83, where much the same point is made.
84 Quoted in Michèle le Doeuff, *Hipparchia's Choice*, trans. Trista Selous, Blackwell, Oxford, 1991, p 98.
85 See, for example, Manning, 'Thinking the Other Without Violence?', p 137; Alison Ainley, 'Amorous Discourses: "The Phenomenology of Eros" and "Love Stories"', Robert Bernasconi and David Wood (eds), *The Provocation of Levinas*, p 74. It should be noted, though, that Ainley herself adds a question mark to this particular idea. See also p 73.
86 'Violence and Metaphysics', p 315; 'Violence et métaphysique', p 228.
87 Derrida, 'At This Very Moment in This Work Here I Am', trans. Ruben Berez-divin, Robert Bernasconi and Simon Critchey (eds), *Re-Reading Levinas*; 'En ce moment même dans cet ouvrage me voici', François Laruelle (ed.), *Textes pour Emmanuel Levinas*, Editions Jean-Michel Place, Paris, 1980.
88 Derrida, 'At This Very Moment', p 40; 'En ce moment même', p 52.
89 *Totality and Infinity*, p 277; *Totalité et infini*, p 310.

Chapter Three Paternal Fecundity: Sons and Brothers

1 In the French, *'cet "autre genre"'*, Levinas draws attention with his *guillemets* to the felicitous double meaning of *genre*, both 'kind' and 'gender' (primarily, 'kind').
2 Levinas, interview from 1985 (for the Zurich weekly *Construire*) reprinted in Levinas *et al.*, *Répondre d'Autrui: Autour d'un entretien avec Emmanuel Levinas*, Edition de la Baconnière, Boudry-Neuchâtel (Suisse), 1989, p 10.
3 See also 'Philosophy, Justice and Love', *Entre Nous: Thinking-of-the-Other*, trans. Michael B. Smith and Barbara Harshav, Athlone Press, London, 1998, p 113; 'Philosophy, Justice et Amour', *Entre Nous: essais sur le penser-à-l'autre*, Grasset, Paris, 1991, p 131: 'Before [*autrefois*], I used to think that alterity begins in the feminine' (t.m.)
4 Tina Chanter, *Ethics of Eros: Irigaray's Rewriting of the Philosophers*, Routledge, London, 1995, p 203.
5 *Time and the Other*, p 89; *Le temps et l'autre*, p 82.
6 See Critchley, *The Ethics of Deconstruction*, p 228.
7 'And God Created Woman', p 170, t.m.; 'Et Dieu créa la femme', p 137.
8 *De l'évasion*, p 392.
9 See, for example, *Totality and Infinity*, p 310; *Totalité et infini*, p 269.
10 Tina Chanter, for example, does not separate out femininity and fecundity, but rather sees the latter as an aspect of the former: 'Associated with the relation of love is the movement of eros, a movement which takes place both as voluptuosity and as fecundity. It is in the difference between these two planes, voluptuosity on the one hand, and fecundity on the other, that the equivocation of the feminine is

produced.' That is to say, the relation with the feminine in voluptuosity is one of immanence, but in fecundity one of transcendence; in fact Chanter goes so far as to say that the transcendence of the erotic relation accomplished as fecundity is identified *as* feminine. Chanter 'Feminism and the Other', pp 43, 45.

11 *Totality and Infinity*, pp 276–7; *Totalité et infini*, pp 309–10.
12 *Existence and Existents*, pp 95–6, t.m.; *De l'existence à l'existant*, pp 163–5.
13 *Totality and Infinity*, p 274, t.m.; *Totalité et infini*, p 306.
14 Ibid., pp 254, 271; pp 285, 304.
15 Ibid., p 272; p 304/5. See also p 254/5; p 285: 'love also goes beyond the beloved. This is why through the face filters the obscure light coming from beyond the face, from what *is not yet*, from a future never future enough, more remote than the possible.'
16 See also *Totality and Infinity*, p 266; *Totalité et infini*, p 298/9: 'The relation with the child . . . . We are here before a new category.'
17 *Time and the Other*, p 90/91, emphasis added; *Le temps et l'autre*, p 85.
18 *Totality and Infinity*, p 274, t.m.; *Totalité et infini*, p 306/7.
19 *Time and the Other*, p 91; *Le temps et l'autre*, p 85/6. Much of these passages from *Time and the Other* is echoed word for word in *Totality and Infinity* (for example, at p 277; p 310). Even where words differ, the essential meaning is the same.
20 *Totality and Infinity*, pp 267, 269, 271, 273; *Totalité et infini*, pp 299, 301, 304–5, 306.
21 Ibid., p 26; p 11.
22 Ibid., pp 268, 271, 278, 282; pp 300, 301, 304, 310, 314.
23 *Time and the Other*, p 36; *Le temps et l'autre*, p 14.
24 Levinas, in François Poirié, *Emmanuel Levinas: Qui êtes-vous?*, La Manufacture, Lyon, 1987, p 107, emphasis added.
25 Peperzak, *To the Other*, p 195. Llewelyn makes a very similar point in *Middle Voice*, p 203. See also Llewelyn, *Emmanuel Levinas*, pp 99, 117, 119, 137, 139, 146.
26 *Time and the Other*, p 92; *Le temps et l'autre*, p 87. See also Ludwig Wenzler, 'Postface à l'édition allemande du *Temps et l'autre*, trans. Guy Petitdemange, Catherine Chalier and Miguel Abensour (eds), *Emmanuel Levinas*, p 190.
27 *Totality and Infinity*, pp 276, 277, 279; *Totalité et infini*, pp 309/10, 310, 312. See also ibid., p 306; p 343: 'The biological structure of fecundity is not limited to the biological fact. In the biological fact of fecundity are outlined the lineaments of fecundity in general.'
28 *Time and the Other*, p 37; *Le temps et l'autre*, p 15. *Ethics and Infinity*, p 71; *Ethique et infini*, p 73/4.
29 Levinas, 'Pluralisme et transcendance', E.W. Beth, H.J. Pos and J.H.A. Hollack (eds.), *Proceedings of the Tenth International Congress of Philosophy* (Amsterdam, 11–18 August, 1948), North Holland, Amsterdam, 1949.
30 Etienne Feron, *De l'idée de transcendance à la question du langage*, Editions Jacques Millon, Grenoble, 1992, footnote 88 to p 105.
31 See, for example, *Totality and infinity*, p 39; *Totalité et infini*, p 29.
32 Chanter, *Ethics of Eros*, p 198–9.
33 'Freedom and Command', trans. A. Lingis, *Collected Philosophical Papers*, p 23; 'Liberté et commandement' *Revue de métaphysique et de morale*, juillet–septembre No 3, 1953, p 727.

34 'The Ego and the Totality', trans. A. Lingis, *Collected Philosophical Papers*, p 30; 'Le moi et le totalité', *Entre Nous*, p 32. (Another translation, under the title 'The I and the Totality', is available in *Entre Nous: Thinking-of-the-Other*, trans. Michael B. Smith and Barbara Hershav, Athlone Press, London, 1998. Aspects of this account of love are already to be found in the *Journal métaphysique* of Gabriel Marcel, Librarie Gallimard, Paris, 1927, for example in the questions on pp 217, 227.

35 This idea is also present in *Totality and Infinity* under the heading of 'the work' [*l'oeuvre*]: 'In undertaking what I willed I realised so many things I did not will: the work rises in the midst of the wastes of labour. The worker does not hold in his hands all the threads of his own action.' (p 176; p 191.) See also the section entitled 'Work and Expression', ibid., p 177ff.; p 192ff.

36 'The Ego and the Totality', pp 31, 32; 'Le moi et le totalité', pp 33, 34. Levinas's discussion of love here is also an explicit critique of the Christian (sometimes mystical) ideal of the love of God as intimate union, excluding society. The structure, however, is for Levinas true also of erotic or romantic love.

37 *Totality and Infinity*, p 304; *Totalité et infini*, p 340.

38 Ibid., pp 213 (emphasis added), 214; pp 234, 235/6.

39 Ibid., p 279; p 312.

40 Critchley, *The Ethics of Deconstruction*, p 227.

41 *Totality and Infinity*, pp 280, 215; *Totalité et infini*, pp 313, 236. See also ibid., pp 212–4, 300–1; pp 234–6, 334–5.

42 Ibid., p 300; p 334.

43 Peperzak, *To the Other*, p 181.

44 Indeed, according to *Le petit Robert*, the French word '*sororité*' dates only from 1970, and means only 'solidarity amongst women' (it is, then, a word belonging to a specifically feminist vocabulary, referring to a sexed specificity). Amongst the several definitions of '*fraternité*', on the other hand, none refer to its masculine specificity.

45 'The Ego and the Totality', p 31; 'Le moi et le totalité', p 33.

46 *Totality and Infinity*, p 214, t.m.; *Totalité et infini*, p 235/6.

47 Ibid., p 25; p 10.

48 'The Trace of the Other', p 352; 'La trace de l'autre', p 195.

49 Ibid., p 354; p 197.

50 Levinas, 'Enigma and Phenomenon', trans A. Lingis (revised by Simon Critchley and Robert Bernasconi), *Basic Philosophical Writings*, p 67; 'Enigme et phénomène', *En découvrant l'existence avec Husserl et Heidegger*, p 204.

51 'The Trace of the Other', p 355; 'La trace de l'autre', p 198.

52 'Philosophy, Justice and Love', p 114; 'Philosophie, Justice et Amour', p 132.

53 'Enigma and Phenomenon', p 72; 'Enigme et phénomène', p 211.

54 Davis, *Levinas: an Introduction*, p 62, makes the same point *vis-à-vis* the Other in *Totality and Infinity*: 'to succeed as a philosophy of the Other, it must fail adequately to thematise its subject.'

55 'The Trace of the Other', p 356, t.m.; 'La trace de l'autre', p 199.

56 'Enigma and Phenomenon', p 75; 'Énigme et phénomène', p 214.

57 'The Trace of the Other', p 358/9, 'La trace de l'autre', p 201/2.

58 Levinas, *Otherwise Than Being or Beyond Essence*, trans. A. Lingis, Nijhoff, The

Hague, 1981, p 13, emphasis added; *Autrement qu'être ou au-delà de l'essence*, Nijhoff, Le Hague, 1974, p 28.

59 Ibid., p 16; p 33.

60 Ibid., pp 158, 159, 160; pp 246, 248, 249.

61 See, for example, *Otherwise Than Being*, pp 82, 83, 87, 158,159; *Autrement qu'être*, pp 131, 132, 13, 246, 247/8. Levinas also speaks of 'the human fraternity' (ibid., p 116; p 184), which *is* responsibility, and which is linked in a footnote to the analyses of illeity in 'The Trace of the Other' and 'Enigma and Phenomenon'.

62 See, for example, *Being and Time*, section 69 'The Temporality of Being-in-the-world and the Problem of the Transcendence of the World', p 401ff.

63 Levinas, 'A propos de Buber: quelques notes', *Qu'est-ce que l'homme? Philosophie/Psychanalyse*, Hommage à Alphonse Waelhens 1911–1981, Publications des facultés Universitaires Saint-Louis, Bruxelles, 1982, p 132, my emphasis. It is, for Levinas, because Buber's *je-tu* relation excludes *le tiers*, that it is associated with the description of the erotic relation in his own work: 'The I-Thou in which Buber sees the category of interhuman relationship is the relation not with the interlocutor but with feminine alterity.' (*Totality and Infinity*, p 155; *Totalité et infini*, p 166.) See also *Otherwise Than Being*, p 13; *Autrement qu'être*, p 28, where the difference between Buber and Levinas is once again posed by the latter in terms of illeity, which, he there says, is not only not the '*tu*' of the *je-tu* relation, but is also not the '*il*' of Buber's *je-il* [I-it] relation.

64 *Totality and Infinity*, p 28; *Totalité et infini*, p 13.

65 Ibid., pp 269, 272; pp 302, 305.

66 Plato, *Republic*, 509B.

Chapter Four A Maternal Alternative? Levinas and Plato on Love

1 *Totality and Infinity*, p 172; *Totalité et infini*, p 187.

2 'The Trace of the Other', p 349/50; 'La trace de l'autre', p 192.

3 *Otherwise Than Being*, pp 56 (t.m.), 72; *Autrement qu'être*, pp 94, 116.

4 Ibid., p 74; p 119.

5 See for example, ibid., pp xliii, 37; pp 10, 65, footnote 2.

6 See, for example, ibid., pp 67, 68, 71; pp 109, 111, 114.

7 Ibid., p 25 (t.m); p 46.

8 Ibid., pp 75, 105; pp 121, 167.

9 In Greek mythology Demeter, mother of Persephone and the figure of the Mother more generally, is the symbolic synthesis of the mother and of the earth as providers of nourishment, a connection which Levinas echoes in the twin tropes of food and maternity.

10 The conversation between Luce Irigaray and Hélène Rouch in Irigaray's *Je, tu, nous: Toward a Culture of Difference*, trans. Alison Martin, Routledge, London, 1990, p 88ff. (*Je, tu, nous: pour une culture de la différence*, Grasset, Paris, 1990, p 42ff) seems to affirm the relation between mother and foetus as unique in the way that Levinas had previously described paternity and would later describe responsibility. In what Irigaray and Rouch call the 'placental relation', that which is of the mother or in the mother remains other (a stranger) in a way that provides a model for the post-natal negotiation of self-other relations; as Levinas

would say, 'me a stranger to myself' (*'moi étranger à soi'*) (*Totality and Infinity*, p 267; *Totalité et infini*, p 299).

11 Catherine Chalier, 'Ethics and the Feminine', Robert Bernasconi and Simon Critchley (eds), *Re-Reading Levinas*, pp 123, 127. See also *Figures du féminin*, p 45.

12 'Judaism and the Feminine Element', p 33; 'Le judaïsme et le féminin', p 55.

13 *Totality and Infinity*, p 270; *Totalité et infini*, p 303.

14 *Ethics and Infinity*, p 68 (t.m); *Ethique et infini*, p 71.

15 Chalier, 'Ethics and the Feminine', p 128. The argument is somewhat different in *Figures du féminin*.

16 Monique Schneider, 'En deçà du visage' in Jean Greisch and Jacques Rolland (eds), *Emmanuel Levinas: l'éthique comme philosophie première*, Éditions du Cerf, Paris, 1993 (Actes du colloque de Cérisy-la Salle, 1986), p 149.

17 Found in 1898 at Priene (on the coast of Asia Minor, facing the island of Samos) in the remains of a temple dedicated to Demeter and Kore. See Maurice Olender, 'Aspects of Baubô: Ancient Texts and Contexts', M. Halperin, J. J. Winkler and I. Zeitlin (eds), *Before Sexuality: The Construction of Erotic Experience in the Ancient Greek World*, Princeton University Press, Princeton, NJ, 1990, p 83; Kathleen Freeman, *The Pre-Socratic Philosophers*, Basil Blackwell, Oxford, 1949, p 11.

18 Schneider, 'En deçà du visage', p 150.

19 Ibid., p 151: 'It is because the opening onto the entrails/womb (the opening indicated or prefigured in the mouth) must be banished in the accession of every being called to become a citizen that the memory of this original dwelling can only be derisory.' The only literary illustration of the word '*vulve*' given in *Le Petit Robert* confirms Schneider's point: '*Singes d'hommes tombés de la vulve des mères*', Rimbaud. A literal translation would read absurdly; Rimbaud implies, however, that the unattractive aspect of 'human nature' is of a piece with its maternal origin, reduced here to a crude physical reference. St Augustine's well-known phrase expresses much the same thing: *Inter urinam et faeces nascimur* – we are born between piss and shit.

20 Levinas, Preface to Catherine Chalier, *Les Matriarches: Sarah, Rebecca, Rachel et Léa*, Editions du Cerf, Paris, 1991, p 8.

21 Bernard Forthomme, *Une philosophie de la transcendance: la métaphysique d'Emmanuel Levinas*, Vrin, Paris, 1979, p 332. Peperzak, *To the Other*, p 195, makes much the same point: 'one might maintain that Levinas's description of love, the beloved and the lover are typically masculine. This would certainly not offend an author who does not swear by the neutrality of "formal logic".'

22 Forthomme, *Une philosophie de la transcendance*, pp 382/3.

23 Ibid., p 333.

24 Llewelyn, *Middle Voice*, p 219.

25 Llewelyn, *Emmanuel Levinas*, p 208. Llewelyn echoes Levinas here: 'one has to find another kinship relation than that which ties man to being' ('il faut trouver à l'homme une autre parenté que celle qui attache à l'être'); *Otherwise Than Being*, p 177; *Autrement qu'être*, p 272.

26 Llewelyn, *Emmanuel Levinas*, p 190.

27 Chalier, *Figures du féminin*, pp 95, 109ff.

28 Llewelyn, *Middle Voice*, p 220.

29 Jacques Derrida and Christine V. McDonald, 'Choreographies', *Diacritics*, 12, Summer 1982, p 76.

30 Llewelyn, *Emmanuel Levinas*, p 145.

31 Ibid., p 145, echoing the title of Levinas's *Humanisme de l'autre homme*.

32 Chalier, 'Ethics and the Feminine', p 128. Although it contains internal contradictions, and is therefore not easy to reconstruct with confidence, the reading proposed by Christian Saint-Germain in his *Ecrire sur la nuit blanche* (Presses de l'université du Québec, Québec, 1992) is in many ways consonant with that of Llewelyn. Like Llewelyn, Saint-Germain criticizes the masculinized version of subjectivity in *Totality and Infinity* (pp 258, 260) but then cautions against any interpretative correlation of the feminine in *Totality and Infinity* with the later notion of maternity. In order to sustain the difference between the two without thereby denying that the maternal is, in some sense, 'feminine', Saint-Germain then makes a distinction between the feminine and femininity, where it seems that the former designates that idea as it appears in *Totality and Infinity*, that is, the feminine as sexually differentiated, or as the mark of sexual difference. 'Femininity', on the other hand, is employed in speaking of the maternal and is not exclusive to the female because maternity is not exclusive to the female (p 229; see also pp 219, 268). This perhaps contradicts another concurrent thread in his argument, one that agrees with Chalier, that the feminine is ultimately only ethically respectable as maternity (p 265).

33 *Time and the Other*, p 37; *Le temps et l'autre*, p 15. *Ethics and Infinity*, pp 70/1; *Ethique et infini*, pp 73/4. *Otherwise Than Being*, p 87; *Autrement qu'être*, p 138.

34 Llewelyn, *Emmanuel Levinas*, p 208.

35 The centrality of these concerns to both Llewelyn's *Middle Voice* and his *Emmanuel Levinas* are what make them parts of the same philosophical project.

36 Critchley, *The Ethics of Deconstruction*, p 226; see also pp 223, 229ff.

37 For the idea of the 'justified Said' see ibid., p 229.

38 *Otherwise Than Being*, p 157 (t.m.); *Autrement qu'être*, p 245.

39 Ibid., p 161 (t.m.); p 251.

40 Ibid., p 162 (t.m); p 253. See also 'Philosophy, Justice and Love', p 104; 'Philosophie, Justice et Amour' p 122. On the 'wisdom of love' see Chalier, *L'Utopie de l'humain*, Albin Michel, Paris, 1993, p 119ff.

41 See Critchley, *The Ethics of Deconstruction*, pp 227, 232.

42 See, for example, *Otherwise Than Being*, pp 87, 97, 158, 159, 166; *Autrement qu'être*, pp 138, 154, 246, 247, 258. Critchley is well aware of the patriarchal implications of 'fraternity'; see *The Ethics of Deconstruction*, pp 227–8.

43 *Otherwise Than Being*, p 160; *Autrement qu'être*, p 249.

44 Ibid., p 158 (emphasis added); p 246.

45 Ibid., pp 49, 56; pp 83, 94.

46 *Otherwise Than Being*, pp 192 (footnote to p 89), 176; *Autrement qu'être*, pp 143, 271. See also ibid., p 177; p 272.

47 Ibid., p 123; p 195/6.

48 'God and Philosophy', pp 140, 141; 'Dieu et la philosophie', pp 115,116, 117.

49 Levinas, *Dieu, la mort et le temps*, Grasset, Paris, 1993, p 252.

50 Levinas (avec les études de Guy Petitdemange et Jacques Rolland), *Autrement que savoir*, Editions Osiris, Paris, 1988, pp 64, 74, 77. See also Poirié, *Emmanuel*

Lévinas: Qui êtes-vous?, p 96, where Levinas discusses the same hesitation in his use of the word 'love', and 'Philosophy, Justice and Love', p 103 ('Philosophie, Justice et Amour', p 121), where the word 'love' is said to be 'usé et frelaté', 'worn-out and debased.'

51 'And God Created Woman', pp 170, 172; 'Et Dieu créa la femme', pp 137, 140. In 'Philosophy, Justice and Love', p 113 ('Philosophie, Justice et Amour', p 131), Levinas makes the same point: 'I am definitely not a Freudian; consequently I do not think that Agape comes from Eros.'

52 *Time and the Other*, p 36; *Le temps et l'autre*, p 15.

53 Most commentators signal Levinas's debt (for example Peperzak, *To the Other*, pp 67, 132). Where one might expect to find the most detail, however, in Chanter's *Ethics of Eros*, Plato's *Symposium* is discussed in the context of Irigaray's reading of Heidegger (pp 159–63), and not mentioned in the chapter on Levinas.

54 *Existence and Existents*, p 85; *De l'existence à l'existant*, p 145.

55 *Time and the Other*, p 94; *Le temps et l'autre*, p 89.

56 'Philosophy and the Idea of Infinity', p 57 (t.m.); 'La philosophie et l'idée de l'infini', p 175. In *Totality and Infinity* Levinas repeats the lines from 'Philosophy and the Idea of Infinity' almost word for word with an added caution: 'But love analysed by Plato does not coincide with what we have called Desire. Immortality is not the objective of the first movement of Desire, but the other, the Stranger'. (*Totality and Infinity*, p 63; *Totalité et infini*, p 58.)

57 Unless otherwise indicated all quotations in this section refer to *Symposium*, trans. Walter Hamilton, Penguin, London, 1951, 201A–204E. 'Love', with the upper case initial letter, refers to the name of the god.

58 Or, in W.R.M. Lamb's translation (*Symposium*, Loeb Classical Library, London, 1991), 'Resource the son of Cunning'.

59 *Symposium*, 192E.

60 Empedocles, *The Fragments of Empedocles*, trans. William Ellery Leonard, The Open Court Publishing Co., Chicago, IL, 1908, Fragments 57–61.

61 Gregory Vlastos, 'The Individual as Object of Love in Plato', *Platonic Studies*, Princeton University Press, Princeton, NJ, 1981, p 20. The neo-Platonists, for example Ficino, are a notable exception to this tendency. See Marsilio Ficino, *Commenatry on Plato's 'Symposium'*, trans. Sears Reynolds Jayne, Columbia University Press, Columbia, 1994.

62 *Totality and Infinity*, p 63; *Totalité et infini*, p 58.

63 Alfred Fouillée, *La philosophie de Platon* (Tome Premier), Librarie Philosophique de Ladrange, Paris, 1869, p 331. See also Davis, *Levinas: An Introduction*, p 45, who refers to 'the myth of the Platonic hermaphrodite or the Romantic yearning for fusion.'

64 Sigmund Freud, 'Beyond the Pleasure Principle' (1920), trans. J. Strachey *et al.*, *On Metasychology*, Freud Pelican Library vol 11, Penguin, London, 1984, p 331. In this essay Freud opposes eros to the death drive in a dualistic way. The derivation of the latter from the Aristophanesian account of eros would, however, suggest, as some Freudian theorists would have it, that eros and the death drive are but different aspects of a single drive.

65 Georges Bataille, *Eroticism*, trans. Mary Dalwood, Marion Boyars, London, 1990, p 15; *L'erotisme*, Editions de Minuit, Paris, 1957, p 21–2.

66 See, for example, *Totality and Infinity*, p 292; *Totalité et infini*, p 325: 'The social relation engenders this surplus of the Good over being, multiplicity over the One. It does not consist in reconstituting the wholeness of the perfect being which Aristophanes speaks of in the myth of the *Symposium*.'

67 Wyschogrod, in *Emmanuel Levinas: The Problem of Ethical Metaphysics*, p 116, makes a similar point when she says that Aristophanes' myth reflects a profound understanding of the 'incestuous' nature of one aspect of the erotic, that is, its seeking of what is kindred to it, the same. Like Levinas, however, Wyschogrod seems also to read Aristophanes' myth as the actual reuniting of the two into the whole.

68 Lucretius, *De Rerum Natura*, IV, 1108–14, quoted in Ficino, *Commentary on Plato's 'Symposium'*, p 226.

69 Leone Ebreo (a.k.a. Judah Abravanel), *The Philosophy of Love*, trans. F. Friedeberg-Seeley and J.H. Barnes, Sonano Press, London, 1937, p 345.

70 Origen, for example, thinks that Eros's birth in the garden of Zeus 'seems to bear a certain resemblance to the Paradise of God, and Penia [Poverty], who is like the serpent of the Bible, and Porus [Contrivance] who was conspired against by Penia, who is like the man against whom the serpent conspired.' *Origen Contra Celsum*, trans. Henry Chadwick, Cambridge University Press, Cambridge, 1953, p 215.

71 Ebreo, *The Philosophy of Love*, p 350.

72 In Isaac Preston Cory (ed./trans.), *Ancient Fragments*, William Pickering, London, 1832, p 292.

73 Plato, *Phaedrus*, trans. Walter Hamilton, Penguin, London, 1973. Hamilton translates αμφιβητησιμων as 'ambiguous'; H. N. Fowler (*Phaedrus*, Loeb Classical Library, 1999) has 'doubtful', and 'disputed' would also have been possible. With all three translations, however, it is the meaning or interpretation of the word or the thing that is at issue.

74 *Phaedrus*, 266A.

75 Unless otherwise indicated all quotations in this section refer to *Symposium*, 205–12.

76 *Phaedrus*, 261A/B.

77 Hamilton's translation was slightly coy; the Greek names 'philosophy' at 210D.

78 See, for example, Seth Benardete, *On Plato's Symposium* (held at the British Library, no publication details given), lecture at the Carl Friedrich von Siemens Foundation, June 1993, pp 41, 43.

79 *Symposium*, 181B–C. Both Plotinus and Ficino, the latter probably influenced by the former, explain the purity of unmothered Heavenly Aphrodite through a false etymological connection between 'mother' (*mater*) and 'matter'. Despite the fact of this mistake, the assumption behind it shores up the point Plato is making. See Plotinus, *Enneads*, Third Ennead, Fifth Tractate, p 172; Ficino, *Commentary on Plato's Symposium*, Chapter VII, p 142.

80 H.A. Mason, 'Plato's Comic Masterpiece', *Fine Talk at Agathon's: a Version of Plato's 'Symposium'*, Cambridge Quarterly, Cambridge, 1992, p 47.

81 See Shelley, 'A Discourse on the Manners of the Antient Greeks Relative to the Subject of Love', *Plato's Banquet*, Curwen Press, London, 1931.

82 Mason translates the passage as follows: 'if the lover is confronted with an ugly

body, he feels instantly saddened and depressed, he draws in his horns, his organ shrinks to nothing, he turns his back on the ugly body, and no impregnation occurs. He then suffers great pain from the retention of his seed. But when he is with a beautiful body, he experiences wonderful relief from the pain of a swollen and congested organ.' (p 93) Mason admits that he has been even plainer than Diotima in his translation, presumably to convey that the Greek words make it plain that it is being looked at 'from the male end', as he says (p 47).

83 *Phaedrus*, 251B–E. G.R.F. Ferrari, in *Listening to the Cicadas: a Study of Plato's 'Phaedrus'*, Cambridge University Press, Cambridge, 1987, p 265, says that the Greek word used for the shoot or the stump of the feather also occurs in ancient medical literature as a term for 'penis'.

84 *Symposium*, 219C. Lamb's translation has 'truly spiritual and miraculous'.

85 *Phaedrus*, 250E/251A.

86 Of course, the dependency of the description of this alleged spiritual purity on the imagery of erection and ejaculation clearly shows that it remains *in fact* essentially ambiguous. The importance of this for Levinas's Platonic account of love is discussed in the following chapter.

87 *Symposium*, 183D.

88 This is a charge, incidentally, from which even Socrates was not immune, as in Lucian's 'The Auction of the Philosophers', in which he sarcastically has Socrates sell himself thus: 'I dote upon boys and am wise in love matters . . . . I'm not in love with their bodies. It's their souls that I regard as beautiful.' Lucian, *Dialogues*, trans. Winthrop Dudley Sheldon, Drexel Biddle, Philadelphia, 1901, p 409.

89 *Symposium*, 192C.

90 Ibid., 195E, 196E.

91 Thus Levinas's refusal to contemplate the divinity of (physical) love is the core of Irigaray's critique in both 'The Fecundity of the Caress' and 'Questions to Emmanuel Levinas' (subtitled 'On the Divinity of Love').

92 *Totality and Infinity*, p 254 (t.m.); *Totalité et infini*, p 284/5.

93 'God and Philosophy', p 140; 'Dieu et la philosophie', p 115.

94 *Totality and Infinity*, p 114; *Totalité et infini*, p 118.

95 Ibid., pp 63, 282, 56, 268; pp 58, 314, 49, 301. See also ibid., p 282; p 315: 'The discontinuous time of fecundity makes possible an absolute youth and recommencement . . . . This recommencement of the instant, this triumph of the time of fecundity over the becoming of the mortal and aging being, is a pardon, the very work of time.'

96 William S. Cobb, *The 'Symposium' and the 'Phaedrus': Plato's Erotic Dialogues*, State University of New York Press, Albany, NY, 1993, p 75/6.

97 Lamb translates as follows: 'Every mortal thing is preserved in this way; not by keeping it exactly the same for ever, like the divine, but by replacing what goes off or is antiquated with something fresh, in the semblance of the original. Through this device, Socrates, a mortal thing partakes of immortality, both in its body and in all other respects; by no other means can it be done.'

98 In Lamb's translation 'many fair fruits of discourse and meditation in a plentious crop of philosophy'.

99 Peperzak, *To the Other*, p 199. See also Llewelyn *Middle Voice*, p 203.

100 Poirié, *Emmanuel Lévinas: Qui êtes-vous?*, p 109.

101 The word translated here as 'goodness' is *arete*; previously (for example at 206A: 'love is desire for the perpetual possession of the good') the word is *agathos*, as it is in the *Republic* 509B when Plato speaks of the Good beyond being. Levinas's word '*bonté*' is, one presumes, a reference to the latter. But as what Plato means by the 'Good beyond being' and what Levinas means by '*bonté*' are both anti-pathetic to precise determination, trying to establish any strict parallelism would be senseless.

102 *Totality and Infinity*, pp 269, 272; *Totalité et infini*, pp 302, 305.

103 Arlene W. Saxonhouse, 'Eros and the Female in Greek Political Thought: an Interpretation of Plato's *Symposium*', *Political Theory*, 12, No 1, February 1984, especially pp 21–2. Whilst not agreeing entirely with Saxonhouse, Wendy Brown is similarly sympathetic, reading Plato as locating philosophy in the realm of love, nurturance and procreation, such that '[t]rue being, philosophy, and wisdom are depicted as female just as it is a woman, Diotima, who taught Socrates what he knows about the relationship between Eros and wisdom.' (Wendy Brown, ' "Supposing truth were a woman": Plato's Subversion of Masculine Discourse', *Political Theory*, 16, No 4, November 1988, p 608.)

104 Irigaray, 'Sorceror Love: a Reading of Plato's *Symposium*, Diotima's Speech', trans. Eleanor H, Kuykendall, Nancy Fraser & Sandra Lee Bartky (eds), *Revaluing French Feminism*, Indiana University Press, Bloomington, IN, 1992, p 64; 'L'amour sorcier, lecture de Platon (*Le Banquet*, 'Discours de Diotime')', *Éthique de la différence sexuelle*, p 27.

105 Adriana Cavarero, *In Spite of Plato*, trans. Serena Anderlini-D'Onofrio and Åine O' Healy, Polity Press, Cambridge, 1995, pp 93, 94.

106 A.W. Price, *Love and Friendship in Plato and Aristotle*, Clarendon Press, Oxford, 1988, pp 15/16.

107 *Theaetetus*, 148E, 150C/D.

108 Cavarero, *In Spite of Plato*, p 93.

109 *Theaetetus*, 150B/C.

110 Cavarero, *In Spite of Plato*, p 92.

111 *Phaedrus*, 247C.

112 *Republic*, 508B/C, 506D/E.

113 *Totality and Infinity*, pp 103, 80; *Totalité et infini*, pp 106, 79.

114 Critchley, *The Ethics of Deconstruction*, p 129ff. reads Derrida's 'At This Very Moment' in terms of 'How Levinas's Work does not Work' (one of Critchley's subheadings).

Chapter Five Affectivity and Meaning: The Intelligibility of Transcendence

1 Plato, *Republic*, trans. Robin Waterfield, Oxford University Press, Oxford, 1994; Plato, *Republic*, trans. Paul Shorey, Loeb Classical Library, 1999.

2 *Otherwise Than Being*, pp 183, 123; *Autrement qu'être*, pp 281, 197.

3 *Phaedrus*, 255–6.

4 *Totality and Infinity*, p 266; *Totalité et infini*, p 298.

5 Ibid., pp 258–60; pp 288–90.

6 Ibid., p 110; pp 112–13.

7 Ibid., p 135; p 143.
8 Ibid., p 115; p 118.
9 Ibid., p 112; p 115.
10 Ibid., p 118; p 123.
11 '*Jouissance*' may mean 'sexual pleasure'. The verb, *jouir*, may mean 'to come'.
12 *Totality and Infinity*, p 114; *Totalité et infini*, p 117–18.
13 Ibid., p 133; p 141.
14 *Existence and Existents*, p 43; *De l'existence à l'existant*, p 66.
15 *Totality and Infinity*, p 187, emphasis added; *Totalité et infini*, p 204.
16 Existence and Existents, p 43; *De l'existence à l'existant*, p 66.
17 *Totality and Infinity*, p 187; *Totalité et infini*, p 204.
18 Ibid., p 188; p 204.
19 Ibid., p 193; p 211.
20 Ibid., p 197; p 215.
21 Ibid., p 179; p 195–6.
22 'The Desirable does not gratify my Desire but hollows it out, and somehow nourishes me with new hungers.' Levinas, 'Meaning and Sense', *Basic Philosophical Writings*, p 52; 'La signification et le sens', *Humanisme de l'autre homme*, p 49.
23 *Totality and Infinity*, p 200; *Totalité et infini*, p 219.
24 'Enigma and Phenomenon', pp 67/8; 'Énigme et phénomène', p 205.
25 Ibid., p 71, emphasis added; p 210.
26 'Meaning and Sense', p 60; 'La signification et le sens', p 63.
27 See, for example, *Otherwise Than Being*, pp 89, 177; *Autrement qu'être*, pp 143, 273; 'God and Philosophy', pp 139–141; 'Dieu et la philosophie', pp 115–7; *Autrement que savoir*, p 64.
28 *Otherwise Than Being*, pp 82, 75; *Autrement qu'être*, pp 131, 121.
29 Ibid., pp 192 footnote, 90; pp 143, 144.
30 Ibid., pp 123, 176–7; pp 195, 271–3.
31 *Otherwise Than Being*, p 87 footnote, t.m.; *Autrement qu'être*, p 19.
32 Ibid., pp 49, 56, 64, 15; pp 83, 94, 104, 31.
33 Ibid., pp 49, 50, 55; pp 83, 85, 92–3.
34 Ibid., p 87, footnote 222 p 192; p 138. Plato, *Phaedrus* 251A.
35 *Otherwise Than Being*, p 75; *Autrement qu'être*, p 121, t.m. See also ibid., pp 67, 71, 76, 79, 106; pp 109, 114, 122, 127,168.
36 Ibid., p 63; p 102.
37 Ibid., p 198 fn.; p 222.
38 *Totality and Infinity*, p 188; *Totalité et infini*, p 204.
39 'God and Philosophy', p 142; 'Dieu et la philosophie', p 119.
40 Ibid., p 190 footnote, emphasis added; p 117.
41 *Otherwise Than Being*, pp 63–4, t.m; *Autrement qu'être*, p 103–4.
42 See Derrida, 'Violence and Metaphysics', pp 112–3; 'Violence et métaphysique', pp 165–7.
43 *Otherwise Than Being*, p 64; *Autrement qu'être*, p 104.
44 Kant, *Critique of Pure Reason*, pp 65–91; Heidegger, *Being and Time*, section 29, pp 175–179.
45 'God and Philosophy', p 189 footnote; 'Dieu et la philosophie', p 106.
46 Ibid., p 130; p 100.

47 Ibid., p 131; pp 101–2.
48 'Meaning and Sense', *passim*.
49 Ibid., p 47; p 40.
50 Ibid., p 41 and *passim*; p 27.
51 'God and Philosophy', p 134; 'Dieu et la philosophie', p 107.
52 Ibid., p 140; p 115: 'Diotima . . . will find love to be indigent, needy, and subject to vulgarity. The celestial and the vulgar Venus are sisters.'
53 Ibid., p 135; p 107.
54 Ibid., pp 139, 140; pp 113, 114.
55 Ibid., p 139; p 114.
56 Ibid., p 139; p 114. Cf. *Existence and Existents*, p 66; *De l'existence à l'existant*, p 43.
57 'God and Philosophy', p 142; 'Dieu et la philosophie', p 118.
58 'Violence and Metpahysics', pp.109, 141–3; 'Violence et métaphysique', pp 161, 208–212.
59 Ibid., pp 147, 151; pp 219, 224.
60 *Otherwise Than Being*, pp 54, 122/3; *Autrement qu'être*, pp 91, 195.
61 'Violence and Metaphysics', pp 148, 153; 'Violence et métaphysique', pp 220, 228.
62 See *Totality and Infinity*, p 214; *Totalité et infini*, p 236.

Coda: Metaphysics and Feminism

1 *Totality and Infinity*, p 79; *Totalité et infini*, p 77.
2 Ibid., p 78; p 77.
3 Ibid., p 79, p 77.
4 Derrida, *Adieu to Emmanuel Levinas*, p 21; *Adieu à Emmanuel Levinas*, p 49.
5 Ibid., p 20; pp 45/6.
6 Ibid., pp 22–5; pp 51–5.
7 Ibid., pp 28–34; pp 59–68.
8 Ibid., p 28; p 59.
9 *Totality and Infinity*, pp 24/5, 27, 78; *Totalité et infini*, pp 10, 12, 77.
10 Levinas (in conversation with Bracha Lichtenberg-Ettinger), *What Would Eurydice Say?/Que dirait Euridice?* (bilingual text), *BLE* Atelier, Paris, 1997, p 22 (from p 10), t.m.
11 Ibid., Lichtenberg-Ettinger.
12 Luce Irigaray, *This Sex Which is Not One*, trans. Catherine Porter, Cornell University Press, Ithaca, NY, 1985, p 74 (t.m.); *Ce sexe qui n'en est pas un*, Editions de Minuit, Paris, 1977, p 72.
13 Irigaray, *This Sex*, p 74; *Ce sexe*, p 72.
14 Irigaray, *An Ethics of Sexual Difference*; *Ethique de la différence sexuelle*, p 13; see also *Je, tu, nous: Toward a Culture of Difference*, p 15; *Je, tu, nous: pour une culture de la différance*, p 13.
15 Plato, *Republic* 620A–C.
16 Adriana Cavarero, *In Spite of Plato*, p 27.
17 Ibid., p 50.
18 Ibid., p 53.

19 Ibid., p 52.

20 Plato, *Timaeus and Critias*, trans. Desmond Lee, Penguin, London, 1971, 90E/ 91A.

21 Despite the fact that Irigaray is the (mostly unnamed) theorist of 'feminine specificity' against whom much of Michèle le Doeuff's *Hipparchia's Choice* is directed, le Doeuff's definition of 'masculinism' is strikingly similar to this Irigarayan definition of 'the masculine'. For le Doeuff 'masculinism' is a 'particularism'; masculine specificity masquerading as universality. See, for example, pp 42, 78, 96, 97. Also, despite Irigaray's identification of Simone de Beauvoir as *the* exponent of 'equality feminism' (as opposed to the feminism of difference, which sees the aim of the achievement of equality as an attempt to make women the same as men), Irigaray's definition of the masculine is remarkably similar to some of de Beauvoir's comments in the Introduction to *The Second Sex*: 'The terms *masculine* and *feminine* are used symmetrically only as a matter of form, as in municipal registers and declarations of identity. The relation of the two sexes is not like that of two electrical poles: man represents both the positive and the neutral, as is indicated by the way one says in French "*les hommes*" to designate human beings in general and in the assimilation of the particular meaning of the word "*vir*" to the general meaning of "*homo*". Woman appears as the negative, such that all determination is understood in relation to her as limitation, without reciprocity.' (p 15, t.m.; *Le deuxième sexe*, p 14.)

22 Tina Chanter's work on Levinas and the feminine has sometimes argued for this reading. See, for example, 'Feminism and the Other', p 52: 'Levinas's account of the Other provides feminism with a voice that many feminists have already begun to seek', and 'Antigone's Dilemma', in Robert Bernasconi and Simon Critchley (eds), *Re-reading Levinas*, p 134: 'By singling out the feminine Levinas makes clear that he is concerned to wrest it from the oblivion to which it has been subjected, and to invest it with a positive significance.' In her most recent contribution to this debate, Chanter's conclusion is substantially unchanged, although the way to it is more critically nuanced. See *Ethics of Eros*, p 234: 'the feminine functions at the order of the saying in Levinas' text, which remains, in its external appearance, at the order of the said, thoroughly male.'

23 *Time and the Other*, p 87; *Le temps et l'autre*, p 79.

24 Manning, 'Thinking the Other Without Violence?' (p 136), for example, argues *contra* de Beauvoir that Levinas's descriptions of 'the feminine' are not an attempt to 'label' or 'define', that is, assume the right to name, 'what is female and feminine'. On the contrary: 'This is, in fact, exactly what Levinas's idea of the absolute alterity of every Other, which he describes through the alterity and mystery of the feminine, is attempting to oppose.' Manning assumes that the gendered discourse of 'the feminine' is reversible. He fails to account for the very specificity of 'the feminine' which he claims to defend here by assuming that the details of its description may be transferred to 'the masculine' 'from the female perspective' (p 135). (He does not, however, grant this possibility to the gendered discourse of 'paternity', and (p 139) chides Chanter for not being critical enough.) His opposition to de Beauvoir's critical comments on Levinas are informed, he admits, by a knowledge of the development of Levinas's 'ethical philosophy' that was unavailable to de Beauvoir, but still does not take into account the

qualification of the alterity of the feminine in Section II of *Totality and Infinity*, for example (and knowledge of the feminist critiques which *have* done so *was* available to Scheffler Manning).

25 Irigaray, 'The Fecundity of the Caress', p 235, 'Fécondité de la caresse', p 177.
26 Ibid., p 233; p 175.
27 Ibid.
28 Irigaray, 'Questions to Emmanuel Levinas', p 109.
29 Ibid., p 113.
30 Ibid.
31 Derrida, *Adieu to Emmanuel Levinas*, p 44; *Adieu à Emmanuel Levinas*, p 83.
32 For a fuller discussion of these translation problems, specifically in relation to the Anglophone reception of Simone de Beauvoir's *The Second Sex*, see Stella Sandford, 'Contingent Ontologies: Sex, Gender and "Woman" in Simone de Beauvoir and Judith Butler', *Radical Philosophy* 97, September/October (1999).
33 Derrida, *Adieu to Emmanuel Levinas*, pp 43, 44; *Adieu à Emmanuel Levinas*, pp 81/2, 84.

Bibliography

Works by Levinas

Levinas, Emmanuel, *Alterity and Transcendence*, trans. Michael B. Smith, Athlone Press, London, 1999; *Altérité et transcendence*, Fata Morgana, Montpellier, 1995.

Levinas, Emmanuel, 'And God Created Woman', trans. Annette Aronowicz, *Nine Talmudic Readings*, Indiana University Press, Bloomington, IN, 1990; 'Et Dieu créa la femme', *Du sacré au saint: cinq nouvelles lectures talmudiques*, Editions de Minuit, Paris, 1977.

Levinas, Emmanuel, 'A propos de Buber: quelques notes', *Qu'est-ce que l'homme? Philosophie/Psychanalyse*, Publications des Facultés Universitaires Saint Louis, Bruxelles, 1982.

Levinas, Emmanuel, 'Au-delà de l'essence' *Revue de métaphysique et de morale*, juillet–septembre, 1970, n. 3.

Levinas, Emmanuel, *Autrement de savoir* (with Guy Petitdemande and Jacques Rolland), Editions Osiris, Paris, 1988.

Levinas, Emmanuel, *Basic Philosophical Writings*, Adriaan T. Peperzak, Simon Critchley and Robert Bernasconi (eds), Indiana University Press, Bloomington, IN, 1996.

Levinas, Emmanuel, 'Beyond Intentionality', trans. Kathleen McLaughlin, Alan Montefiore (ed.), *Philosophy in France Today*, Cambridge University Press, Cambridge, 1983.

Levinas, Emmanuel, *Collected Philosophical Papers*, Nijhoff, Dordrecht, 1987.

Levinas, Emmanuel, *De l'évasion*, *Recherches Philosophiques*, 5, 1935–6.

Levinas, Emmanuel, *Dieu, la mort et le temps*, Grasset, Paris, 1993.

Levinas, Emmanuel, 'The Ego and the Totality', trans. A. Lingis, *Collected Philosophical Papers*, Nijhoff, Dordrecht, 1987 (another translation, under the title 'The I and the Totality', is also available in the English *Entre Nous: Thinking-of-the-Other*, trans. Michael B. Smith and Barbara Harshav, Athlone Press, London, 1998); 'Le moi et la totalité', *Entre Nous: Essais sur le penser-à-l'autre*, Bernard Grasset, Paris, 1991.

Levinas, Emmanuel, *En découvrant l'existence avec Husserl et Heidegger*, Vrin, Paris, 1994.

Levinas, Emmanuel, 'Enigma and Phenomenon', trans. A. Lingis (revised by Simon Critchley and Robert Bernasconi), Adriaan T. Peperzak, Simon Critchley and Robert Bernasconi (eds), *Basic Philosophical Writings*, Indiana University Press, Bloomington, IN, 1996; 'Enigme et phénomène', *En découvrant l'existence avec Husserl et Heidegger*, Vrin, Paris, 1994.

Levinas, Emmanuel, *Entre Nous: Thinking-of-the-Other*, trans. Michael B. Smith and

Barbara Harshav, Athlone Press, London, 1998; *Entre Nous: Essais sur le penser-à-l'autre*, Bernard Grasset, Paris, 1991.

Levinas, Emmanuel, *Ethics and Infinity*, trans. Richard A. Cohen, Duquesne University Press, Pittsburgh, PA, 1985; *Ethique et infini: Entretiens avec Philippe Nemo*, Fayard, Paris, 1982.

Levinas, Emmanuel, *Existence and Existents*, trans. A. Lingis, Kluwer Academic, Dordrecht, 1988; *De l'existence à l'existant*, Vrin, Paris, 1993.

Levinas, Emmanuel, 'Freedom and Command', trans. A. Lingis, *Collected Philosophical Papers*, Nijhoff, Dordrecht, 1987; 'Liberté et commandement', *Revue de métaphysique et de morale*, juillet–septembre 1953, n. 3.

Levinas, Emmanuel, 'God and Philosophy', trans. A. Lingis (revised by Robert Bernasconi and Simon Critchley), Adriaan T. Peperzak, Simon Critchley and Robert Bernasconi (eds), *Basic Philosophical Writings*, Indiana University Press, Bloomington, IN, 1996; 'Dieu et la philosophie', *Le nouveau commerce*, Printemps, Paris, 1975, Cahier 30–31.

Levinas, Emmanuel, *Humanisme de l'autre homme*, Fata Morgana, Montpellier, 1972.

Levinas, Emmanuel, 'Is Ontology Fundamental?', trans. Simon Critchley *et. al.*, Adriaan T. Peperzak, Simon Critchley and Robert Bernasconi (eds), *Basic Philosophical Writings*, Indiana University Press, Bloomington, IN, 1996 (another translation is also available in the English *Entre Nous: Thinking-of-the-Other*, trans. Michael B. Smith and Barbara Harshav, Athlone Press, London, 1998); 'L'ontologie est-elle fondamentale?', *Entre Nous: Essais sur le penser-à-l'autre*, Bernard Grasset, Paris, 1991.

Levinas, Emmanuel, 'Judaism and the Feminine Element', trans. Edith Wyschogrod, *Judaism*, vol 18, No 1, 1969; 'Le judaïsme et le féminin', *Difficile liberté*, Albin Michel, Paris, 1976.

Levinas, Emmanuel, 'Martin Heidegger et l'ontologie', *En découvrant l'existence avec Husserl et Heidegger*, Vrin, Paris, 1994.

Levinas, Emmanuel, 'Meaning and Sense', Adriaan T. Peperzak, Simon Critchley and Robert Bernasconi (eds), *Basic Philosophical Writings*, Indiana University Press, Bloomington, IN, 1996; 'La signification et le sens', *Humanisme de l'autre homme*, Fata Morgana, Montpellier, 1972.

Levinas, Emmanuel, 'L'ouevre d'Edmund Husserl', *En découvrant l'existence avec Husserl et Heidegger*, Vrin, Paris, 1994.

Levinas, Emmanuel, *Otherwise Than Being or Beyond Essence*, trans. A. Lingis, Nijhoff, The Hague, 1981; *Autrement qu'être ou au-delà de l'essence*, Nijhoff, Le Hague, 1974.

Levinas, Emmanuel, 'Philosophy and the Idea of Infinity', trans. A. Lingis, *Collected Philosophical Papers*, Nijhoff, Dordrecht, 1987; 'La philosophie et l'idée de l'infini', *En découvrant l'existence avec Husserl et Heidegger*, Vrin, Paris, 1994.

Levinas, Emmanuel, 'Philosophy, Justice, and Love', trans. Michael B. Smith and Barbara Harshav, *Entre Nous: Thinking-of-the-Other*, Athlone Press, London, 1998; 'Philosophy, Justice et Amour', *Entre Nous: Essais sur le penser-à-l'autre*, Bernard Grasset, Paris, 1991.

Levinas, Emmanuel, 'Pluralisme et transcendance', E.W. Beth, H.J. Pos and J.H.A. Hollack (eds) *Proceedings of the Tenth International Congress of Philosophy* (Amsterdam, August 1948), North Holland, Amsterdam, 1949.

Levinas, Emmanuel, 'Preface to the German Edition of *Totality and Infinity*', *Entre*

Nous: Thinking-of-the-Other, Athlone Press, London, 1948; 'Preface à l'édition alle-mande', *Totalité et infini: essai sur l'extériorité* (Livre de Poche), Nijhoff, Le Hague, 1971.

Levinas, Emmanuel, 'Questions et réponses', *Le nouveau commerce*, Printemps, Paris 1977, Cahier 36–37.

Levinas, Emmanuel, 'Reflections on the Philosophy of Hitlerism', trans. Seán Hand, *Critical Enquiry* (Autumn 1990); 'Quelques réflexions sur la philosophie de l'hitlérisme', Catherine Chalier and Miguel Abensour (eds), *Emmanuel Levinas*, Les cahiers de l'Herne, Paris, 1991.

Levinas, Emmanuel, *Répondre d'Autrui: Autour d'un entretien avec Emmanuel Lévinas*, Edition de la Baconnière, Baudry-Neuchâtel, 1989.

Levinas, Emmanuel, 'Résumé of *Totalité et infini*', *Annales de l'université de Paris* [*Sorbonne, Paris V*], 31 (1961), n 3, pp 385–6.

Levinas, Emmanuel, 'Signature', trans. A. Peperzak, *Research in Phenomenology* VIII, 1978; 'Signature', *Difficile Liberté*, Albin Michel, Paris, 1976.

Levinas, Emmanuel, *The Theory of Intuition in Husserl's Phenomenology*, trans. André Orianne, Northwestern University Press, Evanston, IL, 1989; *La théorie de l'intui-tion dans la phénoménologie de Husserl*, Vrin, Paris, 1970.

Levinas, Emmanuel, *Time and the Other*, trans. Richard A. Cohen, Duquesne University Press, Pittsburgh, PA, 1987; *Le temps et l'autre*, Quadrige/Presses Universitaires de France, Paris, 1994.

Levinas, Emmanuel, *Totality and Infinity: an Essay on Exteriority*, trans. A. Lingis, Duquesne University Press, Pittsburgh, PA, 1992; *Totalité et infini: essai sur l'extéri-orité* (Livre de Poche), Nijhoff, Le Hague, 1971.

Levinas, Emmanuel, 'The Trace of the Other', trans. A. Lingis, Mark C. Taylor (ed.) *Deconstruction in Context*, Chicago University Press, Chicago, IL, 1986; 'La trace de l'autre', *En découvrant l'existence avec Husserl et Heidegger*, Vrin, Paris, 1994.

Levinas, Emmanuel, 'Transcendence and Height', trans. Simon Critchley; Adriaan T. Peperzak, Simon Critchley and Robert Bernasconi (eds), *Basic Philosophical Writings*, Indiana University Press, Bloomington, IN, 1996; 'Transcendance et hauteur', Catherine Chalier and Miguel Abensour (eds), *Emmanuel Levinas*, Les cahiers de l'Herne, Paris, 1991.

Levinas, Emmanuel, (with Bracha Lichtenberg-Ettinger), *What Would Eurydice Say?/ Que dirait Euridice?* (bilingual text), *BLE* Atelier, Paris, 1997.

Works by other authors

Ainley, Alison, 'Amorous Discourses: "The Phenomenology of Eros" and "Love Stories"', Robert Bernasconi and David Wood (eds), *The Provocation of Levinas*, Routledge, London, 1988.

Allen, Michael B., *Icastes: Marsilio Ficino's Interpretation of Plato's Sophist* (translation and commentary), University of California Press, Berkeley, CA, 1989.

Aristotle, *Metaphysics*, trans. Hugh Tredennick, Loeb Classical Library, London, 1933.

Aristotle, *On Sophistical Refutations*, trans. E.S. Forster, Loeb Classical Library, London, 1933.

Atkinson, Michael, *Ennead V, 1: A Commenatry*, Oxford University Press, Oxford, 1983.

Bailhache, Gérard, *Le sujet chez Emmanuel Levinas: fragilité et subjectivité*, Presses Universitaires de France, Paris, 1994.

Bataille, Georges, *Eroticism*, trans. Mary Dalwood, Marion Boyars, London,1990; *L'érotisme*, Editions de Minuit, Paris, 1957.

Beauvoir, Simone de, *The Second Sex*, trans. H.M. Parshey, Picador, London, 1988; *Le deuxième sexe*, Gallimard, Paris, 1949.

Benardete, Seth, *On Plato's Symposium*, lecture at the Carl Friedrich von Siemens Foundation, June 1993, held at the British Library, no publication details given.

Bernasconi, Robert and Critchley, Simon (eds), *Re-Reading Levinas*, Athlone Press, London, 1991.

Bernasconi, Robert and Wood, David (eds), *The Provocation of Levinas*, Routledge, London, 1988.

Bloy, Léon, *Lettres à sa fiancée*, Delamain, Boutelleau, Paris, 1922.

Bluck, Richard S., *Plato's 'Sophist': a Commentary*, Manchester University Press, Manchester, 1975.

Bono, P. and Kemp, S. (eds.), *Italian Feminist Thought: a Reader*, Blackwell, Oxford, 1991.

Brochard, Victor, *Etudes de philosophie ancienne et de philosophie moderne*, Librarie Felix Alcan, Paris, 1912.

Brown, Wendy, '"Supposing Truth Were a Woman": Plato's Subversion of Masculine Discourse', *Political Theory*, 16, No 4, November 1988.

Brumbaugh, Robert S., *Plato on the One: the Hypotheses in the 'Parmenides'*, Yale University Press, New Haven, CT, 1961.

Cavarero, Adriana, *In Spite of Plato*, trans. Serena Anderlini-D'Onofrio and Åine O'Healy, Polity Press, Cambridge, 1995.

Cavarero, Adriana, 'The Need For a Sexed Thought', P. Bono and S. Kemp (eds), *Italian Feminist Thought: A Reader*, Blackwell, Oxford, 1991.

Chalier, Catherine, 'Ethics and the Feminine', Robert Bernasconi and Simon Critchley (eds), *Re-Reading Levinas*, Athlone Press, London, 1991.

Chalier, Catherine, *Figures du féminin*, La nuit surveillée, Paris, 1982.

Chalier, Catherine, *Les Matriarches: Sarah, Rebecca, Rachel et Léa*, Editions du Cerf, Paris, 1991.

Chalier, Catherine, *l'Utopie de l'humain*, Albin Michel, Paris, 1993.

Chalier, Catherine and Abensour, Miguel (eds), *Emmanuel Levinas*, Les cahiers de l'Herne, Paris, 1991.

Chanter, Tina, 'Antigone's Dilemma', Robert Bernasconi and Simon Critchley (eds), *Re-Reading Levinas*, Athlone Press, London, 1991.

Chanter, Tina, *Ethics of Eros: Irigaray's Rewriting of the Philosophers*, Routledge, London, 1995.

Chanter, Tina, 'Feminism and the Other', Robert Bernasconi and David Wood (eds), *The Provocation of Levinas*, Routledge, London, 1988.

Cobb, William S., *The 'Symposium' and the 'Phaedrus': Plato's Erotic Dialogues*, State University of New York Press, Albany, NY, 1993.

Cohen, Richard A (ed.), *Face to Face with Levinas*, State University of New York Press, Albany, NY, 1986.

Comte, Auguste, *Introduction to Positive Philosophy*, trans. Frederick Ferré, Bobbs-Merrill, Indianapolis, IN, 1970.

Cornford, F.M., *Plato's Theory of Knowledge*, Kegan Paul, Trench & Trubner, London, 1935.

Cory, Isaac Preston (ed. and trans.), *Ancient Fragments of the Phoenician, Chaldean, Egyptian, Tyrian, Carthaginian, Indian, Persian, and Other Writers*, William Pickering, London, 1832.

Coxon, A.H., *The Fragment of Parmenides* (translation and commentary), Van Gorcum, Assen, 1986.

Critchley, Simon, *The Ethics of Deconstruction*, Blackwell, Oxford, 1992.

Davis, Colin, *Levinas: an Introduction*, Polity Press, Cambridge, 1996.

Deleuze, Gilles, *Difference and Repetition*, trans. Paul Patton, Columbia University Press, Columbia, NY, 1994.

Derrida, Jacques, *Adieu to Emmanuel Levinas*, Stanford University Press, Stanford, CA, 1999; *Adieu à Emmanuel Levinas*, Editions Galilée, Paris, 1997.

Derrida, Jacques, 'At This Very Moment in This Work Here I Am', trans. Ruben Berezdivin, Robert Bernasconi and Simon Critchley (eds) *Re-Reading Levinas*, Athlone Press, London, 1991; 'En ce moment même dans cet ouvrage me voici', François Laruelle (ed.), *Textes pour Emmanuel Levinas*, Editions Jean-Michel Place, Paris, 1980.

Derrida, Jacques, (with Christine V. McDonald), 'Choreographies', *Diacritics*, 12, Summer 1982.

Derrida, Jacques, 'Violence and Metaphysics', trans. Alan Bass, *Writing and Difference*, Routledge, London, 1990; 'Violence et métaphysique', *L'écriture et la différence*, Editions de Seuil, Paris, 1967.

Descartes, René, *Discourse on Method and the Meditations*, trans. F.E. Sutcliffe, Penguin, London, 1988.

Diès, Auguste, *Le définition de l'être et la nature des Idées dans le 'Sophiste' de Platon*, Paris, Vrin, 1932.

Doeuff, Michèle le, *Hipparchia's Choice*, trans. Trista Selous, Blackwell, Oxford, 1991.

Ebreo, Leone (a.k.a Judah Abravanel), *The Philosophy of Love*, trans. F. Frideberg-Seeley and J.H. Barnes, Sonano Press, London, 1937.

Empedocles, *The Fragments of Empedocles*, trans. William Ellery Leonard, The Open Court Publishing Co., Chicago, IL, 1908.

Feron, Etienne, *De l'idée de transcendance à la question du langage*, Editions Jacques Millon, Grenoble, 1992

Ferrari, G.R.F., *Listening to the Cicadas: a Study of Plato's 'Phaedrus'*, Cambridge University Press, Cambridge, 1987.

Ficino, Marsilio, *Commenatry on Plato's 'Symposium'*, trans. Sears Reynolds Jayne, Columbia University Press, Columbia, NY, 1994.

Forthomme, Bernard *Une philosophie de la transcendance: la métaphysique d'Emmanuel Levinas*, Vrin, Paris, 1979.

Fouillée, Alfred, *La philosophie de Platon* (Tome Premier), Librarie Philosophique de Ladrange, Paris, 1869.

Freeman, Kathleen, *The Pre-Socratic Philosophers*, Blackwell, Oxford, 1949.

Freud, Sigmund, 'Beyond the Pleasure Principle', trans. J. Strachey *et.al.*, *On Metapsychology*, Freud Pelican Library vol 11, Penguin, London, 1984.

Freud, Sigmund, 'On the Universal Tendency to Debasement in Love', trans. J. Strachey et al., *On Sexuality*, Freud Pelican Library Vol. 7, Penguin, London, 1977.

Gallop, David, *Parmenides of Elea: Fragments*, University of Toronto Press, Toronto, 1984.

Goethe, Johann Wolfgang Von, *Faust* (Part Two), trans. Phillip Wayne, Penguin, London, 1959.

Gould, Thomas, *Platonic Love*, Routledge & Kegan Paul, London, 1963.

Guibal, François, . . . *Et combien de dieux nouveaux: Levinas*, Aubier-Montaigne, Paris, 1980.

Halperin, David, 'Why is Diotima a Woman?', *One Hundred Years of Homosexuality, and Other Essays*, Routledge, London, 1990.

Handelman, Susan A., *Fragments of Redemption: Jewish Thought and Literary Theory in Benjamin, Scholem and Levinas*, Indiana University Press, Bloomington, IN, 1991.

Hegel, G.W.F., *Lectures on the History of Philosophy* (vol II), trans. E. Haldane, Kegan Paul, Trench & Trubner, London, 1892.

Hegel, G.W.F., *Phenomenology of Spirit*, trans. A.V. Miller, Oxford University Press, Oxford, 1977.

Hegel, G.W.F., *Science of Logic*, trans A.V. Miller, Allen & Unwin, London, 1969.

Heidegger, Martin, *Being and Time*, trans. John Macquarrie and Edward Robinson, Blackwell, Oxford, 1990.

Heidegger, Martin, 'On the Essence of Truth', trans. John Sallis, David Farrell Krell, *Basic Writings* (ed.), Routledge, London, 1993.

Hume, David, *Enquiries Concerning Human Understanding and Concerning the Principles of Morals*, Clarendon Press, Oxford, 1988.

Husserl, Edmund, *Cartesian Meditations*, trans. Dorion Cairns, Nijhoff, Dordrecht, 1988.

Irigaray, Luce, *An Ethics of Sexual Difference*, trans. Carolyn Burke and Gillian C. Gill, Athlone Press, London, 1993. *Ethique de la différence sexuelle*, Editions de Minuit, Paris, 1984.

Irigaray, Luce, 'The Fecundity of the Caress', trans. Carolyn Burke, Richard A. Cohen (ed.), *Face to Face with Levinas*, State University of New York Press, Albany, NY, 1986; 'La fecondité de la caresse', *Ethique de la différence sexuelle*, Editions de Minuit, Paris, 1984.

Irigaray, Luce, *Je, tu, nous: Toward a Culture of Difference*, trans. Alison Martin, Routledge, London, 1990; *Je, tu, nous: pour une culture de la différence*, Grasset (Livre de Poche), Paris, 1990.

Irigaray, Luce, 'Questions to Emmanuel Levinas', trans. Margaret Whitford, Robert Bernasconi and Simon Critchley (eds), *Re-Reading Levinas*, Athlone Press, London, 1991.

Irigaray, Luce, 'Sorcerer Love: A Reading of Plato's *Symposium*, Diotima's Speech', trans. Eleanor H. Kukendall, Nancy Fraser and Sandra Lee Bartky (eds), *Revaluing French Feminism*, Indiana University Press, Bloomington, IN, 1992; 'L'amour sorcier, lecture de Platon (*Le Banquet*, 'Discours de Diotime')', *Ethique de la différence sexuelle*, Editions de Minuit, Paris, 1984.

Irigaray, Luce, *This Sex Which is Not One*, trans. Catherine Porter, Cornell University Press, Ithaca, NY, 1985; *Ce sexe qui n'en est pas un*, Editions de Minuit, Paris, 1977.

Kant, Immanuel, *Critique of Pure Reason*, trans. Norman Kemp Smith, Macmillan, Hampshire, 1990.

Libertson, Joseph, *Proximity: Levinas, Blanchot, Bataille and Communication*, Nijhoff, The Hague, 1982.

Lingis, Alphonso, 'Emmanuel Levinas and the Intentional Analysis of the Libido', *Philosophy in Context*, 8, 1978.

Lingis, Alphonso, *Libido: The French Existential Theories*, Indiana University Press, Bloomington, IN, 1985.

Llewelyn, John, *Emmanuel Levinas: The Genealogy of Ethics*, Routledge, London, 1995.

Llewelyn, John, *The Middle Voice of Ecological Conscience*, Macmillan, Hampshire, 1991.

Locke, John, *An Essay Concerning Human Understanding*, Everyman, London, 1988.

Lucian, *Dialogues*, trans. Winthrop Dudley Sheldon, Drexel Biddle, Philadelphia, PA, 1901.

Manning, Robert John Scheffler, 'Thinking the Other Without Violence? An Analysis of the Relation between the Philosophy of Emmanuel Levinas and Feminism', *Journal of Speculative Philosophy*, V, No 2, 1991.

Marcel, Gabriel, *Journal métaphysique*, Gallimard, Paris, 1927.

Mason, H.A., 'Plato's Comic Masterpiece', *Fine Talk at Agathon's: a Version of Plato's 'Symposium'*, Cambridge Quarterly, Cambridge, 1992.

Mirandola, Pico della, *Of Being and Unity*, trans. J.W. Miller, Marquette University Press, Milwaukee, WI, 1943.

Mortley, Raoul (ed.), *French Philosophers in Conversation*, Routledge, London, 1991.

Nye, Andrea, 'The Hidden Host: Irigaray and Diotima at Plato's *Symposium*', Nancy Fraser and Sandra Lee Bartky (eds), *Revaluing French Feminism*, Indiana University Press, Bloomington, IN, 1992.

Olender, Maurice, 'Aspects of Baubô: Ancient Texts and Contexts', M. Halperin, J.J. Winkler and I. Zeitlin (eds), *Before Sexuality: the Construction of Erotic Experience in the Ancient Greek World*, Princeton University Press, Princeton, NJ, 1990.

Origen, *Origen contra Celsum*, trans. Henry Chadwick, Cambridge University Press, Cambridge, 1953.

Owen, G.E.L, 'Plato on Not-Being', Gregory Vlastos (ed.), *Plato: a Collection of Critical Essays I: Metaphysics and Epistemology*, University of Notre Dame Press, Indiana, 1978.

Parmenides, *Fragments*; see Coxon *The Fragments of Parmenides* (translation and commentary), Van Gorcum, Assen, 1986.

Peperzak, Adriaan (ed.), *Ethics as First Philosophy: the Significance of Emmanuel Levinas for Philosophy, Literature and Religion*, Routledge, London, 1995.

Peperzak, Adriaan *To the Other*, Purdue University Press, Indiana, 1993.

Petrosino, Silvano and Rolland, Jacques, *La vérité nomade: Introduction à Emmanuel Levinas*, La Découverte, Paris, 1984.

Plato, *Lysis*, trans. W.R.M. Lamb, Loeb Classical Library, London, 1991.

Plato, *Parmenides*, trans. H.N. Fowler, Loeb Classical Library, London, 1991.

Plato, *Phaedo*, trans. Hugh Tredennick, *The Last Days of Socrates*, Penguin, London, 1988.

Plato, *Phaedrus*, trans. H.N. Fowler, Loeb Classical Library, London, 1999.

Plato, *Phaedrus*, trans. Walter Hamilton, Penguin, London, 1973.

Plato, *Republic*, trans. Desmond Lee, Penguin, London, 1988.

Plato, *Republic*, trans. Paul Shorey, Loeb Classical Library, London, 1999.

Plato, *Republic*, trans. Robin Waterfield, Oxford University Press, Oxford, 1994.

Plato, *Sophist*, trans. H.N. Fowler, Loeb Classical Library, London,1987.

Plato, *Symposium*, trans. Walter Hamilton, Penguin, London, 1951.

Plato, *Symposium*, trans W.R.M. Lamb, Loeb Classical Library, London, 1991.

Plato, *Theaetetus*, trans. H.N. Fowler, Loeb Classical Library, London, 1987.

Plato, *Timaeus and Critias*, trans. Desmond Lee, Penguin, London, 1971.

Plotinus, *Enneads*, trans. Stephen Mackenna, Penguin, London, 1991.

Poirié, François, *Emmanuel Lévinas: Qui êtes-vous?*, La Manufacture, Lyon, 1987.

Pollock, Griselda, 'What's Wrong With Images of Women?', Rosemary Betterton (ed.), *Looking On: Images of Femininity in the Visual Arts and Media*, Pandora, London, 1987.

Price, A.W., *Love and Friendship in Plato and Aristotle*, Clarendon Press, Oxford, 1988.

Ricoeur, Paul, *Etre, essence et substance chez Platon et Aristote*, Société d'éditions d'enseignement supérieur, Paris, 1982.

Rijk, L.M. de, *Plato's Sophist: a Philosophical Commentary*, North-Holland, Amsterdam, 1986.

Rolland de Renéville, Jacques *L'un multiple et l'attribution chez Platon et les sophistes*, Vrin, Paris, 1962.

Rosen, Stanley, *Plato's 'Sophist': the Drama of Original and Image*, Yale University Press, New Haven, CT, 1983.

Saint-Germain, Christian, *Ecrire sur la nuit blanche*, Presse de l'Université du Québec, Québec, 1992.

Sandford, Stella, 'Contingent Ontologies: Sex, Gender and "Woman" in Simone de Beauvoir and Judith Butler', *Radical Philosophy* 97, September/October 1999.

Sandford, Stella, 'Plato and Levinas: the Same and the Other', *Journal of the British Society for Phenomenology*, 30, No 2, May 1999.

Sartre, Jean-Paul, *Being and Nothingness*, trans. Hazel Barnes, Routledge, London, 1989; *L'être et le néant*, Gallimard, Paris, 1994.

Saxonhouse, Arlene W., 'Eros and the Female in Greek Political Thought: an Interpretation of Plato's *Symposium*', *Political Theory*, 12, No 1, February 1984.

Schneider, Monique, 'En deçà du visage', Jean Greish and Jacques Rolland (eds), *Emmanuel Levinas: l'éthique comme philosophie première*, Editions du Cerf, Paris, 1993.

Seligman, Paul, *Being and Not-Being: an Introduction to Plato's 'Sophist'*, Nijhoff, The Hague, 1974.

Shelley, Percy Bysshe, 'A Discourse on the Manners of the Antient Greeks relative to the Subject of Love', *Plato's Banquet*, Curwen Press, London, 1931.

Shorey, P., *What Plato Said*, University of Chicago Press, Chicago, 1933.

Smith, Steven G., *The Argument to the Other: Reason Beyond Reason in the Thought of Karl Barth and Emmanuel Levinas*, California Scholars Press, Chico, CA, 1993.

Vlastos, Gregory, 'The Individual as Object of Love in Plato', *Platonic Studies*, Princeton University Press, Princeton, NJ, 1981.

Vlastos, Gregory (ed.), *Plato: a Collection Of Critical Essays 1: Metaphysics and Epistemology*, University of Notre Dame Press, Indiana, 1978.

Wahl, Jean, *Etude sur le Parménide de Platon*, F. Ridier, Paris, 1926.

Wahl, Jean, *Existence humaine et transcendance*, Editions de la Baconnière, Neuchâtel, 1994.

Wenzler, Ludwig, 'Postface à l'édition allemande du *Temps et l'autre*', trans. Guy Petitdemange, Catherine Chalier and Miguel Abensour (eds), *Emmanuel Levinas*, Les cahiers de l'Herne, Paris, 1991.

Whitford, Margaret, *Luce Irigaray: Philosophy in the Feminine*, Routledge, London, 1991.

Whittaker, Thomas, *The Neo-Platonists*, Cambridge University Press, Cambridge, 1918.

Wyschogrod, Edith, *Emmanuel Levinas: the Problem of Ethical Metaphysics*, Nijhoff, The Hague, 1974.

Ziarek, Ewa, 'Kristeva and Levinas: Mourning, Ethics, and the Feminine', K. Oliver (ed.), *Ethics, Politics, and Difference in Julia Kristeva's Writing*, Routledge, London, 1993.

Index